Project Planning
and Management

Pergamon Policy Studies on Socio-Economic Development

Carman Obstacles to Mineral Development
Golany Arid Zone Settlement Planning
Goodman/Love Management of Development Projects
Goodman/Love Project Planning and Management
Gould Bureaucratic Corruption and Underdevelopment in the
  Third World
Stepanek Bangladesh — Equitable Growth?

Related Titles

Goodman/Love Biomass Energy Projects
Goodman/Love Food Projects
Goodman/Love Geothermal Energy Projects
Goodman/Love Small Hydroelectric Projects for Rural
  Development

Related Journals*

Regional Studies
Socio-Economic Planning Sciences
World Development
        *Free specimen copies available upon request.

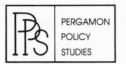

PERGAMON POLICY STUDIES ON SOCIO-ECONOMIC DEVELOPMENT

Project Planning and Management

An Integrated Approach

Edited by
Louis J. Goodman
Ralph N. Love

Published in cooperation with the
East-West Center, Hawaii

Pergamon Press
NEW YORK • OXFORD • TORONTO • SYDNEY • FRANKFURT • PARIS

Pergamon Press Offices:

U.S.A.   Pergamon Press Inc., Maxwell House, Fairview Park,
                Elmsford, New York 10523, U.S.A.

U.K.   Pergamon Press Ltd., Headington Hill Hall,
                Oxford OX3 0BW, England

CANADA   Pergamon of Canada, Ltd. Suite 104, 150 Consumers Road,
                Willowdale, Ontario M2J 1P9, Canada

AUSTRALIA   Pergamon Press (Aust.) Pty. Ltd., P.O. Box 544,
                Potts Point, NSW 2011, Australia

FRANCE   Pergamon Press SARL, 24 rue des Ecoles,
                75240 Paris, Cedex 05, France

FEDERAL REPUBLIC   Pergamon Press GmbH, Hammerweg 6, Postfach 1305,
OF GERMANY   6242 Kronberg/Schönberg, Federal Republic of Germany

Library of Congress Cataloging in Publication Data

Main entry under title:

Integrated project planning and management.

  (Pergamon policy studies)
  Bibliography: p.
  Includes Index.
  1. Industrial project management—Addresses,
essays, lectures. I. Goodman, Louis J.
II. Love, Ralph Ngatata. III. East-West Center.
HD69.P75I57 1980   658.4'04   79-25990
ISBN 0-08-024667-2
ISBN 0-08-025962-6 pbk.

**The East-West Center gratefully extends special
acknowledgment to the Exxon Education Foundation
for its grant to support the case studies on
development projects.**

Printed in the United States of America

Contents

List of Tables
and Figures

Preface and Acknowledgments

Development to increase economic growth and improve the quality of life has been a major objective of all countries over the last two decades. The pace of development, however, has not always been matched by the ability to manage the process itself. Both developing and developed countries have experienced a shortage of project-oriented managers who can provide unified control of development projects and development problems as a whole.

Traditional management education and training programs have not provided enough skilled managers for the vast number of development projects that continue to be implemented in the world today. Because of the urgency of this global problem, the East-West Center has been working cooperatively since 1972 with senior scholars and practitioners from over fifty institutions in fifteen countries in Asia, the Pacific, and the United States to design and develop curriculum materials based on the conceptual framework of an integrated project planning and management cycle (IPPMC). The significant direct results of their combined effort are reflected in a new project management series published by Pergamon Press, Inc. in cooperation with the East-West Center. Project Planning and Management: An Integrated Approach is the second in a series of books. The first book, Management of Development Projects: An International Case Study Approach (1979), is a collection of case histories analyzed within the framework of the integrated project planning and management cycle. Subsequent books will be case-history compendiums on the planning and management of alternative energy systems projects, also viewed within the IPPMC framework. The third book in the series will cover geothermal energy projects; the fourth, biomass energy projects; the fifth, small hydroelectric projects for rural development; and sixth, planning and management of food projects.

Each book seeks to present case histories from widely different socioeconomic settings within the IPPMC conceptual framework, in-

ix

cluding an introductory chapter on the theory and practice of the alternative energy system in question and a final chapter emphasizing policy issues and lessons to be learned from each of the cases.

The intent of the present book is to fill serious gaps in the literature on theory and practice of project planning and management from start to finish. It examines in detail the major phases of the integrated project planning and management cycle, the tasks within each of the phases, and the overall dependency on central policy relationships.

Introduction to the Curriculum describes the development of the integrated project cycle as a working concept and its use as a teaching tool for educating and training project managers in seven countries in Asia, the United States, and the Pacific. Students as well as teachers may find this account of interest, as today's trainees are often tomorrow's trainers.

Chapter 1 introduces readers to the concept of the integrated project cycle and its four phases in the context of the history of development projects. Chapter 2 focuses on the crucial figure of the project manager and the complex role the manager plays in the course of a project's lifetime. The project manager must identify goals, break them into operational objectives, and assemble, develop, and utilize resources – both material and human – for their efficient and effective attainment. This involves planning, organizing, budgeting, personnel management, information systems, evaluation, and other tasks. During the project cycle – depending upon socioeconomic circumstances and the specific project – accomplishing these duties may involve managers at many levels (for example, at the central government level – including staff managers – at departmental/firm levels, at regional/local levels – including staff managers – at the project level, etc.), and the identification of specific managers and their activities at various stages of the project cycle.

Phase 1: Planning, Appraisals, and Design specifically examines, task-by-task, the issues and factors that affect a project in its first inception.

Chapter 3 discusses the identification of projects and sources of project ideas – private business firms, private not-for-profit agencies, educational institutions, existing government agencies, planning units, international agencies, etc., and specific organizational arrangements for ensuring the identification of more and better projects under varying socioeconomic circumstances.

Chapter 4 examines the formulation and preliminary design of projects: arranging to get good project ideas formulated – including designs – for further consideration; assignment of responsibility and resources for this formulation; use of specialists (for example, consultants); and improved organizational-budget-personnel methods to improve the amount and quality of this work.

Chapter 5 discusses feasibility and appraisal: based on preliminary formulation and design work, project feasibility (that is, whether it can be carried out with the technical, material, human, financial, and organizational resources in the environment) and whether the project offers net benefits adequate to justify the use of scarce resources, with due regard given to possible long-term environmental changes (both material and cultural), must be determined; responsibility for making this determination will have to be assigned; and techniques for making this determination selected and used.

Phase 2: Selection, Approval, and Activation addresses salient problem areas and the issues.

Chapter 6 discusses selection and approval: related to appraisal work, a process for selecting and giving formal approval to projects must be developed; the process as based on cost-benefit analyses; the process as influenced by political/leadership considerations; the process as influenced by scheduling considerations; the role of planning, budgeting, executive-legislative agencies and activities in this process.

Chapter 7 takes up the activation of projects, which requires: 1) identification of project manager; 2) approval of broad project organization as required via legislation, executive order, unit organization chart, or the like; 3) development of detailed organization initially required; 4) initial budget request; 5) recruitment and assignment of core staff; and 6) statement of minimal internal operative rules.

Phase 3: Operation, Control, and Handover addresses the major issues from project implementation to evaluation. Chapter 8 discusses project implementation. The project – as a relatively narrow, specifically approved, limited-life activity – may be able to make particular use of newer organizational forms (for example, matrix organizations, systems structures, and so forth), newer budget systems (for example, PPBS), more flexible personnel systems, etc., all of which are opportunities that should be explored. Scheduling techniques are particularly important. Accomplishment of objectives via contract is likely to be particularly important, and thus contracting policies and procedures are given special attention.

Chapter 9 deals with the issues of project supervision and control: outline techniques such as, 1) accounting statements by budget categories, 2) manpower reports by cadre categories, 3) activity statements by scheduling technique category, 4) statistical reports by output categories, and 5) special research reports; report forms; staff meetings; field contract; and feedbacks.

Chapter 10 discusses project completion and assimilation: projects have limited life, but what they have produced (presuming a successful project) continues to be usefully embedded in physical facilities or operating modes of continuing organizations or social structures; selection of the relevant continuing organizations and structures and the means of transfer; problems of maintaining momentum; and budget and personnel problems.

Phase 4: Evaluation and Refinement brings the project to its natural conclusion.

Chapter 11 addresses project evaluation and such factors as relationships of success or failure to project supervision and control. In terms of effectiveness, was the ratio of marginal benefits to marginal costs equal to that obtainable if resources were used alternatively? In

terms of efficiency, were costs minimized for outputs actually produced? And if effectiveness and efficiency were low, where did the
fault lie? Why did project supervision and control not correct the
problem? Can procedures for correction be generalized? How?

Chapter 12 discusses the all-important and often neglected factor:
how best to incorporate the lessons learned from evaluation and the
project as a whole into future project structures.

The final part of the book, Overview: Projects and Policy, is a
general discussion of policies to ensure effective projects: overall
governmental policies – often formulated without particular regard to
projects – impact importantly on the shaping and effectiveness of
projects. Chapter 13 gives a systematic indication of this process, the
policy context within which all development projects operate.

As can be seen from the foregoing brief descriptions of the
chapters, development project management is a complex and demanding
subject. The writing of this book would not have been possible without
the collaboration and cooperation of many senior scholars and practitioners and their institutions in Asia, the Pacific, and the United States.
We wish to convey warmest thanks and deepest appreciation for the
many contributions. Space does not permit adequate acknowledgment
of each person and institution involved in this international, cooperative
project effort at the East-West Center, but special thanks are due to
the authors of the various chapters and to their institutions for the
splendid cooperation received. In addition, a special note of thanks must
go to Vicki Nelson for her invaluable advice in working closely with us
in the professional editing of the manuscript. Also, thanks are extended
to RSI writer/editor Barbara Yount for her advice regarding the overall
manuscript and to Jim Mack for his reviewing of certain chapters.

We hope that the impact of this cooperative project will have
profound implications in the context of international efforts to improve
the planning and management of development projects for all sectors of
the economy and society. This should result in more efficient and
effective use of critical resources for the mutual benefit of many
countries and the well-being of their people.

Introduction to the Curriculum

For the past two decades, educational planners and policy makers in both developed and developing nations have sought to utilize formal and nonformal education as a means to promote "national development." In this context, it has become increasingly clear that, although development is generally pursued through projects that emphasize the technological components of increasing productivity (for example, the projects that stress technological innovations in developing agriculture, forestry, raw materials, energy, etc.), the success of these projects is in many ways related to effective preparation and utilization of human resources through which both formal and nonformal education are the primary media. Foreign technical assistance programs, of course, have played a significant role here, especially as they have related to the printing of instructional materials, training of teachers and administrators, and providing expatriate consultants and management experts. Many governments, however, now see the need to utilize foreign technical assistance primarily as a temporary measure to generate projects and programs.(1)

In Indonesia, for example, educational planners have identified several national educational priorities related to overall development goals and objectives. One of the highest priorities is the development of indigenous programs appropriate to the training of personnel in the areas of administration and project management.(2) In the Philippines, educators have reached similar conclusions and have stressed the fact that overemphasis has been placed on capital accumulation and foreign technical assistance, resulting in a lack of appropriate indigenous training for personnel, especially in such areas as project management.(3) The list could go on.(4) The overall conclusion seems to be that both academic universities and applied training programs must take a more active role in developing and conducting appropriate training curriculums. Until this occurs, it will be difficult to provide the kinds of personnel essential to successfully implement the many development projects currently underway. In particular, there will be problems in training project managers, upon whom the success or failure of development projects depend.

Several problems hinder the development and implementation of appropriate project management curriculums. Project management training should increase the capacity for both theoretical analytic thinking as well as practical implementation skills.(5) What is lacking, however, are innovative instructional programs that provide coherence and workable instructional strategies for the training of project managers. In this very important area, a recent bibliography of project management studies listed over ninety citations, none of which focused on the educational or curricular features of project management education.(6)

Another problem is that many management-education techniques are uncritically transferred from the developed nations to less developed national settings. A recent Rockefeller report suggested that a major priority in this area is the development of experimental curricular programs that emphasize genuine cross-national participation. Immediate involvement of participant nations in the design, refinement, and eventual implementation of management curriculums is seen as an essential ingredient to the successful adoption of new programs. The Rockefeller report further suggested that it was precisely in the realm of short-term project management education that gaps existed, and that an effective way to approach this problem was through the judicious use of case studies.(7)

Finally, it is clear that one important dimension, still insufficiently explored, has hindered the development of appropriate project management curriculums. That is the need to promote "localization" in decision making, especially in developing new curricular models.(8)

In summary, recent studies appear to confirm that there is:
1. A need for more effective management education specifically focused on development project management.
2. A lack of appropriate curricular materials, including case histories, and consequently a lack of appropriate curricular packages.
3. A need for genuine collaborative development of project management curriculums.
4. A need for "localization" in developing project management curricular materials and curricular packages.

The Public Policy Implementation and Project Management (PPIPM) project has responded to these issues in both theory and practice. The PPIPM project team – an international collaborative team composed of scholars and practitioners from Asia, the Pacific, and the United States – cooperated in designing a prototype curriculum especially for project managers. Not only did project-team members develop the curriculum from an appropriate concept, the Integrated Project Planning and Management Cycle (IPPMC), they also developed appropriate curricular materials. These materials included a recommended set of readings selected from over 2,000 books and articles on project management, development project case studies written especially to enhance the study of project management, and a teachers' guide on the use of case studies. Collectively embodying the concept of the integrated project cycle, the materials have been packaged into a sixteen-week (six hours/day, five days/week) curriculum, for which a detailed syllabus was prepared. However, as will be indicated later, flexibility was built into the package, thus allowing individual users to adapt the materials to region-specific needs.

CASE HISTORY APPROACH

Perhaps the most innovative feature of the PPIPM curriculum is its systematic use of case histories organized around a coherent conceptual framework: the integrated project cycle. The case method for management training has a long history, perhaps most distinguished by the Harvard Business School.(9) The use of the case method in the social sciences reveals a number of strengths to this approach. Individuals are allowed to think about and analyze the subject matter in the context of all the complexity and difficulties of the real world. Case materials force the learner to think purposefully and constructively, and allow freer channels of communication among students, as well as between students and teachers. Students are no longer cast in their habitual role of passive receivers of information but are placed in a situation requiring independent, willful, active thought. This process promotes mature behavior in individuals who are likely to be in future leadership and policy-making positions. Case histories are often more interesting than more abstract text material (though they do not by any means replace formal text material) in the sense that they are experiential and ideally represent real-life situations. Finally, perhaps the strongest characteristic of the case method is that it puts the student in the position of learning to utilize theories and facts and take responsibility for action. This action component is missing in, for example, the lecture-discussion method.

All the foregoing does not mean that the case method lacks problems or weaknesses. In the first place, it is often initially frustrating for students who have been spoon-fed with the lecture method to be suddenly thrown into the presence of a situation that demands action-oriented analytical thinking. Students also find out very quickly that they cannot always think of all of the aspects of a particular case, and they also discover that each individual perceives the cases differently. Often the student's first impression is that the material is too complex, and some lack of motivation may result. This situation, however, is ideal for bringing the notion of teamwork and cooperation into the class, a concept also rather alien to the ordinary classroom setting. The point can be made that most work in the development sector today involves teams of individuals, and that a start can be made in this direction during the training period through the effective use of case histories.

But perhaps the most serious problem revolves around the linkages between the case materials and materials auxiliary to the entire course. Experience with the use of case materials on educational planning and policy making clearly demonstrates the need for some sort of organizing framework ideally applied to the case materials before their preparation. In short, the ideal curricular situation would be a conceptual framework uniformly applied to the development of the case histories as well as a framework to organize discussion and analysis of the case studies. In this context, the PPIPM project is innovative. The integrated project planning and management cycle utilized by both case-history writers and teachers provides the kind of coherence and organization lacking in so many other case-method texts. This fact brings up the issue of curriculum development in general and the question of developing innovative curricular and instructional models.

PPIPM: CURRICULUM AND INSTRUCTION

It is highly likely that most development projects in the future will contain an instructional component. Increasingly, national governments, funding agencies, and educational institutions are requiring that a development project contain a mechanism to disseminate the most successful aspects of the project. The emphasis is on replicating appropriate and workable projects rather than on pigeonholing the project as an end in itself. Translated into educational terms, this means curriculum development and instructional design. Because the PPIPM program is essentially an instructional and training model, and because the process of the development of this curricular package contains some important and interesting features, this section will explore the major curricular and instructional lessons of the PPIPM program, some of which may be useful for others who are embarking on a curriculum and instructional development program. The discussion will be in the context of current thinking and experience in the fields of curriculum and instruction; those elements that have emerged as most innovative will be identified and analyzed. There are several levels that could be explored; for the purposes of this section, however, we will concentrate on curricular theory, curriculum planning, curriculum design, instructional design, and, finally, some implications for implementation.

The field of curriculum theory is recognized as undeveloped and theoretically weak. Yet some advances have been made in the past few years(10) drawing upon models adapted from the physical and social sciences. Most prominent among these models is the systems approach. While few curriculum theorists actually utilize a strict systems model, many of them employ several elements of this approach.(11) Grossly simplified, a systems approach to curriculum development takes into account input factors (student needs translated into goals and objectives), influenced by environmental factors, (for example, legal, cultural, national specific, international, etc.), processed by a curriculum model (for example, the IPPMC) to put into operation the goals and objectives, leading finally to the output of learners, with specific levels of skills to be evaluated and fed back through workshops, conferences, and other meetings for continuous revision and redevelopment. Again, it should be stressed that not all writers would include all these steps, but many now agree that for curriculum theory to develop more rigor, some form of systematic approach to development must emerge. As will be seen later in the discussion of planning, the PPIPM program indeed did satisfy many of the requirements of the systems approach, and in this sense the continued development and refinement of the integrated project cycle model will contribute to curriculum theory in general and to training curriculum in particular. The key to this approach remaining innovative is that the system remain flexible in curriculum ("a grouping of learning opportunities planned to achieve a single major set of closely related educational goals with corollary subgoals and specific objectives").(12) If flexibility exists here, then the international impact of the project will be more meaningful, as each national setting will be able to develop its own personalized curriculum domain.

To translate basic theoretical precepts into a usable curricular product, some form of curricular plan must be followed. The conventional approach has generally involved completing four major tasks: selection and identification of learning objectives, selection and creation of appropriate learning experiences, the organization of learning experiences to achieve maximum cumulative effects, and the evaluation of the product for revision and improvement. More recently, however, curriculum planners have developed more sophisticated approaches that go conceptually beyond these four tasks. Curriculum planning can thus be viewed as a process involving the determination of precise boundaries for the instructional unit, systematic identification of subject matter, transformation of the subject matter into learning materials, and providing more or less precise guidelines for the instructors. Furthermore, this process can be delineated in the format of a plan: "a plan for providing sets of learning opportunities to achieve broad goals and related specific objectives for an identifiable population served by a single (instructional) center."(13) Conceptualizing curriculum development as a plan is a much more functional approach for many nations already engaged in national and local level planning. Indeed, the PPIPM program was developed in a planning mode. Step-by-step procedures were followed in utilizing expert judgment to determine the boundaries of the subject matter, selected criteria were utilized for grouping the subject matter (focusing conceptually on the IPPMC model), and the subject matter was appropriately aligned with specific methods of instruction. Planning was a major factor here in assuring that the various components were appropriately sequenced and that various points of view were reflected in the construction of the materials.

A second innovative feature related to curriculum planning was the effective development and use of cooperative networks. The East-West Center as an institution and the PPIPM project represent a useful example of the utilization of networks for cooperative curriculum planning. The essence of this approach involves several basic aspects that can be summarized as follows: 1) utilizing the network to seek common goals; 2) assuring that all groups involved in the implementation of the final product are adequately represented; 3) providing competent group leadership which shifts periodically among the membership; 4) utilizing alternative forms of communication through the use of workshops, conferences, on-site meetings, etc.; 5) providing adequate time and facilities for planning. The seven-nation network established at the outset of the project and the institutional facilities of the East-West Center satisfied the basic requirements of effective network utilization and contributed to the curriculum project as a whole.

It is important to remember, however, that planning models only provide a basis for launching a curriculum development project. The next critical step, involving a process rarely followed by most curriculum projects, is to choose an appropriate curriculum design. With regard to design choices, a rather doctrinaire approach has been utilized by many curriculum projects whereby models that worked for certain courses of study have been transferred uncritically to other subject matter with little or no analysis. In PPIPM, several planning models were considered, the additional elements discussed earlier were analyzed, and the relationships among these elements were explored. Following this process, answers were sought to questions raised in each of four areas: 1) objectives, exploring such considerations as cultural constraints, learner characteristics, and institutional objectives; 2) curriculum experience, focusing on the nature of the knowledge to be transmitted in terms of resources available to each of the participant nations; 3) organizational centers for curriculum, with decisions made on field of study, identification (how broadly to define project management) and method of integrating the learning experiences; 4) determination of scope and sequence, with organization of subject matter sequentially and cumulatively characterizing the final design stage. The concluding step in the process involved integrating a variety of design approaches into one overall design appropriate to the integrated project cycle (for example, the discipline approach, social activities and problems, process skills, individual needs and interests were all integrated through the use of case histories and the IPPMC model). This unique blending of design approaches that are normally kept separate represented the concluding stage of the design process for the PPIPM program.

Finally, having completed the planning and design modes, the PPIPM curriculum project began a process of choosing the most appropriate instructional design. This area shows two basic considerations. The first is the question of who designs the instructional system. Problems in the past have been with the uncoordinated effort of individuals in the curriculum project in planning, designing, and implementing an instructional system. Gagne points out that the ideal instructional design model for the future is the consortia arrangement of representatives of the various parties involved in the final implementation of the product.(14) The PPIPM network represented such a consortium effort and thus from the start avoided many of the problems of lack of coordination.

The second basic consideration of instructional design involves the twelve basic steps considered essential for effective instructional design and development. These steps, while similar to those identified for curriculum development, are now to be viewed in terms of instructional design development. Briefly, they are:

1. Analysis and identification of instructional needs.
2. Definition of instructional goals and objectives.
3. Identification of alternative ways to satisfy the needs.
4. Effective design of the instructional system components.
5. Accurate analysis of material and human resources required, resources available, and constraints on resources.
6. Construction of an action plan to remove or modify resource constraints.
7. Selection and development of actual instructional materials.
8. Design of student assessment procedures.
9. Field testing, teacher education, and formative evaluation of the product.
10. Revision, adjustment, and further evaluation of the product.
11. A more complete summative evaluation.
12. Final operational installation in an institutional setting.

Most curriculum projects, it should be noted, do not attend to all these steps and in fact rarely focus on more than two or three. In the case of the PPIPM projects, only three of the steps outlined were not followed, and it is important to discuss why this decision was made. Steps 5, 6, and 8 were deliberately excluded from the planning design of the broad network of cooperative institutions that comprised the curriculum team, for the following reason: in cross-cultural, international curriculum development projects, the gravest problems arise from the difficulties a curriculum team has in making an accurate assessment of the broad area of resource and resource constraints and the sensitive issue of learner assessment. These areas are best left to the individual consumers of the curriculum product – in this case, the national institutions that implement the project. The PPIPM project follows this policy, and initial findings indicate that the project has taken hold and has become more effective as a result.

IMPLEMENTATION OF THE PPIPM PROTOTYPE CURRICULUM

The PPIPM project, however, did not stop with the international collaborative development of the prototype curriculum. The curriculum was actually implemented in seven nations. Conducting the implementation in their own countries, project team members employed "localization in decision making" by modifying the prototype curriculum to their nation's particular needs and experiences. As a result, each national program was slightly different. Some programs added materials, some deleted materials, and some developed materials more appropriate to their needs. Some programs employed the curriculum in university or other academic settings, and others adopted components of the curriculum for short-term training purposes. In all cases, the basic organizational device was the integrated project cycle.

In 1978 programs were implemented in seven nations and their outcomes were reported at a workshop held in September, 1978 at the East-West Center in Honolulu. The seven countries reported program results as follows:

New Zealand

The local agency spearheading the development of project management courses was the Management Education and Development Centre at Massey University. Academic courses on Project Management at the Master in Business Administration level commenced in 1979.

A training course for the Pacific Region was held in early 1978 and was evaluated at the workshop. A variety of faculty was utilized to present effectively the many specialized topics in the curriculum. Faculty were generally ranked high by the students. Those who were more involved in on-the-job training, however, experienced some difficulty. A total of eighteen participants, from several Pacific Islands, and six observers, took part in the course. The methodology utilized was lecture-discussion. There was a total of thirty-eight sessions, one per topic, and the sessions varied from two hours to two days with an evaluation per session. Use of test items was found to positively motivate the participants, who as a result took the course of study very seriously. Readings included twenty-five set readings and three PPIPM case studies: Pacific Island Livestock Development; Way Abung Transmigration; and Laguna Rural Social Development.

Malaysia

The National Institute of Public Administration, Malaysia (INTAN) was the local agency responsible for developing and conducting a training program on project planning and management. This course of study was based both upon the PPIPM project and the United Nations Asian and Pacific Development Administration Centre (APDAC). The training course required eight weeks; six weeks full-time for class work and two weeks for field work. A group of twenty-four were selected out of thirty-three applicants who came primarily from public sector middle management levels (for example, from the Ministry of Agriculture, Public Works, etc.). A minimum of three years' working experience was required of the participants. A variety of teaching techniques was utilized in the course, such as lecture-discussion, exercises, locally produced case studies, and group discussions and presentations. International collaboration occurred with visiting lecturers from the Philippines. A total of fifteen lectures was presented. Course content included the following modules:

- Development planning and administration   1½ weeks
- Project planning and analysis   2 weeks
- Project organization and management   2½ weeks
- Field work   2 weeks

Selected PPIPM readings and articles were included in the course of study.

United States

The country reports for the United States came from the Department of Public Administration of the University of Arizona and the Department of Education of the University of California, Los Angeles. At the University of California, the IPPMC model and curriculum guide was utilized in a graduate-level seminar on "Education and National Development." Students were asked to utilize the materials to analyze selected case histories of educational projects in Africa, Asia, and Latin America. The cases were critiqued in class and revised according to the IPPMC model. At the end of the ten-week session the model, curriculum guide, and cases were evaluated and found to be an effective approach to gaining experience in educational project planning and practice.

An academic course on project management was conducted at the University of Arizona for one semester, three hours a week. Participants or students in the course were mostly graduate students from a variety of professional backgrounds (for example, engineering, anthropology, education). A total of fifteen students was enrolled in the course. The basic teaching methodology used was lecture-discussion. The course was taught primarily by one individual, but experts were utilized on occasion for specific technical subjects. In identifying projects to analyze, this course provided an interesting balance between public and private sector projects and technical and social ones. Reading materials used were two textbooks, PPIPM readings, articles, and several case histories.

Philippines

In the Philippines, a major step forward in institutional cooperation was taken in 1979 when the University of the Philippines and De La Salle University signed a consortium agreement to allow their respective programs, the Administrative Development Center and the Project Management Center, to offer joint academic and training courses in project management.

An academic course on project management was conducted for one semester, three and a half hours a week, at the De La Salle Graduate School of Business. This program would lead to an M.B.A. in the Project Management degree program. The course of study was divided into three segments: Management – twenty-seven units; Project Management Electives – twelve units; Thesis – six units. Seventy percent of the participants were directly involved in project management activities divided equally between the public and private sectors. Teaching methodology included lecture-discussion, exercises, case histories, group presentations and management games. Materials used were a compilation of readings and exercises. Academic courses on project management were scheduled to be offered at the College of Public Administration and Engineering, University of the Philippines, in 1979.

A training course entitled Project Development and Management was conducted at the Administrative Development Center. Participants engaged in a full seven weeks of study and the course was fully funded by each participant's agency. Those participants who passed a final exam were given six units of credit. A total of thirty-nine participants completed the course, eleven from engineering, ten from economics, and eighteen from a variety of other fields. Most of the participants came from the middle-level management sector. Methodology for conducting the sessions included lecture-discussion, case histories, panel work, exercises, games, and fieldwork. In the area of fieldwork, participants attended projects at the national computing center and visited the largest dam and irrigation project in Asia for several days. Course content included six modules:

- Introduction to project development and management
- Project planning and design
- Management tools and other techniques
- Project implementation
- Human behavior in project management
- Project evaluation

A significant feature of this course was the wide range of faculty resources involved. Thirty-seven specialists provided lectures and exercises for the participants, including a visiting specialist from Malaysia. Evaluation of this curriculum was conducted on three occasions. In addition to the activities listed, an in-plant training program was conducted for the government-owned energy company. Pre-workshop meetings held with top management personnel proved to be an essential element in successfully implementing the program. The faculty consisted of subject specialists, all of whom had teaching experience. Outside specialists were also brought in. The participants were required to have college degrees, actual project responsibilities, and basic skills in such areas as network modeling. The training course lasted two weeks and consisted of fifteen project managers and officers. Teaching methodology included lecture-discussion, exercises, games and case histories. Course content included:

- Project planning and preoperating activities
- Tools in project management

● Project implementation/completion/evaluation

Other institutes and agencies, having heard about the East-West Center's PPIPM project materials, also adopted the cycle concept and utilized some PPIPM materials. These included: the University of the Philippines Institute for Small Scale Industries, Bancom Institute for Development Technology, Fund for the Assistance to Private Education, Development Academy of the Philippines, and Private Development Corporation of the Philippines. Future plans for 1979 included another workshop and a case history writing workshop.

Indonesia

The local institution involved in conducting the training course related to project management was the Institute for Economic and Social Research, University of Indonesia. Because of a policy decision in 1970, Indonesia's National Development Planning Agency (Bappenas) embarked on a program to provide increased numbers of planning officers and project managers. In cooperation with the Faculty of Economics of the University of Indonesia, Bappenas established a training course called National Development Planning Program (PPN). PPN has designed a thirty-two-week (eight-month) course of which two and a half weeks were devoted to development administration and project management. Forty-five participants attended the course in 1978; they were from middle-management sectors and averaged thirty-five years of age. Participants were required to have a minimum of two year's work experience, a university degree, facility in English, high motivation, and work in areas that were project-oriented. The methodology used for conducting the course was lecture-discussion. Course materials were textbooks and readings, and course instructors included both permanent staff and several guest specialists. Areas of emphasis in the course were:

● Monitoring, evaluation, control and termination
● Direction of operations and personnel
● Planning techniques
● Organization techniques
● Acquisition of resources

Taiwan

In Taiwan, a course on project management was offered by Professor Huang Ta-chou of the Department of Agriculture, National Taiwan University. Participants were fifteen graduate-level degree students who enrolled in the course for one semester (sixteen weeks). The course utilized the integrated project cycle and several readings from the course syllabus. An innovative method was utilized to overcome obvious language difficulties by requiring that students who were fluently bilingual read intensively and translate three to five of the readings in the PPIPM syllabus into Chinese to facilitate future use of the total curriculum. It was projected that within two years the majority of the curriculum would be in Chinese and thus available to a much wider audience.

Iran

Shiraz University, Department of Civil Engineering, was the site for curriculum implementation in Iran. The integrated project cycle was used as an organizing concept for a class in engineering. Attempts were made to translate relevant portions of the curriculum, but this experiment met with some difficulty and was not continued. It was decided to require English as a prerequisite for the course. A sixteen-week curriculum with resource officials from the government was planned for implementation in 1978 along with a nine-week winter course. This was intended to be a program for both training purposes and professional development as well as academic training of students at the graduate level. It was also planned to conduct an organizing seminar in Tehran with senior government officials who will conduct a needs analysis and initiate a strategy for wider dissemination and diffusion of the PPIPM concept.

IMPLICATIONS FOR CURRICULUM DEVELOPMENT IMPLEMENTATION

The PPIPM project presents some interesting examples of both the problems and potential of jointly-developed curriculum designed to be implemented on a national-specific scale (see tables I.1, I.2, I.3). One important feature was the early formation of a truly international project team that followed the project through the various stages of needs assessment, development of a theoretical foundation (the integrated project cycle), determination of instructional goals and objectives, identification of an instructional audience, actual product development, and refinement and revision.

Another feature of the project was the actual implementation of the prototype curriculum through a collaborative effort that emphasized the particular needs of each nation. The important ingredient here was the coherence provided by the integrated project cycle, which was flexible enough to allow maximum adaptability by each participant. Finally, the initial implementation was followed up with an evaluation workshop to share experiences, to engage in refinement, and to proceed to the next stage of implementation. The lessons of the project appear to be in at least three areas.

First, the success of the project is linked directly to the fact that the curriculum team was composed of key individuals working in a genuine atmosphere of cooperation and collaboration. This was not a top-down curriculum development project with the "transfer" of a model from one sector to another. Second, unlike many such projects in

Table I.1. Courses in Project Management in
Different Countries*

Country	Academic Course	Training Course
New Zealand	X	X
Malaysia		X
United States	X	
Philippines	X	X
Indonesia	X	X
Taiwan		
Iran		X

*Courses offered at the institutions represented by the workshop
participants.

Table I.2. Comparison of Training Courses Offered

	New Zealand	Malaysia	Philippines	Indonesia
1. Agency	University	Government Planning	University	University
2. Duration	12 weeks	8 weeks	7 weeks 2 weeks (in-plant)	32 weeks
3. Number of Participants	18	24	39 15 (in-plant)	45

Table I.3. Comparison of Academic Courses Offered

	New Zealand	United States	Philippines
1. Name of University	Massey University*	University of Arizona University of California, Los Angeles	University of the Philippines De La Salle University
2. Type of University	Public	Public	Public/ Private
3. Program/ College	MBA	MPA/Ph.D.	MPA/ME/ MBA

*Programs will start in 1979.

which content may be first-rate and materials well conceived but coherent organizational format is lacking, the PPIPM project provided the participants (and those instructors who will increasingly utilize the curriculum package) with an innovative, flexible organizational device: the integrated project cycle. Finally, the most important lesson has to do with the dissemination and diffusion features of the project. By developing a curriculum team composed of key individuals in each of the participant nations, the project was assured of widespread implementation and experimentation. In short, it did not simply remain on the drawing board, as has been the fate of many such projects.

It should be remembered that although the PPIPM project has satisfied many of the criteria of a well-conceived development project, many problems still remain and will continue to emerge during the course of future implementation. Problems related to language of instruction, appropriate case history development, differential levels of course participants, and adequacy of teaching faculty will continue to provide challenges to the curriculum team. These problems have been frankly discussed by all participants and plans are underway to develop strategies to overcome them in the future. In the end, it is clear that this project, along with the many others that are currently being developed and implemented, must be discussed and shared as widely as possible, for a critical reason: the developmental questions raised earlier continue to pose difficulties for national planners and are not likely to disappear in the near future.

NOTES

(1) Commonwealth Consultative Committee on South and Southeast Asia, Special Topic Papers: United Kingdom, Vietnam, Thailand, Philippines, Pakistan, Malaysia, Korea, Indonesia, India, Burma (Manila: 1970).

(2) Ibid., p. 2.

(3) Ibid., p. 1.

(4) See Ibid., complete reports in series.

(5) Yat Hoong Yip, Role of the Universities in National Development Planning in Southeast Asia (Singapore: Regional Institute of Higher Education and Development, 1971), p. 35.

(6) Lee Dyer and Gar D. Paulson, Project Management: An Annotated Bibliography, Cornell Industrial and Labor Relations Bibliography Series, no. 13 (New York: Cornell University Press, 1976).

(7) Laurence D. Stifel, James S. Coleman, and Joseph E. Black, Education and Training for Public Sector Management in Development Countries (New York: Rockefeller Foundation, 1977), p. 48.

(8) Donald Adams, "Development Education," Comparative Education Review 27, no. 2/3: 310.

(9) M. McNair, ed., The Case Method at the Harvard Business School (New York: McGraw-Hill, 1954), p. 54.

(10) For a more complete discussion, see J.G. Saylor and W.M. Alexander, Planning Curriculum for Schools (New York: Holt, Rinehart and Winston, 1976); and J.R. Gress and D.E. Purpel, Curriculum: An Introduction to the Field (Berkeley: McCutchan, 1978).

(11) Saylor and Alexander, Planning Curriculum.

(12) Ibid.

(13) Ibid.

(14) R.A. Gagne and L.J. Briggs, Principles of Instructional Design (New York: Holt, Rinehart and Winston, 1974).

Basic Concepts

1 Development Projects and the Integrated Project Planning and Management Cycle (IPPMC)*

PROJECTS AND DEVELOPMENT

Development is normally defined in two ways: in economic growth and in social progress. In economic terms, development is the process by which a country reaches the position where it can provide for its own growth without relying on special arrangements for the transfer of resources from other countries – where, in short, its growth becomes self-sustaining on a reasonable level, enabling it, through its own efforts, to secure the benefits of industrial and technological progress for its people.(1) In terms of social progress, development means improving the quality of life for the mass of people. Stable and healthy development in a country should provide two important things: 1) an equitable distribution of wealth, and 2) a broad popular participation in the political and economic life of the country. There are several social dimensions to the development process. Development implies change and the transformation of society. The process may bring about changes in a society's fundamental attitudes to life and work. Often development means changes must be made in social, cultural, and political institutions.(2) The development process can also be viewed as a path moving away from "underdevelopment" or rising out of poverty. .

Development then basically relates to selected changes in the social and economic structures of society in an effort to reach predetermined objectives acceptable to society as a whole. Where the development process and consequent changes are not acceptable to society, discontent can lead to overthrow of the authorities in charge of development.

---

*Portions of this chapter were adapted from Louis J. Goodman and Ralph N. Love, Management of Development Projects (New York: Pergamon Press, 1979), chapter 1.

3

Development, as narrowly defined in economic aggregate terms, is not always synonymous with equitable economic growth. In some developing countries, for example, average gross national product (GNP) per capita might rise while income inequality increases – the poor become poorer and the rich become richer.

The interdependence among economic, social, and political elements in society have brought new variables into focus in recent times. New nations pursuing rapid development through the instruments of formal plans have recognized the limitation of economic indicators as measurements of development. The problem of reconciling economics with social dimension in development plans and translating them into programs and projects is a complex task for planners and policy makers. The need to identify quantitative indicators of what are essentially qualitative phenomena involves indirect measures and successive approximations and refinements. The planning of development is, therefore, always a learning process.

Development planning in most countries is concerned with both long- and short-term objectives. The long-term objectives normally encompass sustained economic growth, a more equitable distribution of national products and services, and improved allocation of the country's resources. Determination of priorities and emphasis is dependent upon political perspectives, the social structure of the country, and the shape and level of economic activities currently taking place. The short-term goals generally involve the maintenance of a high level of employment, the stabilization of the level of forces and the promotion of a favorable balance of payment. Material plans for economic growth have been likened to national flags and national airlines as essential items in the paraphernalia of nation states.(3)

The long-term development plan and objectives of countries are, however, rarely achieved in full. Priorities may change during, say, a five-year planning period. Economic and political circumstances within a country or a region can also alter development objectives dramatically. Problems of implementing plans are also common in developing countries. Lack of well-qualified personnel and appropriate organizations to implement development schemes can hamper the achievement of planning goals.

Many approaches are adopted to deal with shortfalls in attaining the stated goals and objectives of national development plans, programs, and projects. These range from comprehensive reforms of the civil service to the strengthening of planning, implementation, and evaluation capabilities of economic and social planning bodies, the sectoral ministries, state and regional machinery, and local governments.

Some of the changes and reforms introduced are structural or organizational; for example, creation of centralized bodies for overall planning, organizing planning units from ministerial, departmental, bureau levels to regional/state, provincial and municipal levels, state/regional, and local levels. Other reforms focused on improving technical and management capability for formulation and implementation, such as improving the statistical and data base for planning, forecasting, monitoring, and evaluating development programs and projects through employment of both "hardware" components (computers and EDP) or "software" (MIS, data banks, national, and regional accounts).

Translating national development plans into operational programs and investment projects is one of the most critical and difficult tasks facing planners and administrators in developing countries. The problems arise in part from the inability of planners to communicate concisely the investment implication of long-range plans and policies to national ministries, provincial and local governments, autonomous agencies, and private firms with investment resources.(4) The separation between plan formulation and implementation has rendered many plans to be mere statements of intent covering ambiguous objectives without engaging in specific implementation strategy that may provide adequate investment guidelines and possible contingency measures for any foreseen implementation problems. The failure to provide adequate interaction within the planning process among the constituencies of the government, particularly the beneficiaries of socioeconomic projects, has created a huge gap in development.

Effective strategic planning and management for development must take into account the following guidelines: 1) planning must be based on a thorough understanding of the political environment in which policies are made; 2) it must adopt a variety of forms and styles that are directly related to major functions in the policy making process; and 3) it must fashion a variety of intervention and interaction techniques into strategies for influencing not only the choice of alternatives but also the implementation of selected policies.(5) An examination of the broad development themes of the seventies in developing countries shows that they have concentrated on rural development, issues of poverty, social equity, and balanced growth. The development of the rural sector has assumed particular attention in Third World countries, as these countries are predominantly agricultural and rural in character. The development and progress achieved since the United Nations Planning Decade of the fifties and the First Development Decade of the sixties, with their concern for industrial development, has generally not benefited the vast majority of people, particularly the rural poor.

Various programs and projects costing billions of dollars have been undertaken in many Third World countries principally aimed at reducing poverty, modernizing the agricultural sector, and accelerating rural development through infrastructural facilities (for example, irrigation, dams, roads, and bridges) and rural services (such as health, education, credit, and family planning). Although the main development thrust has been the development of the rural sector, the overall impact of international assistance and lending programs has not sufficiently altered the basic landscape of rural poverty and underdevelopment.(6)

One viewpoint suggests that the existing socio/economic and political structures and processes tend to skew or bias development in favor of urban, commercial, and industrial sectors (7) thereby further perpetuating the imbalanced growth patterns – inherited from centuries of colonial rule – between the modern and developed metropolitan/urban centers on one hand and the underdeveloped agricultural and rural communities on the other.

Although governments in Third World countries have actively espoused through national policies and development plans the concept of balanced growth, social justice, and equity, and the accelerated development of agriculture and the rural sector, the actual flow and allocation of resources from domestic and international sources to the rural sector have not been of such scale as to match and sustain the priority rating generally given to rural development. This fact may partly be traced to conditions in some countries where the larger proportion of development resources are controlled by the private sector enterprises whose policies and activities in pursuit of profits and returns on investment are often not aligned (or cannot be closely redirected) to achieve national development priorities to accelerate rural development. An example is the failure of the industrial dispersal program from urban/commercial and industrial centers to underdeveloped regions of the country, despite the priority given to this policy by some Third World governments. In some cases, government programs and projects for agriculture and rural development tend to favor the relatively economically well-off members of the rural community, thereby excluding from the development process a large number of economically disadvantaged and poorer members of the rural community.

Out of the euphoria for the promise of planning the United Nations Planning and First Development Decades of the fifties and sixties emerged strong voices for post-mortems and analyses of what went wrong in development strategies. Even in the late fifties and mid-sixties, serious questions were already raised concerning the efficacy of comprehensive planning in countries where the administrative infrastructure to carry out such plans is weak. Some questioned the apparent preoccupation of developing countries for macro and comprehensive planning and the consequent neglect and lack of priority attention given to the development of feasible and viable projects (macro planning) as a base for comprehensive plans. It has been mentioned that the administrative and management capability for plan implementation often poses serious obstacles for the implementation of comprehensive plans for development. As a result, implementation became a catchword and priority concern in the UN development strategy for the Second Development Decade of the seventies;(8) this concern will extend through the eighties as well.

Shortfalls in expected benefits from development programs and projects resulted in the broadening of criteria used by international funding institutions through the incorporation of noneconomic factors in evaluating and appraising developing project proposals from the developing countries.(9) The administrative capability for plan formulation and plan implementation was incorporated as a variable when appraising projects for foreign and domestic funding. Evaluation of projects equally receive national and international attention and interest be-

cause of the concern not only for efficiency but also for the effectiveness of the projects for achieving the desired results.(10)

International funding institutions such as the World Bank, together
with national socioeconomic planning bodies, recognize that the huge
financial investment in large infrastructure projects in developing
countries needs specialized administrative support. The need to develop
administrative capability through strengthening both planning as well as
plan implementation capability for development programs and projects
is now well recognized. The interest in implementation problems to
redress the preoccupation in planning has added a vital dimension to the
management of development projects, particularly rural development
projects. Planning and implementation should be viewed as being part of
an inseparable process. Many implementation problems can therefore be
traced to the planning process. Plans must, if they are to be effective,
be continually adjusted to account for actual conditions. Questions of
project implementability have sensitized the planning process to the
need to examine a variety of factors and variables which could impede
successful implementation. The variables include political, economic,
administrative, and sociocultural factors that relate to the projects.(11)

When the planning process has been finalized, implementation at the
broad sector program level must be undertaken. A development program consists essentially of an interrelated series of development
projects. A road-building construction program, for example, can involve a string of road construction projects, linked in time, proximity,
and function. Implementation of plans and programs to be successful
must therefore be successful at the grassroots level – the project level.
Projects are thus the "building blocks" of development. Without properly implemented projects, development plans become only empty
objectives remaining forever elusive. A thorough understanding of the
role, status, procedures, and methods relating to projects is therefore
very important for those charged with the responsibility of implementing and managing development projects.

To clarify the mass of procedures, methods, and possibilities relating to the management of projects, it is useful to have a framework
within which to view projects. In fact, there is an underlying unity of
process that is the same in all projects, even though each one is
different.   This unity of process can be understood through using the
concept of the integrated planning and management cycle (IPPMC).

THE INTEGRATED PROJECT PLANNING AND MANAGEMENT CYCLE

The integrated project planning and management cycle (IPPMC) is a
conceptual tool for observing and analyzing the single process that
constitutes the life of a development project (fig. 1.1). It is a
framework developed to clarify the mass of procedures arising out of
this process.   The IPPMC may be divided into four major phases: 1)
planning, appraisal, and design; 2) selection, approval, and activation; 3)
operation, control, and handover; and 4) evaluation and refinement.
Specific tasks may be further identified within these four phases.

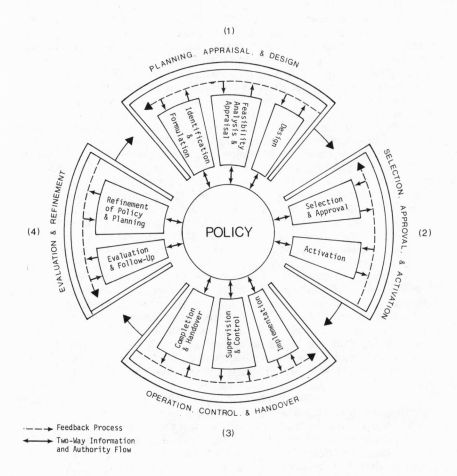

(1)

PLANNING. APPRAISAL. & DESIGN

Identification & Formulation

Feasibility Analysis & Appraisal

Design

SELECTION. APPROVAL. & ACTIVATION

Refinement of Policy & Planning

POLICY

Selection & Approval

Activation

(4)   (2)

EVALUATION & REFINEMENT

Evaluation & Follow-Up

Completion & Handover

Supervision & Control

Implementation

OPERATION. CONTROL. & HANDOVER

·——→ Feedback Process
◄———► Two-Way Information
and Authority Flow

(3)

Fig. 1.1. Integrated project planning and management
cycle: the four phases.

Figure 1.1 illustrates the relationships among the phases of the
project cycle, the tasks within each of the phases, and the overall
dependency on central policy issues. It must be emphasized that the
project cycle is an ideal model; not every project will conform exactly
to it. The tasks of the cycle, furthermore, are not necessarily sequential – they may take place at the same time or in a different order
– nor are all of them necessarily required. For example, the head of a
country might decide that a dam is needed for a hydro-electric project.
The leader decides to have it built and instructs subordinates according-

ly, thereby bypassing the first two tasks in Phase I of the cycle. A continual feedback and dependency relationship does exist among the tasks, however. Each task is dependent upon and is influenced by the others.

There is a two-way flow of information between those responsible for policy and those responsible for managing each of the project tasks. This feedback to policy makers and management's response is an important part of the integrated project cycle. Decisions on project implementation, though in the hands of the manager on a day-to-day basis, are closely linked to the policy framework in which the project operates. Thus, all tasks within the four phases of the IPPMC are tied together by policies emanating from the various authorities concerned with the projects.

The IPPMC framework emphasizes the interdependent and cyclical nature of projects. However, because each task within the four phases of the cycle is distinct and must be examined as an individual entity proceeding in an orderly time sequence the cycle must also reflect this linear progression. The IPPMC matrix in Table 1.1 illustrates the linear organization of several actual projects, examined in case histories in the first book of this series, evaluating how well the tasks for each project were performed.(12) The IPPMC matrix is useful in analyzing how well the various phases and tasks of a project were undertaken. Furthermore, an analysis of performance that is broken down in this manner can sometimes indicate whether or not a weakness during one phase of a project caused difficulties in the implementation of other phases.

Some projects, it should be noted, may not proceed beyond the first phase. After the tasks within the planning, appraisal, and design phase have been completed, the information fed back to policy makers may lead to a decision to scrap the project. In certain cases, however, for economic, technical, or other reasons, it may not be desirable to stop a project once the first phase has been completed.

With this overview of the integrated project planning and management cycle, we can proceed to examine each of the four phases and their tasks in turn.

Phase 1: Planning, Appraisal, and Design

The first phase of the project is planning, appraisal, and design. There are three basic tasks in this phase: 1) the identification and formulation of the project, 2) the feasibility analysis and appraisal of the project, and 3) the design of the project. The first joint task, identification and formulation, involves the actual conception or identification of a project, which may occur in several ways. Basic needs within a country will induce the implementation of projects to satisfy these needs. The planning process often identifies project possibilities for each sector in society.

Table 1.1. The IPPMC Matrix

Project	Phase 1		Phase 2				Phase 3		Phase 4	
	Identification & Formulation	Feasibility Analysis & Appraisal	Design	Selection & Approval	Activation	Implementation	Supervision & Control	Completion & Handover	Evaluation & Follow-Up	Refinement of Policy & Planning
Bangkok Water Improvement	FS	FW	W	W	FW	FW	FS	W	W	W
Laguna Social Development	FS	FS	FS	FW	FW	W	W	W	W	W
Pacific Islands Life Stock Development	FS	FW	W	FW	FS	FW	W	W	W	W
Way Abung Transmigration	FS	FW	FW	FS	FS	FW	FW	FW	W	W
Malia Health Project	FS	W	W	W	W	FW	W	W	FS	S

Strong = S
Fairly Strong = FS
Fairly Weak = FW
Weak = W

The major source of projects in developing countries, however, will be the existing departments or ministries, including central planning agencies. Projects may be identified by political parties or government officials. In this case, the motivation to undertake a project may be political, such as an attempt to gain the support of particular constituents. In some countries, private entrepreneurs or multinational corporations will identify projects that meet the criteria established by government.

International agencies have their own procedures for identifying projects. The World Health Organization, for example, describes a step-by-step approach to problem analysis in its manual on project preparation. It suggests that the problem be viewed in terms of consequences, critical elements, objectives, and targets, followed by the identification of potential obstacles. The World Bank identifies projects through a "repeater" system whereby new opportunities develop out of ongoing development programs and projects. Thus existing projects lead to the identification of other projects, and a piggy-back system operates where, as part of one project, funding may be obtained for feasibility studies for subsequent projects. The identification of projects, then, is a process that must take into account various needs, preconditions, and policies if the project idea is to proceed to operational reality.

After a project has been identified, its parameters must be defined. This is part of the formulation task. The formulation of a project involves developing a statement in broad terms which shows the objectives and outputs of the project and also provides an estimate of the various resources required to achieve the project's objectives.

The second set of tasks in the first phase, feasibility analysis, and appraisal, are critical ones that, in effect, involve two distinct operations. A prerequisite of this set of tasks is the development of preliminary designs for the project. The early designs must be detailed enough so that cost estimates and decisions on various aspects of the project can be made.

Feasibility analysis is the process of determining if the project can be implemented. Appraisal is the evaluation of the overall ability of the project to succeed. Projects will proceed to the feasibility stage only if decision makers find them desirable.

While the feasibility analysis and appraisal are being conducted, several critical decisions need to be made. These decisions will determine first, if the project is capable of achieving its objective within the limits imposed by decision makers and second, whether it will proceed. Preliminary estimates of the resources required, and basic decisions about size, location, technology, and administrative needs must be made.

Feasibility and appraisal should be approached systematically and deliberately; time spent in researching the feasibility of a project is usually time well spent. Moreover, the findings at this point of the project's life will be useful during other phases of the project, particularly in Phase 3.

Determining project feasibility depends on the accuracy of the information received. Even though the final detailed design of the project can be undertaken only after approval has been given, the preliminary designs determine the base upon which future decisions will rest. Most developing countries have to contend with a shortage of both design and research and development capabilities. The result may be a lack of attention to critical aspects of the project. When decisions have been made on the overall project concept, its dimensions and parameters, it is then possible to determine the feasibility of the project in the terms required by the policy makers and the funding agents.

Some projects may require a pilot study as part of the feasibility process. Pilot studies provide data to enable more meaningful decisions to be made about larger projects. The appraisal process may require a comparative study to determine the merits of one project over another. Although the project identified may be feasible to implement, a comparative study determines whether resources are best used in the project or in some other form.

Many governments and international agencies have imposed rigid procedures to be followed when their funds are required. While actual details vary from project to project and from organization to organization, a trend over recent years is for more sophisticated and more systematic project-related studies. For example, to receive a recommendation from the United Nations Development Programme (UNDP) for industrial projects, prospective borrowers must undertake market analyses that provide overall national trends in production, foreign trade, consumption, consumer prices, together with details about output type and use, cost of production, and estimated sales. Other agencies have brought in new dimensions to their studies, such as the impact of projects on the social and cultural life of the community, as well as the environmental and ecological impact of the project.

Numerous components of the project can be dealt with in the feasibility report. Studies can relate to the feasibility of the technical, economic, commercial, financial, administrative/managerial, and organizational aspects of the project. Additionally, political, social, environmental, and cultural factors that affect the project may also be included. Various technical alternatives must also be studied to ensure the suggested approach fulfills project requirements.

Economic studies examine the overall sector into which the project falls and consider how the project fits into the broader sector and the national planning framework. Related to economic feasibility studies, commercial studies may be necessary to determine the overall competitive nature of the proposed project. They will examine the market demands for the output of the project, consider the costs of production, and look at all aspects of the project to determine if it is a viable proposition.

Financial studies determine how much capital is required to complete the project. These studies determine whether the project can sustain its financial obligations, have adequate working capital, and generate enough funds to ensure adequate cash flow to keep the project operational.

Administrative/managerial studies determine the adequacy of procedures to control and direct the project. Studies in this area are not always undertaken, even though all projects would benefit from them. Their objective is to determine whether a project that is economically, financially, and commercially sound can be properly implemented by available managerial and administrative procedures. Many countries suffer from a lack of management and administrative capacity to direct projects. Related to this problem is a lack of ability to ensure that a project can be administered effectively within an appropriate agency or organization. Because administration of a project differs from normal departmental procedures, a careful assessment of the operational methods of existing units is necessary to ensure that a project's unique features can be catered to. Even though a project may be conceived and sponsored by an existing department, the department itself may not be the appropriate body to administer it. This is especially the case when the involvement of a wide group of outside personnel and agencies is necessary, since existing departmental procedures are often unable to provide the necessary flexibility.

Once the feasibility studies have been completed, a meaningful appraisal of the project is possible. Policy and decision makers and lending institutions may carry out the appraisal. They satisfy themselves that the project meets the conditions that enable it to proceed. Their concern is to determine whether or not the project is the best means of reaching the objectives they have set. They may review the project itself and alternative means of reaching the objective.

Potential lending institutions may undertake their appraisal with a healthy skepticism toward all phases of the project. They attempt to determine whether or not the project is intrinsically sound and whether or not all the circumstances that surround it are viable.

The last task within this phase of the integrated project cycle is design. As mentioned earlier, preliminary design criteria must be established before the project feasibility and appraisal task begins. Once it has been determined that the project will continue, the design task proceeds. Design is a critical function. It establishes the basic programs, allocates responsibilities, determines activities and resources, and sets down in operational form the areas of priority and functions to be carried out. All inputs relating to projects, including personnel, skills, technical input, and so on, must be determined at this point. Environmental factors, social criteria, technological requirements, and procedures must be assessed and included.

The design task also includes the preparation of blueprints and specifications for construction, facilities, and equipment. Operating plans and work schedules are prepared and brought together in a formal implementation plan; contingency plans may also be prepared. Designers must bring together the views of policy and decision makers and technical experts in such a way that the design reflects the inputs of all those contributing to the project.

Phase 2: Selection, Approval, and Activation

This phase of the project has two major tasks: 1) selection and approval, and 2) activation. Project selection takes place after the project has been accepted by policy makers and funding organizations as meeting the feasibility criteria. At this point, the design function, including the formal implementation plan, has been completed. The project will be well defined, with key elements identified and the inputs required from organizational personnel, technicians, and outside consultants clearly identified. The selection of one project for implementation over another is made on the basis of several criteria. Policy makers consider the overall feasibility of the project and the priority of the project area. If a project fulfills a major need or contributes to national or sector goals and is politically desirable, it may be selected for implementation over a competing project that is not politically important. Funding agencies, however, have a variety of techniques for determining whether resources will be allocated to a particular project. These techniques may range from cost-benefit to other complex forms of analysis. The overall requirement, however, is that the policy makers and the funding agency conclude that the project itself has a priority claim for resources required for the project. Therefore, the selection process is normally a competitive one.

The selection of a project for implementation requires negotiations to be undertaken to obtain formal approval from national authorities, funding agencies, and others contributing to the project. This requires the finalization of funding proposals, agreements, contract documents, including tenders and other contracts and the introduction by government or some other organization of appropriate regulations.

Activation of the program involves the coordination and allocation of resources to make the project operational. Activation is a complex process in which the project manager has to bring together an appropriate project team which may include professionals, technicians, and resource personnel. Other contributions to the project may come from other groups, such as outside consultants, contractors, suppliers, and policy makers in other agencies. The outside inputs must be coordinated with the work of the project team. Responsibility and authority for executing the project must be assigned at this point. This will include the granting of authority to make decisions in areas relating to personnel, legal, financial, organization, procurement, and administration matters.

The activation task must ensure that planning for all phases is undertaken so that delays in vital inputs do not occur. Organizational and administrative procedures, together with feedback and response to policy makers' decisions, will have an important bearing on implementation. Concern for detail and proper planning during activation can save a great deal of time and resources during later phases of the project. At this point, the actual work of the project is about to begin.

Phase 3: Operation, Control, and Handover

Looking at the development project from the outside, the uninitiated observer might mistake this most visible phase for the entire project itself. As has been indicated, Phase 3 in fact makes up only a small part of the integrated project cycle. This phase of the project has three sets of tasks: 1) implementation, 2) supervision and control, and 3) completion and handover.

Implementation involves the allocation of tasks to groups within the project organization. Implementation of the project will be based on procedures set down during the two earlier phases. At this point, a final review of the project design and timetable will be undertaken, and any necessary changes or adjustments will be included. Decisions about the procurement of equipment, resources, and manpower also need to be made. Schedules and time frames need to be established, efficient feedback, communication, and other management information systems must be set up. The responsibility for implementation falls within the jurisdiction of the project manager. The project manager will need to work with policy makers, authorities, and organizations related to the project as well as with policy makers controlling the project. The manager's task is a complex one, requiring him or her to steer the project through many obstacles.

The second set of tasks in Phase 3 is supervision and control. Supervision and control procedures must be activated to provide feedback to both the policy makers and the project manager. Control procedures must identify and isolate problem areas; the limited time span of a project means that fast action is necessary if costly delays are to be avoided. At this point, specific management tools, such as the critical path method (CPM), the program review and evaluation techniques (PERT), and other forms of network analysis, are particularly useful. These control and supervision techniques break down a project into detailed activities and establish the interrelationships between and among the various activities. This allows the project manager to organize the project into manageable components, to coordinate all activities, and to set a time-sequence schedule for project implementation. Although using such techniques means spending more time prior to implementation, it is time well spent. Not only will these techniques give the project internal coherence, but they will also save implementation time by isolating any problems into their appropriate project components.

In addition to internal control, those providing funding for projects will maintain an independent monitoring and control system for the project. The project manager will therefore have to meet control criteria established by either the government or another controlling agency, or perhaps by the funding institution. This may involve using specified procedures, such as international competitive bidding, for supply contracts. Formal procedures are established by many international organizations for the procurement and control of resources.

Whatever supervision and control techniques are used, they must take into account the changing patterns that occur during the life of the project. These may include changes within the policy and political structures, difficulties with procurement, and poor performances by project-team members and contractors. In many cases, the overall project design will need to be reviewed. Many technicians are involved in the supervision and control processes, and adequate information flow in all directions – from the project manager and from those within his organization assigned with special responsibilities – is essential if these procedures are to be effective. As part of supervision and control, any problems relating to environmental factors must also be identified and appropriate action taken.

Control procedures are useful only if action is taken to correct any deviation. It should also be noted that both personnel and input patterns change naturally as the project proceeds through its four phases. As work on some tasks is completed, other personnel, experts, and contractors move in to begin new tasks. Personnel must adjust to their new environment, and procedures need to be reviewed and updated to meet the changing situation.

Project completion prepares the project for phasing out and handover to another form of administration. These are the third tasks of this phase. Project completion consists of scaling down and dismantling the project organization. It also involves the transfer of project personnel to other areas of operation. Assets and other facilities, including equipment and technology, may not be required by the operational project. Provision for their transference must be made, since it is not always possible to have an automatic transition from the developmental to the operational stage.

The process of completion may take place over a considerable period. As various parts of a project are completed, however, they may be taken over by a new organization, and handover may therefore be accomplished in a piecemeal manner. It is essential that development resource linkages between scaled-down projects and those projects in the elementary stages of implementation be planned systematically to ensure optimal use of limited project resources, particularly in the context of broader development programs. The new project, when operational, will have an effect on other aspects within the sector. As the project becomes operational, the new controlling organization must have the skills, personnel, and technical backup required. Key personnel working in the development stage will often transfer over to the new controlling organization.

In cases where technical, financial, political, or other factors prevent projects from being completed according to the original terms, handover and termination procedures may have to be implemented at an earlier stage. This may involve considerable loss as far as the project is concerned. In this situation, the objective should be to liquidate the project in a way that will obtain the most benefit.

As a project nears completion, special reporting systems should be set up so that full information relating to the project is available.

Completion reports will be prepared for various authorities, including funding organizations and policy makers.

The actual handover of the operation of the project involves finalization of contracts, termination of loan facilities, and so on. Handover also includes the transfer of the project activity and resources to the new administration. This is a critical task. While the development of the project can be viewed initially as a creative phase, once the project is completed, it must be viewed as a long-term operational program.

Phase 4: Evaluation and Refinement

The final phase of the project is the evaluation and refinement of policy and planning factors. The first task is <u>evaluation and follow-up</u>. While it is possible to evaluate project results immediately, actual benefits both anticipated and unanticipated, together with side effects, may not become apparent until the project has been operating for some time. Evaluation thus needs to cover several time periods. Evaluation normally includes a retrospective examination of the project in attaining its intended goals within the framework of both the timetable and the budget. However, experience clearly demonstrates that it is necessary to consider evaluation as an ongoing process integrated with each phase of the IPPMC. For example, evaluation procedures must be designed to analyze and propose solutions to problems that may arise during the tasks of activation, implementation, supervision, and control. Ongoing evaluation, which includes retrospective evaluation, should result in a careful documentation of experiences which can provide both insights and lessons for improving project planning and project management in the future.

Evaluation of a project can take several forms. These include evaluations by those responsible for implementing the project and by others with an interest in the project, including funding organizations and contractors. Those funding the project will undertake a thorough investigation of its financial aspects, including an effectiveness study of goal attainment. The agency responsible for the project will be concerned with determining whether goals have been attained and whether the expected impact on a sector or on national development will be achieved. The studies should also consider, in addition to impact on the target group, the impact of the project on the political, social, cultural, and environmental factors relating to the project. An exhaustive evaluation of each phase to determine its contribution to the project in regard to budget, timetable, and other factors is most desirable. In most cases, however, the project as a whole is evaluated with little effort made to analyze each phase or each task separately.

International agencies, such as the World Bank and the United Nations, have their own procedures for evaluating projects. These may be useful to policy makers, since they provide the opportunity for comparative analysis with similar projects.

Related to and often arising from the evaluation of a project is the need for project follow-up. Follow-up activities may vary from determining how unmet needs can be satisfied to action on project tasks not properly fulfilled. The piggy-back or follow-up projects mentioned earlier may come into play at this point. For a project to achieve its full objective, smaller or related projects may need to be implemented almost immediately. There is then a clear need to relate follow-up action closely to evaluation of projects. Follow-up action is one aspect of the project manager's role which could involve considerably more commitment than the manager initially envisaged. If follow-up action means the difference between the project's being fully operational or not, then it is a wise investment to undertake these activities as quickly as possible. Aspects arising from the follow-up procedures may be useful in the future. If the project is successful, guidelines can be set down for the project to be repeated in another setting.

The second and last task is refinement of policy and planning. Policy makers and managers will need to refine their procedures in the light of each completed project. Experiences and lessons learned should be the foundation on which planning and policy tasks are reviewed. As the essential controlling force, policy procedures must be continually updated to meet challenges in the future. Planning must also be able to meet any new demands or new situations. Refinement of these procedures is an important contribution that the project can make to future development programs.

The IPPMC is a flexible model for all phases of a project from conception through completion. The cohesive force unifying all the phases and tasks of the IPPMC is the power and authority relationship vested in various policy makers, ranging from top government and political decision makers to those in charge of one aspect of the project. The project manager, the staff, and those contributing to the project as consultants or contractors are bound by and exist within the framework of policy decisions. Analysis of these changing relationships through the IPPMC model can provide a comprehensive overview of a development project.

NOTES

(1) Lester B. Pearson, The Crisis of Development (New York: Praeger, 1970), p. 7.

(2) P. Streeten, The Frontier of Development Studies (New York: Macmillan, 1972), p. 30.

(3) Ezra J. Mishan, Technology and Growth: The Price We Pay (New York: Praeger, 1970).

(4) See United Nations Economic Commission for Asia and the Far East, "Criteria for Allocating Investment Resources among Various Fields of Development and Underdeveloped Countries," Economic Bulletin for Asia and the Far East, June 1961, pp. 30-45.

(5) Dennis A. Rondinelli, "Public Planning and Political Strategy," Long Range Planning 9, no. 2 (April, 1976): 75-82.

(6) See, for example, What Now: Another Development, the 1975 Dag Hammarskjold Report prepared for the Seventh Special Session of the UN General Assembly.

(7) Michael Lipton, Why Poor People Stay Poor: Urban Bias in the Third World (Cambridge, Mass.: Harvard University Press, 1977).

(8) United Nations, Second United Nations Development Decade: A System of Overall Review and Appraisal of the Objectives and Policies of the International Development Strategy (New York, 1971). See Gabriel U. Iglesias, "Implementation and the Planning of Development," in Iglesias, ed., Implementation: The Problem of Achieving Results (Manila: EROPA, 1976).

(9) See John A. King, Economic Development Projects and Their Appraisal (Baltimore: Johns Hopkins Press, 1967).

(10) See Oscar Oszlak, "Indication of Bureaucratic Performance in Third World Countries," in Philippine Journal of Public Administration 17, no. 3 (July 1973).

(11) See Albert Waterston, Development Planning Lessons from Experience (Baltimore: Johns Hopkins, 1965) and Bertram M. Gross, ed., Action Under Planning (New York: McGraw-Hill, 1967).

(12) For a detailed discussion of these cases, see Goodman and Love, Management of Development Projects.

SELECTED BIBLIOGRAPHY

Agency for International Development. Elements of Project Management, 1976.

Goodman, Louis J., and Ralph N. Love. Management of Development Projects: An International Case Study Approach. New York: Pergamon Press, 1979.

Goodman, Louis J., Ralph N. Love and Reza Razani. "The Integrated Project Planning and Management Cycle," manuscript, East-West Center Technology and Development Institute, 1977.

Hirschman, Albert O. Development Projects Observed. Washington, D.C.: The Brookings Institution, 1967.

Iglesias, Gabriel U. "Implementation and the Planning of Development." Implementation: The Problem of Achieving Results (Manila: EROPA, 1976).

Jones, Garth N. "Strategies and Tactics of Planned Organizational Change: Case Examples in the Modernization Process of Traditional Societies." Human Organization 24, no. 3 (Fall 1965): 192-200.

Lasswell, Harold D. "The Policy Sciences of Development: Review Articles." World Politics 17, no. 2 (January 1965): 286-309.

Rondinelli, Dennis A. Project Planning and Implementation in Developing Countries: A Bibliography on Development Project Management. Hawaii: East-West Center, East-West Technology and Development Institute, 1976.

Shipman, George A. "Developments in Public Administration." Public Administration Review 29, no. 2 (March/April 1969): 206-13.

United Nations, Second United Nations Development Decade: A System of Overall Review and Appraisal of the Objectives and Policies of the International Development Strategy. New York: United Nations, 1971.

United Nations Series on Community Development. Aspect of National Community Development Programmes in Asia. New York: United Nations, 1959.

Waterston, Albert. "A Hard Look at Development Planning." Finance and Development 3, no. 2 (June 1966): 85-91.

Waterston, Albert. Development Planning: Lessons of Experience. Baltimore: Johns Hopkins Press, 1974.

Wildavsky, Aaron. "Why Planning Fails in Nepal." Administrative Science Quarterly 17, no. 4 (December 1972): 508-28.

Wu, Chi-Yuen. "Public Enterprise as an Instrument of Development," Journal of Administration Overseas 6, no. 3 (July 1967).

2 The Managerial Role

In the project cycle, as in any other activity requiring the work of several people and some resources, the manager of the project is a crucial figure. Project management requires many of the same fundamental skills, approaches, and techniques that characterize the management of any complex undertaking, and yet the unique character of projects often dictates a variation or a special adaptation of this role for project purposes. This chapter will look at the managerial role in project management, identifying both the most useful and most problematic applications.

Unfortunately, the importance of this all-pervasive role is often overlooked. Rondinelli points out that World Bank appraisers give problems of managing a project relatively little attention; instead, they concentrate on financial, economic, and technical feasibility.(1) Powelson, speaking of Latin America, says "development financing institutions often pay little attention to the managerial capabilities of project administrators in that they do not know (or care) whether they possess decision-making skills, whether the proper information systems (for example, budgeting and cost accounting) are instituted or whether the appropriate officials know how to advertise and market their products."(2)

And yet projects inadequately managed continue to fail or be expensively delayed. Evaluators of United Nations Special Fund projects found that half of them ran about a year behind schedule and that final reports were submitted an average of two years after the projects had ended. Finally, there are those projects that fail altogether. Research shows the main reason for failure to be such managerial problems as lack of coordination, inefficient organization, inadequate monitoring, and improper scheduling.(3) Clearly, a closer examination of the managerial role in project management is overdue.

In sections that follow, we will thus consider the basic elements of management, the scope and nature of the managerial role through each phase of the project cycle, the crucial management tasks specific to each of these phases, realistic limitations of the manager, and approaches to improving the management of development projects.

THE BASIC ELEMENTS OF MANAGEMENT

The abundant literature on management shows general agreement on the basic meaning of management as the achievement of objectives by identifying and utilizing material and human resources. The identifying and utilizing functions are traditionally further divided into the planning, organizing, staffing, directing, and controlling functions of management. Supporting the infrastructures for these basic functions and undergirding all of them are the information, communication, and responsibility/authority systems.

These elements are, by and large, present in the management of any undertaking, although their complexity obviously varies depending on the size or scope of the unit managed, and on whether it is a national ministry or merely a subcommittee of a neighborhood association. As these apply to projects, special characteristics and applications deserve special attention.

Planning

As the everyday usage of the term implies, a plan is a reasoning about how an organization will get where it wants to go – or, in the vocabulary of management experts, "the process of preparing for the commitment of resources in the most economical fashion, and, by preparing, of allowing this commitment to be made less disruptively."(4)

Compared with the management of other, more routine activities, project management must devote a disproportionately large amount of time, effort, and expertise to the planning phase. A project occurs by definition within a set time frame, and constitutes therefore a "one-shot" undertaking in a largely unfamiliar area. Because the risks are greater, and because time is highly limited, the need for thorough planning cannot be overstated. In Indonesia, for example, a national development policy to reduce urban congestion and population pressures was translated by government planners into a resettlement program and the identification of several transmigration projects, including the Way Abung project, in which 11,000 families were resettled in Sumatra from a neighboring island over the period 1969 to 1974.(5) A large staff of planners spent several years anticipating the logistical details of this project, aware that once the families had geographically moved, it would be impossible to go back and correct the basic elements of the plan. Even so, as it turned out, problems related to support systems, policy directions, and social-cultural aspects arose, for which remedies, given the one-time nature of the project, were often inadequate. It is not surprising that Paul Gaddis says emphatically, "Advance planning is vital in a project. . . .It is unfortunately true that most crises that arise during the course of a project can be traced to lack of adequate advance planning."(6)

There is another reason why planning is vital to project management. Most managed activities have established their validity, their reason for existing, through successive repetitions of the same obviously necessary activity. Projects often fail to show a similar obvious validity. Planning for projects requires looking into the future to see what new things are needed. Project planning should thus focus much more explicitly on starting assumptions and premises, being much more "planning from the ground up" than standard management planning, which is often more a "planning for improvement." For this reason, the thoroughness of planning required for projects often leads to subcontracting the planning documentation effort to research consulting agencies, or setting up entire feasibility-studies divisions for this purpose. The basis for identifying and selecting projects has not always been sound in the past, and has in fact been identified as a major cause of project management failure. The planners of the Korean family planning project had to decide, for example, on whether to focus efforts on changing values and attitudes regarding family size and age space, or on introducing control methods and distributing devices.(7) The wrong decision at this planning stage would have been fatal to the project.

It is important to remember that planning at the project level must consider the project as merely one of a package of several constituting a major program, which in turn articulates the implementation of an even larger policy. Sound project planning should therefore meaningfully link project objectives with program objectives, which in turn should be linked with the policy goals they support. The same network of objectives at the planning stage linking the project upward to programs and policies must also be worked out downward, so that components and divisions within the project see their work as related in a specific way to the total project. Thus, the central planning and policy context for identifying and selecting appropriate projects is a key area of concern.

Organizing

As a function of management, organizing has to do with "the procurement of human and nonhuman factors, the grouping and alignment of personnel and physical resources, and the delegation of authority and responsibility within the organizational structure."(8)

Organizing for a project is in many ways unique. Because the objectives are temporary, the organization that carries them out must also be temporary. Given that the project was established precisely because standard organizations cannot handle the activity, the organization that handles the project will not resemble the corporate or governmental entity, but will be complex and multidisciplinary. Because the project has a specific output rather than an ongoing activity, the organization will generally be drawn up by task rather than by function.

The Apollo project that put a man on the moon, for instance, brought together, for a temporary period, a complex team of engineers, physicians, mathematicians, physicists, nutritionists, astronomers, and even psychologists – each with a specific role within a common, overall objective. Aligning these human resources and delegating responsibility and authority through a reporting relationship structure had to be done in a manner distinctly different from standard organizational charts. Some of the features that characterized organizing for Apollo and other projects include: the formation of task forces, the evolution of matrix organizations, the informal flexibility resulting from a minimum of standard operating procedures, the use of management by objectives, and the device of subcontracting particular tasks to specific individuals or groups.

A popular manner of organizing for projects was the task force:(9)

It is possible to overcome many of the co-ordination problems characteristic of complex projects by establishing project groups. The design engineers, production facilities and many of the indirect services are formed into a project "task force," preferably placed under the command of one project leader. The life span of the group corresponds to the active duration of the project itself, so that the team is dispersed once the work has been finished.

Task forces have the obvious advantage of being able to pull out various people from various functional specializations and focus them completely on a common problem or purpose, without any distraction from other ongoing responsibility. The disadvantage of task forces lies in the difficulty of relieving good workers of their various responsibilities for any length of time. Moreover, task forces for long and complex projects soon begin to develop lives of their own, with an accompanying self-preservation instinct that strives for an existence longer than necessary. When the task force is drawn from functional departments and agencies, these agencies themselves suffer over time from the depletion of what is often the best expertise.

The necessary compromise, then, between adequate control of project staff on one hand and the need for these same people in functional departments on the other hand is the matrix organization. In this model, project staff assume dual responsibilities and are accountable simultaneously to the functional head and the project head. As Gohre puts it:

The functional departments here have a service relationship to the project managements. They perform the specialist partial activities required to master the projects under contract to the project department. No longer can one talk of a hierarchical authority, exercised step-wise in the matrix organization. This is replaced by equal cooperation in the dynamic field between project and system responsibility on the one hand and specialist responsibility on the other. This dynamic field provides the balance between the project dynamics and the necessary stability in the specialist field.(10)

The balance achieved by the dynamic tension in matrix organizations is, of course, one not easily achieved, hence the need for constant flexibility and adjustments in the light of little previous parallel experience. In standard organizations, this backlog of tradition forms the so-called "standard operating procedures" – something not present in projects.

Another dominant feature of project management is management by objectives (MBO), or a variation thereof. This is a management approach according to which performance is monitored, not by control or reward/punishment mechanisms, but rather by comparing actual output promised by the individual or team itself at the beginning of the performance period. The output and schedule orientation of project management makes this management style particularly appropriate.

On a larger scale, the idea of assigning responsibility, a time schedule, specific set of outputs, and even a budget to a team has taken the form of subcontracting aspects of the project to outside firms, university departments, or ad hoc teams. For example, in the Bidtech community development project launched by a private Philippine investment bank, the project director subcontracted the Statistics and Special Studies Division of the Department of Agriculture to undertake a comprehensive baseline study of the community as a starting benchmark for future evaluation.(11) Thus, the use of contracts – their formulation, bidding, and control – forms an essential part of project-management organizations.

Staffing

The management function of deciding how the human resources are to be organized and what reporting relationships should exist must invariably be accompanied by deciding which persons will assume the various responsibilities and activities within the organization. This is the management function of staffing.

For project management, staffing should be done with an awareness of certain special characteristics that must be found in the project team, and especially in the project leader or manager.

Much research has been done on the characteristics of project managers. Gaddis points to four that seem to characterize the more successful ones: 1) a technical competence from a career in some advanced technology environment, 2) a working knowledge of several fields of knowledge other than the manager's own, 3) an understanding of general management problems, marketing, personnel, cost efficiency, and so on, and 4) an active interest in teaching and developing supervisors.(12)

Interestingly, it is widely recommended that the project manager responsible for the implementation of the project be selected, when possible, from those responsible for the project's planning, or at least that he or she be involved with the planning unit as early as possible. In instances where this is not so, the project manager may lead the project in directions quite different from the original intent of the planners, quite unaware of the background so necessary for the project's success. Such a case occurred, for example, in a project to establish a health center for a rural community in Hawaii. Neither the first project director nor the second, who took over after the first left, had an adequate understanding of the background and rationale of the project. In this respect, neither planning director had adequate knowledge of the basic difference in objectives between the community's Board on one hand, who wanted a surrogate hospital, and the professional planners and consultants on the other, who wanted a basic health delivery system.(13)

The other consideration in the choice of the project manager is his or her seniority in the organization or agency. Because the manager will have a general management role within a well-defined area, he or she should be relatively senior, not necessarily in rank but at least in terms of direct access to and control by senior management. The complexity of the Philippines' rice self-sufficiency project, involving as many government and private agencies as it did, would never have been properly and productively coordinated without the leverage that its project director wielded, not by formal authority but by the influence of working out of the president's office and acting in his name.(14)

The importance of direct access is necessitated by the often accelerated pace of project management; decision making in this environment must take place rapidly. Precisely because of this circumstance, many managers who are successful in functional organizations do not succeed in project management. "Because of the operating style required of him, a man who has been highly successful in a traditional department may not last long in project management. . . .In appointing a project manager, the executive must look not only to the candidate's past achievement, but more importantly to the task ahead."(15) For this reason, the search for a suitable project manager (or any position for which past performance is not an adequate criterion) is more and more accompanied by the assessment center method, which simulates futures and tests applicants' performances in these simulations.(16)

This is not to say that a project manager has nothing in common with other managers. In fact, more similarities than differences obtain between the two, and the fundamental learnable skills — technical, human, and conceptual — are just as necessary for project managers as for other managers. There is, interestingly, a healthy transference of managerial skills from one context to the other. Often someone who has served as a project manager may move either to another project, to general management, or back to a functional or technical area, the individual's broadened experience from the project often making him or her more effective in his or her traditional management job. Many senior people in government and private enterprise first came to national attention by the successful management of a major project.

Another approach to staffing would recognize that not a single manager but a management team should be identified. If this is the case, managers can be selected to complement one another. If the senior manager is a skilled generalist, her or his deputy might be knowledgeable in technology, the planning officer in the local environment, and so on. Taken as a whole, their total capacities should stretch to encompass the range of tasks to be performed.

Directing

The management function of directing represents, in a sense, the core of management, dealing as it does with the day-to-day responsibilities for seeing that the available resources – human, financial, material – are being channeled to meet the task objectives efficiently and effectively. In project management, the directing function translates into project implementation responsibilities, such as scheduling, which will be dealt with in greater detail in Chapter 9. A quick overview of the project implementation phase and the direction function of management in it, however, highlights the problem areas in projects.

A study of 100 project managers revealed that conflict areas during this phase occurred in the following areas, listed in order of "conflict intensity": 1) scheduling, 2) technical matters, 3) manpower, 4) priorities, 5) personalities, 6) costs, and 7) procedures.(17)

The resolution of these conflicts and decision making relative to them constitute much of project direction. The manner in which this direction is provided depends on the project manager's leadership style, which varies significantly among managers and for which no ideal style can be prescribed, dependent as it is on the project environment, the nature of the task, the disposition of the project team, and the skills of the project leader. Obviously, what works with one manager in one culture in a highly technical project will not work with another manager in another culture dealing with a different type of project. Thus, for example, the successful previous experience of expert consultants to a Pacific Island livestock project proved to be no guarantee of success in a different culture with a different administrative machinery.(18)

Controlling

The management function of controlling has been defined as "the process of making events conform to plans, that is, coordinating the action of all parts of the organization according to the plan established for attaining the objective."(19) Unfortunately, there is some confusion in the management usage of this word, because the everday usage connotes holding back or reining in, whereas the management sense, as in the word "controllership," merely implies ongoing monitoring to see that objectives are met and activities are moving along well.

In project management, it is clearly necessary to keep informed of performance in order to meet time schedules and budgets. Standard control mechanisms are useful for project managers, and the use of several data control systems are just as applicable to project management. Included among these are budget control systems, according to which expenditures are compared with originally-planned allocations to spot and correct significant variances. Similarly, humanpower data systems look at the human resources used and keep information on such matters as numbers of people hired for the project. Most important, an output data system, the nature of which varies from project to project, monitors the progress and the quality of the outputs produced as the project continues. For example, one of the projects of the Bangkok's water improvement program in the early seventies had as its objective the repair and increased installation of water meters. Periodically throughout the project, the managers received reports of how many new meters were installed, and these numbers compared favorably with budgeted targets. The project, one of four in the water improvement program, was, however, the last to be completed. It was several years behind schedule because the monitoring system failed to take into account the fact that an additional 900 to 1,000 working meters became defective every month.(20)

Within the operation of a project, control systems are particularly crucial in the beginning stages of implementation. An early warning system, even if informal in nature, can spot potentially large dangers and thus avoid serious difficulties. A manual of the U.S. Department of Agriculture and A.I.D. points out: "A common mistake in control systems is to rely unduly on formal written reports that are too infrequent at the beginning of the activity and too frequent once the operation stabilizes."(21)

Information Systems

Supporting the classically defined management functions are various sytems of which the information system is fundamental. The information system is especially useful in the directing and controlling functions of project implementation.

An information system is a scheme according to which (given the mass of data items possible to accumulate in a project) the right information is provided, in the right amount, to the right persons, at the right time. Determining what information to include and how to package this information depends on the person to whom the information is to be addressed and the reason for which it is given. Thus, an information system carefully distinguishes, for example, between executive reports from the project manager to top management, and daily progress reports the manager receives from the project staff.

The former, though much more succinct and abbreviated than the latter, nevertheless require thorough preparation. And this does not merely mean mechanizing the reporting system by replacing a volume of manually prepared data with a larger volume of computer printouts. What is needed is what Berger calls "key item reporting":

> Such a system should be geared to give the project team and top management only the essential information they need to gain optimum control of the project. It should present information important to the project in a meaningful, timely and decision provoking manner.(22)

These key items would include budget performance to date, progress to date measured against plans, forecasts of costs and output schedule revisions, and problem areas.

Obviously, the information system needed by project managers on a day-to-day basis requires a greater amount of detail. This should be a major concern, for project managers require as much information support as any other manager – more so, in fact, because: 1) the information needs usually have to be filled faster and under greater time pressure, 2) the innovative nature of the project requires information in a different form, or from a different group of people, or with a greater degree of complexity and sophistication, and 3) inadequate information makes the risks already inherent in project management much larger.

A discussion of information systems would not be complete without mention of the increasingly necessary role of computers in retrieving, organizing, and presenting data. Beyond a certain stage of simplicity, the use of the computer, even in developing countries, is almost as inexpensive as a thorough manual information system. The advantages of computer utilization include centralization of data information, security of storage, uniformity of formats, accuracy without tedium on a repetitive basis, and quickness of response and reaction time under pressure.

The basic computer applications that project managers most frequently deal with are: 1) scheduling, 2) financial analyses over time, given a set of premises, 3) modifications in projections, given simulated changes in such variables as market trends, investment incentives, inflation, etc., 4) scientific calculations, both technical (such as load factors) and mathematical (such as linear programming), and 5) various forms of a reportorial management information system.(23)

There are, of course, limits to the use of the computer, even within these applications. The quality of the output of computerized information systems can only be as good as the quality of both the inputs and the design for the system. The common errors are to provide too much information, in formats not useful for managerial or decision-making purposes, at too great a cost, and often too late. There are also limits to computer designs, and modeling and simulation exercises on possible futures have to be understood within the boundaries of their premises.

Communication Systems

<u>Communication systems</u> are closely identified with information systems, the latter focusing on the content, or the "what," and the former focusing on the channels and the recipients, or the "how" and "to whom." In project management, this type of communication is crucial:

> One of the most important responsibilities of a project manager is to ensure that all parties from their respective direct staff, functional operation or subcontract basis have a clear, unambiguous and common understanding on a continuing basis, of the project, its aims and complete purpose and problems. This facet apart from any other is instrumental in ensuring the highest chance of a successful project by encouraging problem solving and system trade-offs.(24)

The communication techniques available to all management (and yet frequently not used to full advantage) have their places in project management. Good communication should be clear, exact, brief, and convincing. Fundamental practices, such as relying on the written note or memorandum more than on the spoken word, meticulously preparing agendas and minutes for meetings, making generous use of audiovisual aids such as charts and graphs, and developing the art of listening and reading as well as talking and writing, are all crucial to sound project management.

The project manager is, in a sense, the center of a hub of communication. The manager's communication must go upward to superiors to notify, report, or receive help; sideways to colleagues for coordination and ensuring; and downward to subordinates, giving plans and schedules and receiving reports.

Downward communication in project management acquires a special character because of the often advanced technical composition of the project team. Establishing the atmosphere and the communication links must therefore be carefully planned and executed right at the start. Only then can cooperation and early warning signals be counted upon. In fact, when shortfalls occur, the manager is advised "to treat shortfalls in performance against target as unemotionally as possible. When one department falls behind, examine the situation critically but constructively. The emphasis should be on helping to overcome the problems and not on allocating blame."(25)

A final note on the communication system: it is equally important for the manager to be aware of communication mechanisms not only within the organization but also between the project and its external environment. This is true, but applies differently, through every stage of the project cycle. In the beginning, a need is articulated and a project is identified from this external environment. Subsequently, it is also largely from the external environment that the various human and other resources needed for the project are drawn. In the course of project implementation, there is constant interaction with the environment and the various public sectors involved. Finally, project evaluation at the end of the project's lifetime looks precisely at its impact on the environment.

Some elements of this external environment are obvious and always present to project managers, but others are less so, even if just as important. The following are some important economic, social, political, and technical elements of this external environment and their linkages for the manager to study closely: 1) supporters and donors, 2) cooperating agencies, 3) in some instances, competitors as well as allies, 4) beneficiaries, both individual and organizational, 5) professionals, 6) political parties and forces, 7) general and special publics.(26)

Responsibility/Authority Systems

A final supportive infrastructure to any management system is the authority and responsibility system:

> Authority and responsibility form the legal framework of management. Authority is defined as the right derived from some legitimate source to direct the efforts of others. It is the power to act.(27)

The acceptance of this authority in an organization, and especially in a project, however, depends on far more than the legal conferment of such authority on the manager. In fact, the project manager is often in a position wherein he or she requires the services and resources of individuals over whom he or she has no formal authority. Studies have shown, however, that due to the central decision-making role in the development process, a project manager is able to exercise a degree of power over and above that granted by the formal authority that accompanies the manager's position. Thus, the project manager has access to:

1. Formal authority: the ability to induce or influence others to meet requests because they perceive the manager as being officially empowered to issue orders.
2. Reward power: the ability to induce others to meet his requests because they value the rewards they believe he is capable of administering.
3. Punishment power: the ability to induce others to meet her requests because they wish to avoid punishments they believe she is capable of administering.
4. Expert power: the ability to induce others to meet his requests because of their respect for his technical or managerial expertise.
5. Referrent power: the ability to induce others to meet her requests because of their feelings of identification with her, with the project, or with the position of project manager.(28)

The best possible situation, of course, is to achieve a healthy balance of these sources. One of Avot's project commandments is precisely this: "Whenever possible, tie together responsibility, performance, and rewards."(29)

The basic responsibilities of the manager in the areas of performance output, budget, and time schedule should best be delegated by tasks to lower levels, creating an appropriate responsibility system and motivating the project team.

One can build motivation in the project team through the combination of these influences. It is important to keep in mind the different character of success motivation in the project individual, as distinct from the career motivation in the organization or bureaucracy individual; the former is driven by a desire for short-term success and achievement, the latter by longer-term security and career aspirations.

THE WIDE SCOPE OF MANAGEMENT IN THE PROJECT CYCLE

With this brief overview of the basic elements of management, let us now look more carefully at how these elements are brought to bear on the project cycle, and the managerial roles played by different individuals and agencies in the different phases of this cycle. For the cycle clearly involves not a single organization, but many; it involves not one manager, but many.

In any project of significance, a variety of agencies, both governmental and private, is likely to be involved in different ways in the phases of the project cycle. This involvement can be one of three possible types: 1) major policy responsibilities, 2) major operating responsibilities, and 3) related cooperative or regulatory responsibilities.

To illustrate these various types of involvement of different agencies, it may be helpful to look at three examples of projects in a particular country setting. It is assumed that the government in this country setting is unitary in form, with a strong central planning agency. It is further assumed that the country is developing and has an active private sector. The three projects might be as follows:

Project 1: A project suggested by an international organization for an experimental dairy farm operation, to be undertaken by a private, not-for-profit boys' residential secondary school financed by the government's development bank (which had been previously assisted by the international organization).

Project 2: A project suggested by the planning unit of a municipal government for an industrial park, to be developed using funds loaned by the Ministry of Commerce and Industry.

Project 3: A project suggested by the Central Planning Agency for a new research institute on cassava, to be located with the State University but operated in cooperation with the Ministry of Agriculture.

Table 2.1 tabulates the involvement, as well as the type of involvement, of a range of entities – international, governmental, private, and
project-based – that have had something to do with each of these three
projects. Thus, for example, in Project 1, on an experimental dairy
farm, table 2.1 shows the involvement through the various stages of the
project cycle of the international funders, the government's legislative
body, the chief executive of the responsible private entity (in this case,
the high school principal), and the project manager.   It further
separates the involvement into major policy responsibilities (**), major
operating responsibilities (*), and related cooperative or regulatory
responsibilities (+). The same is done for the industrial park project, and
then for the cassava research project.

A number of significant implications are suggested by a closer look
at this table.

Extension of the Cycle to Several Management Units

In all these examples, the early tasks of the project cycle (identification, design, appraisal, and selection) occur before a project is specifically organized and before it has identified a project management
team.   Only rarely is the project manager picked out and involved in
these earlier stages. Similarly, the last tasks of the cycle (evaluation
and refinement) occur after the project is completed and after the
project team is disbanded. Again, only rarely is the project manager
involved at this stage.

Thus, it is clear that the project cycle cannot be seen as focusing
only on the project manager and team. The project manager's column in
table 2.1 clearly shows his or her limited responsibility. Management
responsibility for the earlier and later stages of the cycle resides
elsewhere, with other entities. A look at this table also shows, for
example, that the dairy farm project involves, at one time or another in
its cycle, the following management units in a "major operating
responsibilities" capacity:

International agency	Project manager
Central planning unit	Project budget staff
Development bank	Project personnel staff
Chief executive (of the	Project organization and
high school)	methods staff
Private consulting firm	Project management information
	system staff

The other two projects similarly catalogue a large number of management units responsible at various stages of their respective cycles. In
fact, even units traditionally dubbed staff rather than line units
nevertheless undertake important management functions, even if they
are done in the name of the executive. Thus, a management information

Table 2.1. Involvement of Different Agencies with Three Hypothetical Projects

Phase of Project Cycle	International Government — International Agency	International Government — International Consultant	Central Government / Chief Executive Level — Legislative Body	Chief Executive	Central Planning	Central Budget	Central Personnel	Development Bank	Ministerial Level — Minister	Minister of Planning	Minister of Budget	Minister of Personnel	Minister of Resources	Local Level — Provincial Governor	Provincial Planning	Local Head-quarters	Local Planning	Public University	Nongovernment / Responsible Private Agency — Chief Executive	Research + Development	Personnel	Budget	Department Heads	Private Consultant	Private Con-sultant	Private Con-tractor	Private University	Project — Manager	Planning	Budget	Personnel	Organization + Management	Management Information Systems
Project 1																																	
Overall Management	**	+	**	**				**											**														
Identification	**	+	+	**	+			*											**	+				*									
Design	**	+	+	**	+			*											*	+				*									
Appraisal	*	+		+	*	+		*											*	+													
Selection		+		+	*	+		*											*														
Operations		+						*											*														
Supervision & Control		+						**											*	+													
Completion		+																	*														
Evaluation	**	+		**				**											**					*		+							
Project 2																																	
Identification		+			+				+	+						*	*	+	+	+	+	+	+					*	+	+	+	*	+
Design		+			+				+	+					+	*	*	+	+	+	+	+	+					*	+	+	+	*	+
Appraisal		+		*	+	+			+	+	+					*	*		+		+	+	+				+	*	+	+	+	*	+
Selection		+		*	+	+			**	**	+					*	*		**									*	+	+	+	*	+
Organization		+			+	+			+	+	+					*	*		+		+	+	+	+				*	+	+	+	*	+
Operations		+				+			+	+	+					*	*		*		+	+	+		+			*	+	+	+	*	+
Supervision & Control		+				+			+	+	+					*	*	+	*		+	+	+					*	+	+	+	*	+
Completion		+							+	+						+	+		+									*	+	+	+	*	+
Evaluation		+							+	+						+	+	+	+									+					+
Project 3																																	
Identification		+		**	+				**	+					+				+								*	*	+	+	+	*	+
Design		+			+				+	+					+				+								*	*	+	+	+	*	+
Appraisal		+		**	**	+			**	**	+				+				**								*	*	+	+	+	*	+
Selection		+		*	**	+			**	+	+				+				**								*	*	+	+	+	*	+
Organization		+			+	+			**	+	+				+				**								*	*	+	+	+	*	+
Operations		+							+	+					+				*								*	*	+	+	+	*	+
Supervision & Control		+							+	+					+				*								*	*	+	+	+	*	+
Completion		+		**					+	+					+				*							+	*	*	+	+	+	*	+
Evaluation		+							+	+	+		+		+				*								+	*	+	+	+	*	+

* = major operating responsibilities
** = major policy responsibilities
+ = related cooperative or regulatory responsibilities

34

systems unit of a specific project may take responsibility for building and utilizing a control system central to the management of the supervision and control phase of the project cycle.

Absence of a Single Coordinating Administrator

Further study of the three projects illustrated indicates that not only are there several management units involved but these are to a large extent independent of each other. For example, in the dairy farm project, the international agency is clearly independent of any local official, the development bank is likely to have its own board of directors, the school head has substantial room for independent action, the project manager operates with adequate autonomy to perform a required task, and the private consultants and contractors exercise the option to accept only tasks and methods of their choice.

Thus, the units involved in the management of the project cycle are not under the direct control or coordination of a single administrator. Project success and integration must be achieved as a team effort rather than through the unified control of a single, tightly-knit organization all the way through.

The team effort required for project integration would normally involve the following specific means:

The sharing of common goals and objectives, as is evidenced, for example, when an international agency, a development bank, and a private school – consistently with the thinking of the Central Planning unit and the Ministry of Agriculture – all see a dairy farm operation as desirable; common interests ensure a measure of cooperation.

The emergence via consensus of a lead person or agency, based on available time, knowledge, resources, or personality, and on shared goals and objectives, to oversee control, scheduling and cooperation functions.

A decision to form an interagency committee to manage the activity involving two or more separate units.

The development of formalized hierarchies of means of communication arising either out of repeated actions or the specific directives of overall regulating bodies.

Coordination via market or established social relationships.

Coordination and control of the many management units involved in the project cycle clearly are thus not always those of superior-subordinate relationships. Coordination is frequently provided by a complex set of interrelationships always in the process of development and change.

Need for Monitoring Projects

The examples illustrated indicate general overall policy made by the legislator and the chief executive. Therefore, another management unit, such as the Central Planning Unit, must seriously undertake the major responsibility for continuous monitoring. This is particularly important in view of the fact that project cycle management is frequently a many-splintered (as well as many-splendored) thing.

In a larger sense, the key task of overall government is most basically to ensure that the project management process works well rather than to participate directly in any number of specific projects. Thus, the governmental roles played by the legislature, the chief executive, and the central planning unit would be optimized if, without their specific participation, project results are attained because they have structured the processes by which projects successfully develop.

Use of Outside Expertise by Contracting Out

The use of expertise outside the responsible agency or the project staff is a common phenomenon in projects; the dairy farm project contracted out a university; the industrial park project and the cassava research project made use of private consultants. Design work is frequently "contracted out" by agreement or some other arrangement, and is often done by an international agency, another government agency, private contractors, research units, and, of course, academic institutions and private consultants.

THE CRUCIAL TASKS OF MANAGEMENT IN THE PROJECT CYCLE

Thus far, management tasks have been categorized – and discussed – in two ways: 1) by general function – planning, organizing, staffing, directing, and controlling supported by an information system, a communications system, and a responsibility/authority system; and 2) by task of the project cycle – project identification, design, appraisal, selection, organization, operation, supervision and control, completion, and continuation.

The first of these categories, general function, focuses on cohesive operating units, each subject to direct bureaucratic control by a single administrator for the achievement of specific objectives. Discussed under this category are the mechanisms and techniques by which each unit can by managed to achieve its objectives at minimum costs. The items in this category are common to general management, and to a large extent apply to business management, educational management, public administration, and so on.

The second of these categories, tasks of the project cycle, focuses on the coordination and combination of the cohesive operating units over time to produce a completed project. Discussed under this category are the procedures necessary to allow the most effective use of society's resources via a rational sequence of specific organizational activities over the entire project cycle, from the birth of the project to its completion and evaluation. The items in this category are specific to management of projects.

Thus, necessary conditions for a successful project are efficient, coherent operating units acting in a coordinated way over the entire project cycle. Several different functions can play a greater or lesser role throughout each phase in the project cycle.

In these circumstances, there are many potential lapses in management that can doom a project to failure. Only a few of the more important lapses — and possible techniques for their avoidance — can be presented herein. Many more will be identified in the chapter to follow.

Source of Project Ideas

Clearly, any policy pursued that limits the sources of project ideas is likely to result in fewer successful projects than would otherwise be possible. There are many ways in which sources of project ideas are adversely limited. Strong central planning staffs may stunt the growth of ministerial or local planning units. Ideological positions may rule out private ideas, whether they originate in profit or nonprofit units. Preferences for the geographic center may weaken local initiatives. Xenophobic preoccupations may prohibit ideas coming in from the world at large. In these and other ways, the population of project ideas is reduced. With such a reduced population, the likelihood that the best ideas will surface is reduced and choice is limited. In this connection, it may well be true that the major problems revolve around getting enough good project ideas, and not in choosing among existing ideas. Good management would thus seem to require utilization of every source and project idea — and a focus on building policies (and necessary institutions) to expand the number and effectiveness of such sources.

Mechanisms for Processing Project Ideas

Good project ideas are not enough. Sensitive mechanisms that become aware of — and responsive to — the ideas must exist. Indeed, a system that encourages institutions and their staffs to develop project ideas that are then systematically ignored is counterproductive. Ministerial and local planning groups whose projects are not considered, private agencies whose desire to act is consistently stymied, marginal areas that have no representation, international agencies that are ignored, all become embittered opponents of — rather than cooperators in — development. The situation is further aggravated if the projects selected for implementation appear to have been chosen at random and without a sense of priorities, or worse, from motivations of vested interest. In this situation, good management would seem to require a system that provides an overt hearing to all ideas without giving up that control and coordination that ensures, within tolerable limits, only the most effective and efficient projects proceed to implementation. This might well mean the following:

> That subordinate units of government be authorized to identify, design, and approve projects within their spheres of responsibility subject only to budget reviews using budgetary techniques which require benefit to cost calculations demonstrating adequate net social benefits.

> That local units of government be authorized to identify, design, and approve projects within their spheres of responsibility subject (for unified governments) to budget reviews as indicated or (for federal governments) to local decisions in use of their own resources (where all costs, both private and social, need to be considered).

> That private agencies be authorized to identify, design, and approve projects for which they can obtain financing and ensure adequate current cash flows (provided they operate under rules which ensure that all costs, both private and social, are considered).

> That international agencies be given access to appropriate decision makers to suggest projects which then find approval within any of the techniques indicated above.

> That the central planning agency at the national level provide the larger frameworks setting national development priorities without discouraging initiatives from other units.

These recommendations suggest that one of the major tasks of the central planning agency should be to ensure that projects identified, designed, and approved elsewhere are considered under circumstances and using techniques that yield for implementation only those projects that promise to be the most effective and efficient. The planning agency will therefore, to a larger extent, simply be forecasting the results of project activity elsewhere rather than controlling it in detail.

Capability for Project Design

The design of projects – and the preparation of proposals incorporating this design for approval – can frequently not be done "in house" by the identifying agency as it then exists. This will be true if the design and preparation of proposal work requires numbers of personnel who cannot be freed from their existing duties or personal skills and for equipment beyond those available within the agency. The identifying agency will need either to expand its staff, its skills, or its equipment to do this work – or it will need to acquire this capacity temporarily via contract with another government unit, an international agency, a university, or private consulting or contracting agencies (either domestic or foreign). To acquire this capacity requires: 1) authority to do so, 2) budget for the purpose, 3) and a unit in the organization with skills in soliciting, completing, and monitoring the necessary contractual agreements. Acquiring the authority, budget, and organization (including appropriate people) is a managerial task of great importance.

Design of Project Organization and Methods

Project design includes design of the necessary organization – and the methods it will use – for project implementation. This design is frequently passed over in favor of great emphasis on technological, engineering, marketing and economic analysis work – essential work, to be sure, but not necessarily more important than the organizational work.

The organizational design work has many dimensions, including the following:

1. The first decision to be made is whether the project tasks should be done within the existing major unit or agency responsible. If so, then the project unit would be organized as a regular subunit, as a project task force reporting to the agency's chief executive, or as a group working through a manager responsible to a special committee; a large variety of combinations and adaptations is possible. If the tasks are not to be done within the agency, some alternatives would be: an independent agency with its own directors reporting to the chief executive, a separate corporation or quasigovernmental corporation also with its own board, or some other short-term institution to be created specifically for the project.
2. Finding the key manager is of great importance. The project is in some measure a unique venture – a repeated activity in a new area, or a new activity – and thus no completely satisfactory, wholly experienced person or persons will be available. The managerial task of identifying and attracting the best persons available is of great importance.
3. The budgetary position of the project must be clearly articulated. This has many dimensions, and both capital budget and operating budget require specific attention.

   For the capital budget, it must be decided whether the project manager will have the authority to arrange for either borrowing on his or her own or appealing to the organization to which the manager belongs only for supplementary "equity" funds. The extent to which the manager can allocate capital funds, from whatever source, to particular items without specific item-by-item approval must be determined. Also, the arrangements the manager will be able to make for repayment of capital funds to either the government or the lending agency, whether out of project receipts from sale of product or service or from an operating subsidy, must be defined.

Similarly, operating budgets, the method of budget approval, and fund release will have to be defined, whether by line item or as a program with adequate leeway for flexibility among categories. Income generated by efficiencies or productivity must be decided; they could be returned and reverted back to the central agency or the funder, re-budgeted, or "belong" to the project.

4. A crucial and often problematic area in project management is the extent to which project teams conform to or differ from personnel rules applicable to their parent central agencies.

Short-term projects within subunits of central agencies require specific personnel, usually on secondment for a temporary period. One should clearly determine beforehand the extent to which the project can pay a premium for this seconding, the extent to which the usual channels and procedures for selection (advertisement, testing, interviewing, sourcing, recommendations, etc.) can be modified or abbreviated, the extent to which procedures for promotions, transfers, and so on can likewise be made more flexible. Strict conformity may straitjacket and impair project success. Unbridled latitude, on the other hand, may create severe morale problems for the agency and a lack of discipline within the project staff, which may develop a "spoiled child" image.

5. Finally, a number of problems arise regarding the extent to which the project organization, regardless of how it is crystallized, is empowered to devise and use unorthodox organizational models, methods, and motivational techniques to achieve its goals. If, for example, the parent agency is traditionally organized on hierarchical pyramids of authority and motivated by tight reward/punishment control mechanisms, a project team organized within a matrix organization, with motivation by objective-setting and compensation by productivity rather than by hierarchy, may meet with considerable resistance.

In dealing with the elements of organization, leadership, budget, personnel, and methods in project design, the key issue is the extent to which the project is seen as independent and thus not subjected to conventional operating procedures and policies.

Consideration of Project Social Benefits

Projects scheduled for implementation should ideally be those that will return the largest net social benefits. To achieve this objective, managers would need to: 1) develop and adopt conventionally acceptable methods and institutions for measuring both social benefits and social costs, 2) be rewarded for the use of these methods and institutions to the end of maximizing net social benefits (or punished for a failure to use them), and 3) be able to resist special-interest thrusts, including those from legislators and senior executives, to maximize their interests rather than net social benefits.

The responsibility for keeping the social cost-benefit dimension paramount goes beyond the duties of the individual project manager. This responsibility will require above all that the ultimate authority – the legislator or the populace in a constituent responsive society, or the executive in a more centrally guided society – be willing to see itself simply as the instrument for maximizing net social benefits by creating that set of institutions and staffing it with those persons who can acceptably define social costs and benefits and act to maximize the latter.

THE LIMITS OF MANAGEMENT

There is always a temptation at this point to see management as all-encompassing and all-powerful – and therefore, all-responsible for failures to achieve desired objectives. This view overlooks the fact that management _always_ acts within a societal framework that even the most powerful manager can change but little, if at all. Only in fundamentally revolutionary upheavals can a charismatic leader change this framework.

In part, this framework is based on resources and technology – on availability of natural and human resources and available knowledge of how they can be utilized to achieve management's purposes. In part, this framework is a network, even a maze, of institutional patterns of behavior that determine how individuals or groups will respond to changing situations and stimuli. It is essential for the manager to be aware of the various elements in this environmental framework that limit her or his actions.

Administrative Limitations

It is obvious that the first set of limitations arises from the environment of the institution to which the project belongs. From the bottom, lack of unqualified support from project team members and cooperating departments limits the possibilities for success. A division of loyalty, which often plagues matrix organization arrangements, must be explicitly resolved.

From the top, lack of executive management support can be fatal. This support, aside from making available adequate human and non-human resources (not always an easy task), must also be translated into interest, enthusiasm, and response to the project's progress. The project manager will inevitably find himself constantly selling and reselling his project package and its constant modifications, but he must make his "pitch" to a sympathetic audience.

Additionally, the policy and program context of the particular project for which the manager is responsible is often a given, which limits project management. The criteria for policy making and the evaluation of projects are often predetermined, and many change during the course of project implementation. For example, the field project teams in the Laguna rural development project in the southern Philippines found that their reporting mechanisms, evaluation measure, and even operating priorities had been changed when overall responsibility for their project was relinquished by their national organization in Manila and assumed by the funding agency that supported them.(30)

Economic and Political Limitations

Quite apart from scarce resources that may beset its parent agency, the project has to survive and succeed in the context of a sometimes fluid total economic situation. A system of prices, markets, and monetary fluctuations operates to organize individual and group activity in substantial measure independent of conscious management. Management and economic forecasts do not always anticipate the havoc that can be wrought on the most carefully planned project budget.

In the political sphere, individuals and groups interact in uncounted ways to influence a government action that an executive can manage only in part. Political pressures of various sorts constantly influence the priorities, the policies, and the programs on which projects are based, and these influences are not always for the good of the project or its beneficiaries.

There are also instances when the political acceptability of the project identified is not evident to the beneficiaries themselves. In the earlier cited Way Abung Transmigration project in Indonesia, as is common with most relocation projects, the people who were being transported to another island, supposedly with less congestion and a better quality of life, refused to move and did not agree with the wisdom of the transfer as it affected them. The needs analysis which leads to project identification can thus misread the true wants of the ultimate beneficiaries.

Sociocultural Limitations

In the social sphere, traditional institutions such as the family, neighborhood, and church operate to provide welfare and similar services again, in substantial measure, independently of conscious management. In instances when a project sets up goals or employs means perceived to be inimical to or irreconcilable with the cultural values or traditions of the area, it is almost certain that the project will be vigorously opposed. There are countless examples of projects involving physical planning, such as a housing project in east Singapore, a high-rise condominium in Moiliili, Honolulu, and the Anggat dam in the Philippines, where disturbance of traditional burial places brought significant opposition and delays to project implementation.

Another interesting sociocultural limitation is not always perceived by the project manager. That has to do with the occasional inapplicability of specific modern management techniques developed in the West to other cultures. For example, a self-reliant management by objectives system must be carefully introduced to a setting in which the predominant culture is one of paternalism and very strong authoritarianism. Team building and consensus formation may encounter difficulty in cultures with very strong deference and hierarchy patterns. Accountability and reward/punishment mechanisms may mitigate against the implicit trust that is assumed by certain cultures for smooth interpersonal relationships. Motivational schemes may have to put more stock in team than individual effort.

Limitations of Consultant and International Agencies

For international agencies and consultants who assume managerial roles in development projects, special limitations arise. Attitudes to host governments vary significantly from country to country and, correspondingly, so do the freedoms and limitations granted to external agencies and consultants. In a transcultural project setting, a number of key factors that influence successful project management have been identified:

> . . .(i) the largely agricultural society in the underdeveloped world and its behavioral implications, (ii) the process of social change taking place, (iii) the psychological tension in the aid relationships, (iv) the clash of cultures, whether in terms of values or social class differences and (v) the physical environment as it affects the socio-cultural environment.(31)

POLICY TO ENSURE EFFECTIVE PROJECTS

All of the foregoing – sometimes implicitly, sometimes explicitly – note that society (with its governmental units playing a significant role) establishes the framework within which projects can be effectively defined, activated, developed, and evaluated. By the same token – if this framework is inappropriate – it can just as certainly lead to project failures.

If the societal framework is in fact so crucial, a "Policy to Ensure Effective Projects" should be at the center of thinking about the project cycle. At every turn of the project cycle, such a policy – effected both through the basic fabric of society and through specific governmental policies, programs, and projects – would set the framework that will encourage or allow effective management of projects.

Thus, the success of project management is in many ways pre-determined by the policy setting within which the project takes place. In this sense, there is a second level of management that requires attention beyond the level of managing specific projects. It is management at a supraproject level that deals with the formulation and implementation of policies that define project settings. This activity often takes place at national levels where, more than direct concern for particular projects, the primary task, as alluded to earlier, is to create the atmosphere, processes, and structures that ensure — through policy — that optimum projects are developed and successfully carried out. Chapter 13, which presents a policy view of the project cycle, will deal with issues related to this wider managerial role in greater detail.

NOTES

(1) Dennis Rondinelli, "International Assistance Policy and Development Project Administration: The Impact of Imperious Rationality," International Organization (in press), p. 5.

(2) Rondinelli, "International Assistance Policy."

(3) Albert Waterson, Development Planning: Lessons of Experience (Baltimore: The Johns Hopkins University Press, 1968), pp. 249-67.

(4) E. Kirby Warren, Long Range Planning: The Executive Viewpoint (Englewood Cliffs: Prentice-Hall, 1966), p. 21.

(5) See Bintoro Tjokroamidjojo, Way Abung Transmigration Project (Honolulu: East-West Center, 1977). Reprinted in Louis J. Goodman and Ralph N. Love, eds., Management of Development Projects (New York: Pergamon Press, 1979), pp. 52-96.

(6) Paul Gaddis, "The Project Manager," Harvard Business Review May/June 1959, p. 93.

(7) See In-Joung Whang, Korean National Family Planning Program (Honolulu: East-West Center, 1977).

(8) David I. Cleland, and William R. King, Systems Analysis and Project Management (New York: McGraw-Hill, 1968), p. 5.

(9) Dennis Lock, Project Management (London: Gower Press, 1968), p. 6.

(10) Heinz Gohre, "Introduction of Project Management Methods — A Project in Itself" (Unpublished paper from Messerschimitt Bolkow/Blohm GabM; Ottobrunn, Munchen, W. Germany), p. 9.

(11) See Victor Ordonez, Bancom Institute of Development Technology (Honolulu: East-West Center, 1978).

(12) See Gaddis, "Project Manager," p. 95.

(13) Nancy Crocco and Tetsuo Miyabara, The Malia Coast Comprehensive Health Center (Honolulu: East-West Center, 1978). Reprinted in Goodman and Love, Management of Development Projects, pp. 176-234.

(14) See Gabriel Iglesias, The Philippines Rice Self-Sufficiency Program (Honolulu: East-West Center, 1977).

(15) Ivar Avots, "Why Does Project Management Fail?" California Management Review, Fall 1969, p. 79.

(16) Douglas Bray, The Assessment Center Method (Pittsburgh: Development Dimension, Inc., 1976).

(17) Hans J. Thamhain and David L. Wilemon, "Conflict Management in Project Life Cycles," Sloan Management Review, Spring 1975, pp. 38 f.

(18) See Ralph N. Love, Pacific Island Livestock Development (Honolulu: East-West Center, 1977). Reprinted in Goodman and Love, Management of Development Projects, pp. 14-51.

(19) Cleland and King, Systems Analysis, p. 6.

(20) See Chakrit Noranitipadungkarn, Bankok Metropolitan Immediate Water Improvement Program (Honolulu: East-West Center, 1977). Reprinted in Goodman and Love, Management of Development Projects, pp. 145-175.

(21) United States Department of Agriculture and A.I.D., Elements of Project Management (An international training manual, 1976), p. 45.

(22) W. Grafton Berger, "What a Chief Executive Should Know about Major Project Management," Price Waterhouse and Company Review, Summer/Autumn 1972, p. 19.

(23) Ibid., pp. 240-44.

(24) W.F. Taylor and T.F. Watling, Practical Project Management (New York: Halsted Press, 1973), p. 106.

(25) Ibid., p. 106.

(26) Raymond Radosevich and Charles Taylor, "Management of the Project Environment" (Graduate School of Management, Vanderbilt, February 1974).

(27) Cleland and King, Systems Analysis.

(28) Gary Gemmill and David L. Wilemon, "Power Spectrum in Project Management," Sloan Management Review, Fall 1970, p. 16.

(29) Avots, "Why Does Project Management Fail?"

(30) Ernesto Garilao, Laguna Rural Social Development Project (Honolulu: East-West Center, 1977). Reprinted in Goodman and Love, Management of Development Projects, pp. 97-144.

(31) Albert Gorvine, "Socio-Cultural Factors in the Administration of Technical Assistance Programs," International Review of Administrative Success 28, 3 (1962): 282.

SELECTED BIBLIOGRAPHY

Cleland, David I. "Understanding Project Authority: Concept Changes Manager's Traditional Role." Business Horizons 10 (Spring 1967):   63-70.
Cleland, David I. and W.R. King. System Analysis and Project Management. New York: McGraw-Hill, 1968.
Gaddis, Paul. "The Project Manager." Harvard Business Review, May/June 1959, p. 89-97.
Gemmill, Gary and David L. Wilemon. "The Power Spectrum in Project Management." Sloan Management Review 12, no. 1 (Fall 1970):   15-25.
Lock, Denis. Project Management. London: Gower Press, 1966.
Thambain, Hans L. and David L. Wilemon. "Conflict Management in Project Life Cycle." Sloan Management Review, Spring 1975, pp. 31-50.
Wilemon, David L. and J.P. Cicero. "The Project Manager – Anomalies and Ambiguities." Academy of Management Journal 13, no. 3 (September 1970): 269-82.

Phase 1 –
Planning, Appraisal,
and Design

3 Identification

The first task within Phase 1 of the project cycle is simply to identify the project area. Ideally, projects should be a response to a readily apparent need or shortfall in the development process. Identification of projects results from multiple strategies developed at the official, local, and personal levels within communities to satisfy needs in particular sectors. For example, poor yields in the agricultural sector may be the result of a lack of water for crops; a project to provide irrigation may be seen by farmers as the means of overcoming this problem. High infant mortality in communities can often be overcome by establishing health centers and health education projects. The needs are felt by those living in a community, and are transmitted to officials either through formal channels on one hand or through crises or expressions of discontent on the other.

In all societies, the needs of communities will always surpass available resources. Thus, it becomes essential for government, at the central and local levels, to make choices about the priority of needs. The fact that some needs must be left unsatisfied, however, leads to frustration within the community. Often the choice must be made between resources allocated for defense purposes instead of community development for agricultural, education, or health projects.

Once the broad areas of priority are established by the government, often in the form of a development plan, as many strategies or ideas as possible must be explored to meet the development objectives. During the 1970s and 1980s, dramatic changes in the availability and cost of energy and other development resources have made it even more important for mechanisms to be established for creative and innovative ideas to be explored. Once the broad choices have been made, the identification of projects in this sense involves the selection of appropriate project ideas for realization.

Projects thus begin as ideas, ideas that contemplate movement via concrete actions to new or improved situations to meet selected needs.(1) Because projects are the "action components" of development work, everything depends upon these ideas. It is important that they be put forth in sufficient numbers and be meaningfully and operationally related to the needs of the society in which they appear.

Developing a large number of project ideas is important for two reasons: 1) The more ideas put forth, the more likely it will be that the best idea – that idea that, when implemented, will yield maximum net benefits – will appear.(2) A process of elimination can then weed out the unworthy ideas, or combine the best features of two or more ideas, during the tasks of formulation, design, feasibility work, and selection; 2) The active involvement of many individuals and institutions – of their initiatives, insights, and skills – not only increases their total input on the development process but leads to a broader understanding of – and commitment to – that process. This active participation helps produce the common understanding and unity of purpose successful implementation requires.

Sources of Ideas

The nature of project ideas – as well as how many are generated – depends in considerable measure upon their sources. These sources, in turn, vary greatly in relative importance from place to place. This circumstance is graphically indicated by table 3.1 which notes, for three different types of social and economic systems and by potentially significant source institutions, the numbers and types of projects likely to appear. Results of table 3.1 can be summarized as follows:

1. The traditional and static social and economic system. Project ideas are likely to be relatively few, deriving largely from a chief executive and the central planning body, supplemented by many ideas for smaller projects from international, private, nonprofit, "missionary-type" agencies, a few larger projects from resource-seeking multi-nationals, and a few substantial projects focusing on the small "modern," urban sectors dealing with educational, health, and scientific institutions and emanating from international agencies (3) (both private, nonprofit, and international bodies).

2. The open social and economic system. Project ideas are likely to be numerous and from the private sector, from international agencies, and possibly from decentralized governmental units as well as from the central governmental units. The chief executive and the central planning body will be less concerned with developing ideas and more concerned with developing policies and activities for ensuring the development and processing of ideas from the diverse other sources active in such development. The decentralized development of project ideas suggests that they will be responsive to particular organizational needs (particularly for financial viability) except as the government intervenes through regulations, subsidies, or operations intended to broaden the range of social needs for which responsiveness is sought.

3. The government-dominated social and economic system. With minor exceptions, project ideas will be generated within the executive branch of government, with responsibilities allocated by bureaucratic directions. In the interest of a faster pace of development and greater efficiency that a loosely democratic system cannot give, ideas will tend to flow from research (analysis) modeling of a technologically-conceived system rather than from a variety of more narrowly conceived organizational responses to a wide variety of circumstances.

Characteristic problems of each of the three types of social and economic system examined in table 3.1 can, in turn, be summarized as follows:

1. The traditional and static social and economic system:
   a. Getting enough project ideas is a major problem. Such a system is frequently viewed as being unable to produce "good projects" for which funds (available internationally as well as locally) might reasonably be forthcoming.
   b. Too large a proportion of project ideas focusing on the "modern urban elite," too few projects focusing on the "traditional rural masses." This result is more or less inevitable, since the "traditional rural masses" are seen as – and in some measure are – impenetrably bound by tradition.
   c. Too many ideas are seen by the traditional groups as "foreign" in orientation, since they are generated by the multinationals or by international units private or governmental, or by the modern urban elite, which is seen as "foreign-dominated." Again, this result is more or less inevitable inasmuch as development is change and therefore an encroachment of "outside" ideas.

In any case, as the traditional and static social and economic system moves (as the result of effectively completed projects) to become nontraditional, project ideas grow in number, the "traditional rural masses" are opened to change, and the "modern urban elite," becoming more numerous and influential, comes to represent a new, indigenous group able to replace or to absorb foreign influences.

2. The open social and economic system:
   a. With a very large number of project ideas surfacing in the private sector (local and international, profit and nonprofit), they must be disciplined to meet societal needs. In substantial measure, this control would be left to the operation of the price-market mechanism (the assumption being that a viable project is a socially satisfactory one). Increasingly, however, this price-market discipline is seen as necessarily supplemented by government actions to meet desired societal goals.
   b. With a very large number of project ideas surfacing not only in the private sector but at ministerial and local governmental levels as well, the concern would be to change the role of the chief executive and the central planning body from a project-idea center to a center for ensuring that desirable projects get effectively implemented. This does not mean that these agencies should not ferret out gaps in forthcoming project ideas – nor that

Table 3.1. Sources of Projects by Types of Social and Economic Systems

	Traditional and Static Social and Economic System*	Open Social and Economic System**	Government Dominated Social and Economic System***
Non Government Local, private, for profit	Few small projects – and these largely in the small, trade area – from a business sector dominated by small shopkeepers.	Large number of projects from a dynamic business sector with large as well as small units.	Very few small projects in business areas in which private firms are allowed to operate.
Local, private, nonprofit	Very few projects emanating from authority figures in traditional institutions. Such projects would fit traditional institutions and modes of action.	Large number of projects from a dynamic non-profit sector with large as well as small units. Will include private universities, private agencies, private welfare agencies.	Very few small projects in non-profit areas in which private agencies are allowed to operate.
International, private, for profit	Very few, but large and significant projects, in which foreign businesses overcome traditional concerns in search of valuable resources (e.g., petroleum, tropical farm products, etc.).	Large number of projects from international firms, both large and small. Likely to include firms producing for local markets as well as for export.	Very few tightly controlled projects largely to provide access to needed technology.
International, private, nonprofit	A significant number of "missionary" projects in religious, health, and education areas. A small number of larger projects focused on educational, health, and scientific institutions in the crucial, small but growing, "modern" sector.	Large number of projects from international agencies, both large and small. Many likely to focus on distressed groups and areas as well as on technology transfers.	Very few tightly controlled projects of "cultural interchange" or to provide access to needed technology.
International Agencies (International Bodies; Bilateral Government)	Very few projects largely limited to urban, wealthy areas with more "modern" views and focusing on technology transfers and infrastructure.	Large number of projects. Many likely to focus on distressed groups and areas, on technology transfers, and on local impacts of international problems (energy, environment, etc.).	Very few tightly controlled projects of "cultural interchange" or to provide access to needed technology.
Government Agencies Legislature	Very few from what is likely to be an advisory body of status leaders to a chief executive.	If the open social and economic system is dominated by an individual or group, very few. If the open system is also democratic, a large number of basic ideas formulated by the legislature and detailed for implementation by the bureaucracy.	Very few from a bureaucratically dominated legislature.

52

Table 3.1 (Cont.)

	Traditional and Static Social and Economic System*	Open Social and Economic System**	Government Dominated Social and Economic System***
Chief executive and central planning body	Few – but increasing numbers – as the executive and planners accept – and begin to implement – programs of modern economic and social development.	Large number of projects, but a growing emphasis on influencing, number and quality of projects identified elsewhere in either the private or public sectors. More a policy-making than a project-identifying body.	Large number. Emphasis upon modeling – research – analysis to rationally isolate project ideas.
Ministries and independent agencies	If (1) chief executive and central planning agency are disposed to allow decentralization, and (2) if personnel resources are adequate, then few – but growing numbers – as ministers and planners accept – and begin to implement – programs of economic and social development. Government universities and research agencies are likely to grow in importance.	Large numbers of projects within a policy framework established by chief executive and central planning body. Are likely to make continually growing use of government universities and research agencies.	Large number. Emphasis upon modeling – research – analysis to rationally isolate project ideas in area of responsibility.
Local units	Very few since they are most likely to be dominated by traditional forces.	Unitary government. Depends upon policy and capacity regarding decentralization. If positive, large numbers of projects within frameworks established in chief executive, central planning body, and ministries. Federal government. Large number of projects from a dynamic local government sector with independent resources.	Government will be unitary. If decentralization okayed, will be large number resulting from regional modeling – research – analysis.

*The early-stage, typical underdeveloped society. Such a society has been characterized by very slow change in a tradition-bound system. Likely to be administered by a hereditary monarch with an advisory body of status leaders, including important religious leaders. Table 3.1 catches this society as it is being confronted by aid agencies seeking its modernization, multi-nationals seeking its resources, and a growing bureaucracy seeking social and economic development.

**The later-stage typical developing society that has a strong, self-confident, nongovernmental sector responsive to market alternatives and a government ready both to assist the nongovernmental sector and to supplement or regulate it to broader developmental objectives. This society may or may not be a democratic one in the sense of elected and independent legislative body and an elected chief executive. It is "open" only in the sense that it can tolerate a wide range of relatively independent agencies and ideas.

***The later-stage typical developing society that does not tolerate a strong, self-confident, nongovernmental sector responsive to market alternatives but which sees government agencies as the almost exclusive mechanisms for obtaining economic and social objectives.

they should not be concerned with coordination of forthcoming ideas. Indeed, they should be concerned with gaps and coordination. But this concern should be in the context of building mechanisms for the effective operation of the project cycle throughout the entire system.

c. With large numbers of projects stemming from distinctly different social and economic sources – and with each project claiming its own special interest constituency – it will be difficult to identify and maintain control mechanisms that both choose and implement projects leading to maximized net social benefits and are consistent with the development and maintenance of democratic processes.

3. The government-dominated social and economic system:

a. By sacrificing the added time and effort to sound out and respond to diverse external constituencies, project ideas would come predominantly from internal governmental units, automatically reducing the variety of idea sources. In addition, these ideas would necessarily be generated in a bureaucratic setting, and thus innovativeness and change would be increasingly limited over time.

b. Everything depends upon the quality of the theory within which project ideas will be determined. If this theory is complete and accurate, including an accurate determination of goals, it should effectively generate project ideas. If, however, it is incomplete or inaccurate – or seriously misinterprets goals – it may generate poor projects.

c. Because project ideas arise centrally, problems of motivation may develop among project managers and workers who do not feel the projects are "theirs."

RESPONSIVENESS TO PROJECT IDEAS

Clearly, good project ideas are not enough. Additionally, sensitive mechanisms that recognize and respond to these ideas must exist. Indeed, a system that encourages institutions and individuals to develop project ideas, yet then systematically ignores them, is counterproductive. Ministerial and local planning groups whose projects are not considered, private agencies whose desire to act is consistently discouraged, or international agencies that are repeatedly ignored all become embittered opponents of – rather than cooperators in – development.

Relating Project Ideas to Society

Project ideas can be meaningfully and operationally related to society by two quite different systems. First, they can be related through the operation of an accepted social and economic system that evaluates project ideas and determines their viability and social usefulness without conscious governmental intervention. If this social and economic system is a "static" one that can tolerate only a limited range of ideas or provide viability mechanisms for only a similarly limited range, then a large number of ideas is unlikely, and change – or development – will be limited. On the other hand, if the economic and social system is a "dynamic" one, accommodating a wide range of ideas and searching for new viability mechanisms that yield growing net values of outputs, then a large number of ideas is likely, and change – or development – is likely to be rapid. A strong price market mechanism in a society tends to become such a "dynamic" social and economic system.

Project ideas can, however, be related to society through the operation of a governmental policies/programs/projects/planning system which attempts to devise, evaluate, and determine the validity of project ideas.(4) A static social and economic system needs this kind of system if project ideas are to be at all numerous and growth in net social output is to be possible, for it provides the means for breaking out of the existing stasis. Such a system is also important, although less obviously essential, in more open societies. It is necessary in situations in which the social and economic system is unable to deal with externalities (5) or to undertake specific activities.(6) Finally, this governmental system will be almost exclusively used where – for whatever reasons – government has become virtually the only significant institution through which major decisions are made.

Government Mechanisms for Responding to Project Ideas

In the foregoing situations, good management requires a process in which society hears all ideas without giving up the control and coordination which ensures that, within tolerable limits, only the most efficient projects proceed to implementation. Such a process might require the following:

1. Private units – both profit and nonprofit, national and international – must be authorized to identify, design, and approve projects for which they can obtain capital financing and ensure adequate cash flows, provided they operate under rules that ensure that all significant identifiable cost, social as well as private, are considered.(7) (This possibility is obviously irrelevant to a society that has opted for government as the decision-making institution.) That all social as well as private costs are considered may well require a review like the "environmental impact statement"(8) in the United States, but broadened to include all social costs, not simply narrowly specified "environmental" ones.

It should also be recognized that there will be cases in which 1) social benefits will exceed private benefits (that is, within which the proposed project will yield benefits that cannot be captured by the private agency by sale of its output) with the result that privately generated cash flows may be inadequate (that is, the units suffer a deficit), 2) it is considered that the private agency can provide the output more efficiently than a government unit, and 3) the government decides to subsidize the private unit (either directly, by tax breaks, or otherwise).

2. Local units of government under a federal system (9) should be authorized to identify, design, and approve projects within their sphere of responsibility, subject to local decisions, yielding required capital financing and ensuring adequate cash flows. Private units should operate under rules which ensure that all significant identifiable costs – social (for society at large, not just for the locality) as well as private – are considered. (This possibility is irrelevant to a society that has opted for a unitary governmental system.)

Again, to ensure that all costs to society as a whole are counted, and not just costs to the local area, something like the environmental impact statement might be required. Again, there may be benefits to society as a whole beyond those to the individual community, which might justify a national government subsidy.

3. Each subsidiary unit of government under a unitary government should be authorized to identify, design, and approve projects within its sphere of responsibility subject only to budget reviews (both capital and recurrent), using budgetary techniques that require social benefits to social cost calculations demonstrating net social benefits.

The problem here is that conventional budget procedures are inadequate for the task for reasons which include the following: 1) Their time horizon is too short. The budget is conventionally an annual one, dealing with projects that frequently extend over several years. 2) They are set up to control expenditures for ongoing activities rather than to reallocate resources or to develop resource supplies for new projects. 3) They do not develop measures of social costs and social benefits necessary for a judgment on societal effectiveness.

This problem can be tackled either by developing budget agencies and procedures to overcome these difficulties or by assigning this responsibility to another agency. This agency is frequently a central planning body whose plans include projects (to be implemented by subsidiary government units out of funds approved by conventional budget procedures) according to schedules set by the planning body. Plans thus come to include identified projects with fund allocations to be confirmed over time by the budget process.

4. International agencies should be given access to appropriate decision makers to suggest projects which then find approval within any of the techniques indicated earlier.

5. A central planning body should be authorized to identify and design projects that do not appear under any of the foregoing categories. Indeed, filling project gaps within logically complete programs may well be one of a central planning body's most important functions. These projects – perhaps assigned to other agencies for further work – should, of course, be subject to the same procedures and tests as applied to other sources.

Please note that the central planning body now serves a dual function: 1) It identifies and designs projects, and 2) it assumes the task of ensuring that projects identified and designed elsewhere are considered and approved using procedures and techniques that yield for implementation only those projects that give promise of being efficient and effective. To the extent that it performs the second function, the central planning body will monitor and forecast project activity elsewhere rather than be the project developer for society.

In addition, of course, the legislative body and the chief executive can certainly suggest − or mandate − projects. They may do so by operating within the system outlined earlier. To do so, they would insert their project ideas into the system for approval within any of the techniques previously indicated. They would, of course, do so only if they approved of the system because they established it or concurred in it. They may also do so, however, by ignoring (or bypassing) the system outlined. In this case, they would simply order the project. They might do so because of 1) personal commitments to certain outputs believed important even though they do not pass a net social benefits test, 2) responsiveness to citizen interest believed able to significantly influence election and/or appointment, 3) belief that the project is required to maintain the integrity of the government, or 4) personal advantage.

In the latter case, in which the project is simply ordered, difficult questions arise. If the legislators and the executive are democratically elected, there is a conflict between democracy and rationality − between elected officials and bureaucrats. If there is no legislature (or it is appointed by the executive), there is a conflict between an individual executive's view and rationality − between a dictator and bureaucrats. In either case, the bureaucrat is faced with a moral decision − shall the bureaucrat resign or "go along"?

FROM PROJECT IDEA TO PROJECT FORMULATION

Project ideas (in their pure form, simply "Wouldn't it be a good idea if..." statements) have many possible roads to travel between inception and realization. Some will simply disappear as their proponents forget about them, reevaluate them, or lack the incentive, time, capacities, or resources to formulate them more fully. Some will be formulated by their proponents on their own time and pushed for approval either within their own organization or elsewhere. Some will be picked up − either with or without their original proponents − by an organization and formulated by an interested or designated body (a committee, a planning group, a specifically designated project group) as a part of their assigned work. In this latter case, formulation implies an organizational structure, assigned personnel, and a budget. Since it is probably not wise to depend wholly on the volunteer efforts − or capacities − of project idea proponents working on their own, organizations (private or public) that expect to formulate projects must structure themselves to do so. They will identify the responsible unit, staff it appropriately, and budget it adequately. Such responsible units may be in private agencies, local government, subsidiary government units, in the central planning body, or in international agencies.

Thus to formulate a project is, in effect, to design it in physical, organizational, and personnel terms. It is therefore appropriate that the tasks of formulation and preliminary design are considered jointly in the following chapter. Project formulation must occur before a project can be presented for approval by any of the sources described previously in this chapter – private units, local government, subordinate governmental units, central planning body, legislature, or chief executive.

NOTES

(1) Project ideas may arise in response to <u>problems</u>, situations regarded as inadequate and needing modification. Project ideas may also arise in response to <u>opportunities</u>, situations regarded as adequate but needing improvements. A problem orientation is <u>reactive</u>; an opportunities orientation is <u>affirmative</u>. The former characterizes a society on the defensive; the latter characterizes a society with a growth orientation.

(2) This statement is based on the view that in a significant number of situations, the "best" project will <u>not</u> inevitably emerge from a scientific or rational analysis of a situation. This is especially true if analysis is based on faulty theory or data. Moreover, the analyst may search for description, not projects, or focus narrowly on a single project, not many alternatives. In any event, a publication of the Development Project Management Center, United States Department of Agriculture, entitled <u>Elements of Project Management</u>, notes that: "Numerous experiments indicate that an exclusive concern with getting more ideas without regard for their worth, produces a larger number of better ideas than if the search for ideas is combined with judgment and analysis."

(3) Such large projects arise out of a perceived need to broaden the existing modern nontraditional sector and to provide it with the tools of science available in developed societies. Such projects are of this type even when they focus on agriculture so long as they emphasize the scientific training of an elite group.

(4) As used here, a <u>policy</u> refers to goals made definite by an adopted course of action to be pursued. A <u>program</u> is a cluster of related activities encompassed by a policy. A <u>project</u> is a conceptually discrete activity which is part of a program. A <u>plan</u> is a rationalized course of action incorporating existing, modified, or newly formulated policies, programs, and projects and integrating them into a complete and consistent package explicitly appropriate to the total economy and society.

(5) Externalities are simply societally important benefits or costs that are not conventionally valued by decision makers (governmental as well as private) within the system. External benefits include community gains in output and employment from expanded public or private expenditures, possibly higher productivity and greater personal satisfactions if income rises in lower income brackets rather than in higher, or the esthetic values of an attractive business or governmental facility. External costs, on the other hand, include community losses in output and employment from reduced public or private expenditures, possibly reduced productivity and lower personal satisfactions if income declined in lower income brackets rather than in higher, or wastes are emitted from business or governmental facilities. The policy-program-projects-plan system would adopt the means to ensure calculation and use of these externalities.

(6) Such "desired" activities are those in which benefits are seen as large relative to costs but which nongovernment agencies cannot implement due to inadequate capital, cultural restrictions or inability to claim revenue for the benefits conferred that will adequately cover cash outlays. These activities would necessarily be undertaken by governments.

(7) This policy is noted as possibly applicable to multinational as well as local units.

(8) A study indicating the "costs" of unfavorable environmental effects of any project for which these costs might be significant.

(9) The federal system recognizes a right of local governmental units in defined areas to act independently of the central government in response to the directives of its own citizens, legislative body, or executive. This contrasts with a unitary system, within which local government is simply a decentralized arm of the central government.

SELECTED BIBLIOGRAPHY

Ahmed, Jusuf J. "Project Identification, Analysis and Preparation in Developing Countries: A Discursive Commentary." Development and Change 6, no. 3 (July 1975): 83-91.

Balogh, T. "The Strategy and Tactics of Technical Assistance." Public Administration 37 (Winter 1959): 327-42.

Jones, Garth N. "Change Behavior in the Planned Organization Change Process: Application of Social-Economic Exchange Theory." Philippine Journal of Public Administration 8, no. 4 (October 1969): 442-64.

Pickering, A.K. "Rural Development in Baluchistan: The Works Programme and Ground Water Supplies." Journal of Administration Overseas 7, no. 3 (July 1968): 444-53.

Rondinelli, Dennis A. "Project Identification in Economic Development." Journal of World Trade Law 10, no. 3 (May/June 1976): 215-51.

United Nations, Department of Economic and Social Affairs. Administration of Development Programmes and Projects: Some Major Issues. New York, 1971.

4 Formulation and Preliminary Design

Two closely interrelated and interdependent tasks in the project cycle are those of formulation and preliminary design. Preliminary design, which follows formulation, depends on the project's continued existence past the formulation stage, since project formulation strives to gain enough preliminary formal commitment to the project idea to justify further work on it. Formulation forms the basis of future planning and design of the project. For smaller, simpler, shorter-term projects, this formulation may itself be adequate to claim organization, money, and personnel to carry it out fully. As projects become larger, more complex, and longer-term, however, formulation may only be adequate to claim resources to detail the design more fully.

FORMULATION

While it is difficult to generalize for all types of projects, three steps can approximately be distinguished in the formulation process: an identification of key factors vital to the project, an analysis of the project's various support systems, and a redefinition of the project itself.

Identification of Key Factors

The first step in the formulation of a project is to identify those factors vital to the development of the project and its successful approval and implementation. This process will involve crystallizing the objective and focus of the project and determining its role relative to other priority projects. In this way, conflicts, duplications, and other possible constraints that could affect the project can be taken into account at the early stages. These factors help guide the initial structuring of the project to increase its probability of success.

Project objective

A project must have a clear <u>objective</u>. The objective or purpose is the ultimate goal that the implementation of the project should achieve. To achieve the project objective, it may be necessary not only to encompass a primary goal but also to formulate and achieve a structure of secondary goals and subsidiary objectives and tasks.

For example, a community water supply may come from a nearby river containing contaminants that cause major health problems. The primary goals of a project could be the provision of an adequate, long-term supply of healthful drinking water to the community. A secondary goal could be provision of water for irrigation or for special-purpose industry that could be developed in the community. Attaining these goals, however, would require achieving a number of specific objectives, such as determining the ways potable water could be obtained, completing the prefeasibility studies on options having apparent possibilities for success, selecting which option is to be proposed, and other subsidiary objectives relevant to achieving the option selected for providing the water.

In establishing goals and objectives, long-term goals as well as short-term goals should be considered. In the example of water supply, provision of potable water for drinking might be the immediate, or short-term, goal. But the project might have several goals that would be reached through a sequence of achieving various subgoals and subobjectives to be accomplished, in stages, over a period of several years. Often, the long-term possibilities in a project are overlooked; as a result, dormant opportunities may not be developed because they are not considered in the early planning stages. Long-term goals need to be identified and clearly distinguished from the shorter-term goals. Time considerations and dependency relations (of one objective depending on the achievement of another objective) need to be established and structured.

Finally, in the structuring of project goals and objectives, no vital goals or objectives relevant to the project should be overlooked. The preliminary structure should be examined for gaps and to assure that dependency relations among the various objectives have been recognized and included.

The project focus

The <u>project focus</u> specifies what course the project must take to achieve certain objectives; it orients the team so that the objectives are more likely to be understood and achieved. The focus states what is really important or even strategic to achieve, and may identify certain long-term achievements that the project helps attain.

For example, in the water-supply project, stopping certain contaminants from entering the river water might reduce or eliminate the immediate health problem. That solution, however, might not be applicable as a longer-term approach due to inadequate water (beyond current needs) for development of irrigation, industry, and the community. Therefore, the focus on long-term adequacy of water supply provides perspective for the goals and objectives of the project and also gives direction to selecting the means for achieving them.

Generally, a project is a means of achieving a segment of a larger goal or network of goals, such as a sector development program. Since a project usually has its own management and budget, however, each project must be firmly focused on its own goals and their achievement so that the larger and longer-term goals are effectively accomplished.

Competing Projects

During the process of formulation, formulators may find that their project is competing with other projects for scarce resources. The selection process may eliminate one of the projects, or the competing parties may compile a joint proposal. If a joint proposal is prepared, the formulation process will need to ensure that agreement was not obtained at the expense of project viability, efficiency, or effectiveness.

Project priorities

Projects must be formulated and eventually selected, delayed, or rejected, based in part on priorities. These priorities can range from the personal preference of politicians and policy makers to national strategy considerations. National and regional priorities tend to provide guidelines for establishing local priorities, and all of these influence decisions affecting specific projects.

In the case of the water project example, accommodating the immediate need for potable water could be so strategic to community health that this short-term objective could take top priority in considering all facets of the total project. Provision of water for irrigation, however, could be necessary if the community is to be capable of economically supporting a significant growth beyond its current population. Thus, provision of irrigation water might take a higher priority than expanding the supply and facilities for community potable water after the immediate need is satisfied.

Priorities are based on many factors, and their relative importance can vary from situation to situation and over a period of time. Some projects have a logical location in a sequence of developments, based in part on factors in a cause-and-effect chain relationship. Furthermore, some projects may be less important themselves, but essential to the success of a higher-priority project.

The priority of a project can depend on the exact location where it will be developed or when it will be completed. A project that must be assigned a low priority at one time may be allocated a higher priority at a later date. Since priorities are based on so many factors, many of them changing with time, it is understandable that priorities will change.

Formulating a project definition and its goals and objectives must consider significant priorities and factors that influence those priorities. In this way, projects can be formulated so that their priorities are likely to be higher, or they can be delayed until they are sufficiently high in priority to be approved and funded.

Long-term project viability

Many projects appear to evolve successfully during the development period, but decay or diminish in their results after some stage has been reached or passed. There may be preconditions or prerequisites to the success of a given project, and there may be potential problems that will not surface until the project is implemented. Formulation of the project definition and goals should take into account the full period over which the project must be operational or effective, and must consider those factors strategic to success of the project.

The more obvious factors affecting long-term viability concern the availability of resources throughout the time span of the project. Less visible, but equally important, is support for the project — by the community, political forces, and others who could influence its status. Often, the visible results of a project are so delayed that support for the project diminishes and the project is either cancelled or dwindles in its effectiveness. Especially in long-term projects, where this problem is more prevalent, it is important to achieve an effective flow of information and public visibility for the projected results of the project. Sometimes intermediate results can be programmed into a project as a means of maintaining continued public support until the longer-term results are reached.

Perhaps even more elusive are negative factors that gain in strength or effectiveness and tend to counter the positive forces supporting the project. After a project is well under way, some of the forces that strengthened its early development may be focused on other projects or matters. The long development or operational period of a project may be less dramatic and demand less attention than the earlier stages. During this longer period, negative forces, reinforced by operational problems, can gain strength and eventually exercise dominant influence on the project and its continuation or success.

For example, in the water project, once the popular support for immediate potable water is satisfied, any negative forces (such as those opposing water irrigation development or expansion of facilities for community growth) could predominate over the interests supporting the longer-term goals of the project. Special attention could be directed to neutralizing these negative forces or circumventing them through planning appropriate strategy, sequencing of project components, or public information and relations.

Most projects are concerned with a need for long-term results. Consequently, long-term viability of projects is crucial to effectiveness of such projects and to the long-term benefits to the population affected, directly and indirectly, by those results.

Impact on other projects

Projects are rarely planned and implemented in isolation from other projects. Because of the interrelationships among goals and objectives at all geographic levels, planning of priorities and projects takes into account the interactions among projects and their influence on one another. Consequently, when the project definition and goals are being formulated, the impact on other projects is considered as part of relating each project to the broader development policies and goals.

Such impact can take many forms, and can be positive, negative, or mixed. One project may be necessary before another is feasible; or one may be a catalyst that makes another acceptable. In the water project example, provision of potable water might cause public support for continuing with the irrigation and water supply expansion stages to be either intensified or diminished. Or, taking the potable water from deep wells might make more water from the river available for expanding the irrigation water supply. Further, provision of potable water could directly impact on prospects for attracting or developing industry in the community.

Formulation of the project must consider competition for available resources, and whether the resources used by the project will diminish critical resources required by other vital projects. Sometimes this problem can be avoided or minimized by appropriate timing of each project, so that peak demands on a vital resource coincide with low demand for the same resources in other projects. In fact, projects can be linked by appropriate interrelationships, especially when they are complementary. Through such linkages, the beneficial impact of each project on the other may be strengthened and adverse impact reduced.

Impact can be psychological as well as physiological. The impact of the project for providing potable water on another project for developing a local poultry industry might be quite visible because the physical relationship between the two would be obvious. But if the farmers in the area thought the new deep wells for supplying the potable water were draining water from their irrigation wells, this belief could drive them to oppose strongly any further development involving deep wells. Opinions often overshadow facts in decisions and action. Both should be considered in recognizing the potential impact of one project on another, or of one project on the prospects of creating another.

Influence on national position and prestige

One of the most influential factors in project selection is the expected impact on national position or prestige. The concern here is both positive and negative. In fact, potential negative impact may be a stronger deterrent than potential positive impact is a reinforcement.

In formulating a project, care should be given to molding the project and its goals to yield a strong, positive influence on national (or even local) position and prestige. Although this influence should be a direct result of the project benefits, a secondary goal, with appropriate actions to achieve it, could be to assure and strengthen this influence through effective communications and public relations.

On the other hand, attention also should be directed to potential adverse influence on position and prestige by the success, failure, or partial failure of a project. Fear of failure is a strong deterrent in many types of projects; fear of exposed failure is even stronger, with potential for adverse repercussions in the minds of those who could be so affected. It is prudent to formulate projects so that the potential for significant adverse impact on national position and prestige is minimal, or so that it can be offset with other positive influences from the same or related project.

National position and prestige, where likely to be affected by a project, should be allocated careful attention in project formulation, with appropriate goals, objectives, and tasks encompassed to accommodate this factor.

The Support System

The second step in formulation involves a study of whether the necessary economic, technical, managerial and other support systems will indeed be adequate to support the proposed project. Formulation of a project needs to include concern with the support system in three ways. First, the project may be designed to utilize available resources. Second, it can be analyzed to assure that resources critical to its successful implementation will be available. Third, early development of vital support can be initiated as a part of project formulation.

Often, a project can be formulated so that its requirements do not exceed resources that can be available and justified. This can be achieved through such means as designing the project in line with resource constraints, timing the project or its segments to be consistent with resource flows, or dividing the project into a sequence of sub-projects so that resource scarcities do not block an otherwise justifiable project. In many countries, project priorities are determined, in part, based on how much they rely on local rather than imported materials, as well as on how little they require of materials in short supply or that must be imported with hard currencies.

After early formulation steps are accomplished, the critical requirements should be reexamined to reassure their availability. Even temporary delays in critical resources can cause such immense problems that the project is seriously impaired. It is these "vital few" resources, including the timing of their availability, that should be reexamined.

The third concern with the support system during the formulation stage involves the support structure. Some types of support, such as legalities, need to be assured. But others, such as popular and political support, not only need to be determined, but also can be strengthened by appropriate measures taken in the early formulative stage.

Because project formulation enables early development to occur in line with resources and support, it is a stage not just of screening out projects but of reinforcing those projects that "pass" this stage. This multiple result of formulation is further strengthened by the realization by political and development personnel that effective formulation of projects matches needs and resources. In this way, needs are most effectively served and resources are most effectively used. Components of the support system are detailed in the following sections.

Economic resources

Will the project be funded? Are there other economic resources that will be needed or that could be substituted for part of the required funds? These questions regarding economic resources usually arise early in consideration of potential projects. Not only is funding important; it may be the dominant consideration that determines whether a project can be implemented.

Formulation of a project should consider the likely funding sources. At the formulation stage, the nature of the project can help indicate the prospective sources, since many funding organizations and agencies allocate their funds to certain types of projects. Time can be saved by identifying the likely sources, conferring with them early in the formulation stage to identify which ones may be interested, obtaining their guidelines for problem formulation, and proceeding with formulation encompassing a composite of those guidelines. Or, a specific funding agency might be targeted, and their guidelines used.

Many funding agencies have strict constraints on projects they will support. On the other hand, many other agencies will allow cosponsorship of projects, so that funding from several sources can be merged into a project. Nevertheless, it is wise to know while formulating the project what financial limits, constraints, or restrictions may be imposed. Such factors may necessitate pilot or experimental developments prior to approval of a full project. Or, they may indicate the need for breaking a project into several projects, each seeking funding at a fraction of the total requirements.

Economic considerations are broader than resolving the question of availability of funds. The requirements for hard currencies for use by projects in soft-currency countries; import-export regulation relevant to the project; possibilities for donations or exchanges of facilities, manpower, or counsel that could reduce the level of funds required are all economic factors relevant to project support.

Perhaps also affecting availability of economic support is the economic impact likely to result from the project. Considering a project as an economic investment, an allocation of funds that has a high probability of yielding a high or quick economic return (along with other tangible benefits) may receive a more favorable response than one that is essentially a purchase of benefits by a financial outlay. The former is a type of loan, since the funds support a project that pays for itself and also yields other project goals — a double benefit; the regenerated funds can be used again for other projects. The latter type of allocation yields the goal benefits but does not regenerate the investment. Especially where funds, or hard-currency funds, are tight, this extra economy from higher efficiency of resource utilization can be vital.

Economic support is crucial to most projects. Consequently, formulating the project with this firmly in mind is important to eventual acceptance and efficiency of the project.

Technical resources

Adequacy of financial support does not assure availability of the technical resources required for a project. These resources encompass materials and supplies, equipment, facilities and land, and humanpower. Shortage or delays in availability of strategic technical resources can impair the completion, increase the costs, and reduce the effectiveness of a project.

During project formulation, the technical requirements are identified and sufficiently analyzed to determine which are strategic and, given a limit in quantity or timing, may impair the project. Focusing on those resources and analyzing the need for them in further detail form the basis for exploring their availability with resource suppliers and any government agencies that control their allocation. Tentative commitments of availability may be advisable in certain cases.

Materials and supplies include not only the basic raw materials such as specific types of construction materials and materials used in the production processes of industrial plants; they also include component parts and supplies such as wire, pipe, and fuel. The availability of utilities, such as electricity, water, and transportation can also be crucial, especially in projects remote from urban areas.

Equipment should receive early consideration, especially due to the limited sources of specialized items and the long lead time in producing or receiving them. Some equipment may be especially vital to a project and quick substitutes may be impractical. The status on such items can sometimes dictate the feasibility of a project.

Facilities and land, in essential quantity, quality, and location, can be vital, and sometimes controlling, to a project. Preliminary assurances that necessary land, buildings, and other facility requirements will be available, or can be developed, should be obtained.

Humanpower, including technical advisors, skilled craftsmen, and other specialized personnel, may be limited. The degree to which their limitation is inflexible and critical to the project determines the extent and focus on this resource in the formulation stage.

Technical resources are a concern in the formulation stage to provide assurance and confidence to those who must approve and implement a project. This especially concerns resources that are sufficiently strategic to the project to seriously affect its success.

Managerial adequacies

Project managers deserve special consideration in examining human resources. If knowledgeable, capable managers appropriate for the proposed project cannot be made available or be developed, the successful implementation of the project is placed in question. These requirements, especially the need for key positions in project management, should be an early concern. Furthermore, if possible, the potential manager of the project should be identified early and involved in the project formulation and design.

Often, personnel experienced in management of the specific project area will be unavailable. Nevertheless, by analysis of the qualifications required for these key positions, determination can be made as to which qualifications could be developed by either special training or by experience through participating in early stages of the project cycle of the given project.

While flexibilities may exist in obtaining or developing project managers, recognition should be given to the immense influence of these managers on effectiveness and efficiency of a project. Productivity and other measures of project success are highly contingent on the quality of the project managers. Through their astuteness, severe problems can be solved, constraints diminished, and delicate factors handled.

The absence of this quality in project managers may be difficult or impossible to ascertain in a project in the short-term, as many difficulties can be alleviated by tactics that delay, but not eliminate or reduce, their influence. Consequently, short-sighted managers may achieve an appearance of success, especially in the early stages of implementation and operation, but then they may experience repercussions from accumulated problems that have been thrust aside rather than resolved.

The competencies of project managers and specialized technical personnel have such an influence on final results of most projects that early attention to this need is highly advisable. The types of competencies needed should be noted and assurance obtained that they can be available.

Administrative and political support

Depending on the country and the project, the administrative and political concerns may be separate or substantially the same. If a project is to be privately financed and owned, then its need for political support would be separate (from administrative support) and perhaps less than if it is a public project and/or financed by government funds.

An understanding of the administrative hierarchy and the political system, as these affect the approval, funding, and support of projects, is absolutely essential. Extending this further, knowledge of their procedures, both formal and informal, along with their relative importance, can determine the ultimate support received by a proposed project.

Consideration of administrative and political support actually involves three elements: approval, funding, and general support. Approval is essential from the organizations that will sponsor and/or administer the project; it may also be required from one or more government agencies, especially if it is a public project or requires resources whose availability is subject to government controls. In addition, if there are national policies and priorities concerning development, then the official development organizations would be part of the administrative/political system whose approval may be required or desirable.

Funding may be distinct from project approval; this may be the case even in public projects. Funding, of course, can originate from a wide range of organizations; these may be private or public, internal or external, local or national, regional or international. The logical funding source, or sources, can depend on the project as well as on government policies. Even public opinion and prior experience with certain sources can be relevant to this decision. Often, however, several likely funding sources should be determined and cultivated, so that if one source does not materialize, alternative sources can be considered immediately.

General support by administrative/political forces can be very beneficial to the ease with which a project flows through every stage of the project cycle. Even from sectors whose approval is not required or whose funds are not used, these can exert overt or subtle pressures or remove roadblocks that can determine the destiny of an authorized and funded project. Consequently, understanding the administrative/political system can be strategic to every aspect of a project and especially to its long-term success, viability and influence.

Legal and procedural factors

The legal factors of support relate to or overlap with the political factors, but they may be sufficiently distinct so that special treatment is needed. Similarly, the administrative/political system involves procedures; but so does the legal system. These must not be neglected.

There may be certain requirements, constraints, or provisions imposed by law that are vital to consider in the formulation of a project. Laws concerning safety, pollution, taxes, imports, foreign exchange, building codes, zoning, wage levels, and numerous other factors can be relevant. At the formulation stage, however, it is essential only to find those legal requirements that must be implemented very early in the project cycle and those legal constraints that may have vital influence on the project. The first should be noted for directing necessary actions for compliance, while the latter should be explored further to determine their potential impact and what can be done to satisfy or avoid them.

Many procedures are imposed to provide and administer compliance with laws, regulations, or accepted practice. Procedures can be followed or ignored; also, they often can be evaded in substance while followed to the letter of the law. Avoiding procedure or evading its principle can be risky. While the need or ethical basis of a requirement, legal or otherwise, may be questioned, nevertheless requirements need to be recognized and decisions made concerning them and the project.

Procedure can be burdensome, but failure to comply with certain procedural detail can delay or withhold essential support from even a high-priority project. The formulation stage is not concerned with procedural detail, but it must encompass identification of those strategic legal/procedural matters that are likely to exert a controlling influence on the project.

Social structure and popular support

Understanding the social structure helps to anticipate and assure popular support of a project. This can be important directly, such as in providing needed labor and public resources. In addition, popular support, or animosity, can influence others, especially those in elected political positions, to provide or withhold their support of a project. Popular opinion can be extremely influential; thus, popular support, or at least public neutrality, can be very important to a project.

During project formulation, popular support should be considered, and the definition goals and approach to project implementation should take public opinion and influence into account. To do this, analysis should include the potential social and cultural impact of the project. The likely influence of this impact on public opinion and support should be considered during formulation as a means of anticipating potential vital problems and of formulating the project so that its social/cultural impact will stimulate positive popular support.

Few projects can ignore popular support, especially if the project's life is long or if the dissemination of project results into other projects (such as from pilot or demonstration projects) is strategic. Public opinion often determines whether the results of a project are used, multiplied, or ended when the project is terminated. Long-term results are especially subject to molding by public forces. For this reason, considering popular support and formulating the project to adhere to its influence or to mold needed support can be vital to certain types of projects.

Redefining the Project

After formulation has proceeded through the steps of project definition and checking of the support system, a redefinition may be advisable based on information revealed during these two steps. Under any circumstances, it is prudent to look objectively at the preliminary definition and goals in view of the information now available and to determine if any reformulation is advisable.

Although this final step in project formulation involves an examination of the information developed in the first and second steps, it does so with the attention focused on whether any alternatives should replace or alter some of the project components. Consequently, this step of redefining the project will emphasize the concern with alternatives.

The consideration of alternatives

While minor modifications to the project definition and goals may occur throughout the formulation stage, the primary concern should be focused on dominant or controlling factors. Throughout each element of both prior steps, potential significant influences that might necessitate change in the project and its goals should be noted. These factors provide the basis for reexamining the project.

Such factors should include not only those that may impair the project or its results, but also those that, with modification, could further enhance those results. The completion of physical development and operation, including minimal attainment of goals and objectives, may be sufficient basis for satisfaction. But continued positive impact or exceeding the basic goals can be a very desirable result, and can be a basis for enhanced support for add-on or related projects. Consequently, redefining the project should strive to formulate the project so that the very best results are likely to be attained.

Examining any indicated needs for alternatives can suggest that the project be delayed or cancelled. If, in any of the elemental analyses, any negative factors that prohibit the approval, funding, or success of the project are identified, then project postponement or cancellation may indeed be necessary. Or, based on any of these factors, altering the project and one or more of its goals may be feasible means to salvage or enhance the project. Certainly, any serious impediment to the project should be checked out; however, alternatives that prevent the factor from being an impediment should be considered.

In the water project example, investigation of the support system might reveal that plans exist for constructing a dam across the river far upstream, and that all water will be diverted for use in other sections of the country. Or it may be found that socially ingrained customs would prohibit eliminating the serious pollution within the near future. Neither of these discoveries might change the primary goal of the project, but they might drastically alter the secondary goals and the objectives through which the goals can be accomplished.

Thus, in redefining the project, all the indicated strategic influences should be examined, alternatives considered for each, and the project redefined, if needed, to enhance its probable success.

Preliminary feasibility considerations

One of the implied purposes of project formulation is to provide a form of prefeasibility analysis. As the formulation occurs, those factors especially relevant to feasibility are considered in defining the project and checking it for appropriate resources and support. Consequently, throughout the formulation analyses, the question of feasibility should be implied and considered.

In redefining the project, however, feasibility considerations should be examined further. The feasibility requirements of the likely funding agencies should be reviewed, and the findings of the project formulation compared with those requirements. If major discrepancies occur between project objectives and the expectations of the approval and funding agencies, then an examination of alternatives with greater congruity should be considered.

By encompassing feasibility considerations, including those specifically stated by agencies who must approve or fund the projects, the project can be formulated to maximize the change of this approval and funding. Furthermore, the cost and time delays in redirecting the project emphasis or components in order to meet feasibility requirements can be minimized. Finally, the principal feasibility factors can be encompassed in the project formulation, enhancing its further development and its chances for acceptance.

Reformulation of the project

The final element in project formulation is completing any reformulation needed or appropriate based on all prior analysis. By this time, the preliminary definition and goals of the project have been examined over and over, based on various factors, influences, and constraints. Potential critical problems have been identified and means have been determined for resolving or avoiding them. Alternatives that might salvage or strengthen the project have been explored. And any additional considerations of feasibility have been examined, especially in relation to appropriate approval and funding agencies.

Reformulation revises the project definition and goals, and structures salient information and conclusions of the formulation process into an organized project statement. This formulated statement of the project serves as the starting point for preliminary design. It should contain, in at least elementary form, the following details:

1. A statement of what – and how much – the project is proposed to accomplish.
2. An indication of the nature of the appropriate technology and of its applicability in the particular circumstance of the proposed project.
3. An indication of the availability of the resources in the necessary quantities and qualities required for the project.
4. An indication of the capital expenditures required to bring the project into being. This will include (a) costs of all fixed assets – land, building, machinery and equipment, licenses and goodwill, etc., and (b) all net recurring costs (materials and supplies, labor, rent, etc.) until the project is ready for turnover to regular operations.
5. An indication of likely sources of funds to cover these capital expenditures.
6. An indication of projected sources and uses of funds after the project is turned over to regular operations. An indication of how net cash balances, if any, will be utilized or how net cash deficits, if any, will be covered. The estimation of sources of available funds

will require estimates of sales and other revenue. The estimation of uses of funds will require estimates of all input costs, that is, materials and labor, license taxes or similar payments. A good estimate for the cash-flow situation is important at this early stage of the project.

7. An indication of the project organization that will undertake further studies for project implementation and for subsequent operations should be considered. An indication of how this organization can be expected to work within the financial limitations indicated under (4) is required. If such an organization cannot be operationally projected, the project will not be viable.

8. An indication of the personnel required for project implementation and for subsequent operations needs to be made at this early stage. If the required personnel are not available, the project may not be viable.

9. An indication that the project as presented is socially desirable in keeping with overall national and local development objectives.

Overall, then, the project statement includes a clear, concise description of the project, including its purpose, goals, specific objectives, target dates, and anticipated benefits. How, and possibly by whom, the project will be carried out is clearly indicated. The project statement also includes supplementary information that was used in the formulation analyses, and evidence, if relevant, of options selected among alternatives. This supplementary data must be able to cover preliminary feasibility concerns. If a funding agency has already been selected, this feasibility information could relate directly to the key feasibility requirements of that agency.

Project formulation provides a sound basis for proceeding with preliminary design of a project. In addition, it yields a statement of the problem, with reinforcing information that can be used for early assurances from approval and funding agencies, and as a basis for discussions of other types of support and defense, even before project design is formally begun.

PRELIMINARY DESIGN

After a potential project has been formulated, a decision must be made either to continue developing the project or to terminate it. If the project formulators, who may include the government planning agency, another government agency, or a private group, decide to continue with the project, they must prepare the preliminary design. The preliminary design is the first formal elaboration of the project idea, and its primary purpose is to provide sufficient information to test the proposed project's feasibility. In this context, the format and information required for the preliminary design are set by the requirements of the feasibility study. If, for example, the project proposers desire funding from the World Bank, then they must prepare a prospectus that allows the Bank to analyze the project's technical, economic, financial, and institutional feasibility. The Korean government requires that all proposals for industrial and commercial projects include construction schedules; technical plans, and operating schedules; the Philippine government's National Economic and Development Authority mandates still other criteria.

Elements in the Preliminary Design

Requirements for the preliminary design will thus differ depending on the appraising agency involved. Generally, however, the preliminary design must include:
1. A list of project objectives.
2. An overview summary of the project including various alternatives.
3. A discussion of the technical elements of the projects.
4. The project's management plan, including the operating and implementing strategy.
5. An estimated project budget.

While these criteria force the preliminary design to be fairly detailed and comprehensive, it is by no means the final design. If the project is eventually approved, about ten percent of the total project budget will be spent on planning, but only two to four percent is spent on formulation and preliminary design. The percentage, of course, varies depending on the requirements of the feasibility study. Generally, however, few project proponents are willing to spend large sums prior to a commitment of financial support of the project. Still, if the decision is made to proceed through the feasibility stage, there are potential funding sources. Funding might come internally, if the project proponents are a government agency. The World Bank also aids in preparing projects at this stage with its special Project Preparation Facility; and various agencies such as the World Health Organization or the United Nations Development Program award special grants for prefeasibility project preparation.

Although these sources can be attractive, especially those providing grants, the project proponents must exercise some discretion in seeing that their particular objectives do not become obscured in securing this support. This is especially true if the supporting agency requires that the preliminary design include complex study and analysis. Such preliminary design requirements may force the project proponents to rely heavily upon foreign consultants, who might be unfamiliar with local conditions.

The following, then, are the elements that should be included in the preliminary design:

Project objectives

First, the project objectives must be explicitly stated. If the formulation document is well prepared, it will already have set forth the ultimate objective of the project, the other important objectives, and the long- and short-term goals required to achieve these objectives. The planners must then refine or reformulate each of these and list them formally. In refining the ultimate objective, they must be sure that it is indeed the primary purpose of the project. Upon close examination, some of the other objectives may loom as more important. In this case, whether the project can actually fulfill the primary objective is a question that must be reassessed.

Once the ultimate objective is clearly stated, the other objectives must be stated in order of priority. These objectives should unquestionably fulfill a clear and expressed need in the area the project is to serve. Then the long- and short-term goals must be listed under the appropriate objective; these goals must be stated as specifically as possible so that they can be used to monitor project progress. Finally, this section of the preliminary design must put the project in perspective. The project must be related to a local, regional, or national program or development plan and placed explicitly within this larger context. Also, the project's interrelationship or relevance to other projects must be specified.

Project summary

Although this section of the preliminary design may be combined with the objectives, it provides in addition an overview description of the project activities, usually breaking the project into discrete phases of action. This section should provide a brief narrative review of the project, including a summary of the project budget. The budget should be broken down into the major categories of spending; if there are major cost alternatives, each should be presented as a separate budget option. Since this section is intended for a decision maker or policy maker who requires a quick review of the project but who will not necessarily conduct the detailed project analysis, it should highlight only the major points of the project, and cross-reference the location of the detailed information.

Technical factors

Technical aspects and considerations make up a major section of the preliminary design. Although final specifications and blueprints are not prepared until a later stage, planners and engineers use preliminary field surveys and supplement them with additional data to design a workable basic plan. This basic plan may then be compared roughly with alternatives to accomplish the desired objectives of the project. An estimated time duration for detailed engineering and construction should be designed in this stage. Any major ecological aspects and their implications must be identified in connection with the proposed projects.

Following are two examples: a highway project from the public works sector and a manufacturing plant from the industrial sector, both illustrating technical considerations that go into a formulation study.

For preliminary highway design purposes, essential basic data include width and alignment, grades, intersections, drainage, and miscellaneous structures such as bridges and retaining walls. Included in the preliminary engineering design must be attention to earthwork considerations, such as cut or soil to be excavated to meet grade requirements, and fill or the need to raise the grade by means of adding soil and/or rock to existing grades to meet final grade requirements. The width, alignment, grades and intersections fall in the category of geometric design. Drainage and pavement design are considered to be special topics.(1)

Examples of works that have to be done in preliminary surveys and engineering design for highway projects include:

1. Preliminary alignment map of proposed location based on ground surveys, aerial surveys, topographic map, etc.

2. Preliminary plan-profile drawings with established grades and general drainage schemes and typical cross sections, sufficient to permit reasonably firm estimates of earthwork quantities.

3. Rainfall and run-off data and calculations of streamflow estimates, sufficient to permit rational design or drainage structure.

4. Sketches, diagrams or photographs of typical existing drainage works, bridges, retaining walls, tunnels, etc.

5. Location sketches of new major structures. Preliminary plans for modification of existing structures and for construction of typical new structures, culverts, drainage ditches, etc.

6. Preliminary schedule of drainage structures, giving approximate number and total length of each type and size.

7. Preliminary plans for modification of existing structure and or construction of typical new structures, culverts, drainage ditches, etc., in sufficient detail to permit reasonably close estimates of work quantities.

8. Preliminary plans of any major safety features such as median dividers, grade separations, interchanges, etc.

9. Results of soil and subsurface investigations for determination of quality of foundations for fills and major structures and for location of quarries and borrow pits.

10. Sufficient soil sampling along proposed alignment for deter-
    mination of types, characteristics, and quantities of the soil,
    including excavation material.(2)

Normally, in estimating principal quantities of constructions, the
owner of the project will permit a certain degree of accuracy of final
quantities. The principal quantities of construction will include common
excavation, rock excavation, base and sub-base material, surfacing
material, number and size of principal drainage structures, major
bridges, and other major structures. Preliminary engineering design of
major bridges and other major structures will include determination of
the approximate spans, types of superstructures, and types of foundations. On the basis of this preliminary engineering design, costs of
construction of the highway can be estimated.

In some projects, involvement of contractors and availability of
resources have to be considered. If the project is to be done jointly by
local and foreign contractors, it has to be stated clearly what parts of
construction will be done by each contractor. In this case, the components of foreign and local currency for all proposed construction have
to be identified. For example, the foreign currency component will
include such items as wages of foreign personnel, equipment and
imported materials. The local currency component will include such
things as local materials and supplies, local wages, and taxes. Cost
estimates will be used in the next stage of this phase or the economic
feasibility analysis. After preliminary engineering design has been
planned, an estimated program and time schedule for detailed engineering and construction can be calculated.

For industrial projects, and especially those involving manufacturing
plants, choice of the process is the first step in preliminary design after
the projects have been formulated. The type of process to be used
depends on:
1. The characteristics of the available raw materials.
2. The desired quality or specifications of the end product.
3. The manufacturing costs and the initial investment required.
The selected manufacturing process should be described based on the
advantages and disadvantages of alternative processes. The second step
is to determine the plant capacities and machinery design and specifications. The auxiliary equipment such as transport, material handling,
etc., have to be included in this design. Where major alternatives are
possible, each should be discussed with particular regard for comparative advantages and disadvantages.

Management Plans

The preliminary design must also present a fairly detailed plan for the
overall strategy that will be used to implement and operate the project.
In this section, the planners should include the detailed schedule of
project activities. If construction is to be undertaken, the schedule will

set out construction dates, time to negotiate subcontracts, lead time necessary to procure equipment, and critical times to hire employees. The essential point in planning the schedule is to include all project activities and to allow them adequate time. The more detailed the schedule, the more confidence it will impart in the project's viability.

Also vital to the management plan is the way in which the project will be coordinated and supervised. Since this depends upon the project organization, planners must specify the potential structure of the project and outline the major project participants, assigning each specific responsibilities.(3) In some cases, it is most effective to empower the project manager with overall authority, and at other times it is necessary to assign him a coordinative role with shared authority. Whatever structure of control is used, it is also necessary to specify the control and monitoring procedures that will be used to manage project activities. Other specific management aspects that should be included in the design are criteria for bidding, criteria for evaluating bids, contract and subcontract procedures, and the role of expert consultants in the project. Even though they may be designed in detail during later stages of the project, it is useful to articulate an overall philosophy regarding specific procedures. Not only does this make potential funders more confident that the project proponents are competent, it also makes the preliminary design a more complete document. The specific detail, however, must be kept within the bounds of the budget for the preliminary design.

Personnel data constitute a particularly important aspect of the management plan because they will be needed to estimate a project budget. The planners must include in this section estimates of the required humanpower and projections of the skilled personnel required to implement and operate the project. Since some of this information will be included within the technical section of the design, the planners will have to integrate the two sections carefully to avoid redundancy. The discussion of personnel should also project the number of consultants, with special regard for foreign consultants. Finally, the planners should spell out personnel recruiting procedures, hiring procedures, personnel policies, wages, salaries, other benefits, and personnel requirements and responsibilities.

Estimated project budget

Once the basic elements of the preliminary design have been set forth in sufficient detail, a project budget must be estimated.(4) This will include estimates for the total capital costs, if the project involves construction machinery, the estimates for the operating costs, and estimates for all preliminary work such as planning and mobilizing the project. To obtain reasonably accurate estimates, the planners must rely upon information from the other sections of the preliminary design. For example, if the planners are to estimate the costs of a geothermal power plant, they must know what kinds of turbine generators are being considered so that they can obtain prices from the manufacturers.

They must also have an indication of the number of employees to be hired, their rate of pay and their benefits, so that they can estimate these costs; then more detailed design work must be conducted. In this section, it is also imperative to estimate the costs of major alternatives. The geothermal power plant, for example, could use different cost generators and different cost pollution control systems; since the costs between these systems vary considerably, each must be put down as a major budget option.

In fashioning a preliminary design, there is a premium on preparing the most detailed and most complete plans for the least amount of money. Therefore, it is a common practice for project proponents to hire a consulting firm that specializes in preparing topic-specific preliminary designs. Such firms can produce comprehensive detailed designs rapidly, often using a general preset format but incorporating local information and data into it. Although these preliminary designs may be technically accurate and generally sound, and may be exactly what is required at this point in the project cycle, they often reflect a lack of understanding of special local conditions, particularly if the consulting firm is foreign. Therefore, it is essential for project proponents to carefully scrutinize any such preliminary designs and make modifications that account for local conditions. Although this can be done more carefully after the project is approved, glaring erroneous assumptions should be corrected as the last step in completing the preliminary design.

Once the preliminary design of a proposed project has been completed, it is then possible to examine the viability of that project within a comprehensive framework that analyzes and appraises the various components that constitute project feasibility. This most important set of tasks, feasibility and appraisal, is the subject of the next chapter.

NOTES

(1) Elwyn E. Seelye, Design (New York: John Wiley and Sons, 1951).

(2) Republic of the Philippines, National Economic and Development Authority, A Guide to Project Development (Manila), 1978, p. 180.

(3) East-West Technology and Development Institute, Entrepreneur Development Report, "Prefeasibility Exploration," Initiating Rural Non-Farm Projects: A Working Guide, Report of Inter-Country Research Mission and Workshop on Fostering Local Innovation to Meet Basic Needs, September 1977, p. 34.

(4) Vicente Muro, How to Study and Finance Philippines' Enterprises, (Quezon City, Philippines: Alomar Phoenix Publishers House, Inc., 1972), pp. 79-100.

SELECTED BIBLIOGRAPHY

Basheer, A.M. Steps in Agricultural Project Formulation, FAO/UNDP
    Training Course on Agricultural Project Formulation and Evaluation,
    mimeographed, Document E1-13382, (Rome), 1979.
Cotton, Frank E., Jr. Planning Methods for Administrators in Public
    Offices, Agencies, and Organizations, unpublished manuscript, 1978.
Groenveld, D.R. "The Preparation of Projects for Agricultural Develop-
    ment," East African Journal of Rural Development 2, no. 1 (1969):
    26-34.
Johnson, A.F. "Project Planning." Design of Small Dams. Water Re-
    sources Technical Publication, United States Department of the
    Interior, Bureau of Reclamation, 1960, pp. 1-17.
Muro, Vicente. How to Study and Finance Philippines' Enterprises.
    Quezon City, Philippines: Alomar Phoenix Publishers House, 1972.
Schroder, Harold J. "Making Project Management Work." Management
    Review 59, no. 11 (December, 1970): 24-28.
Seelye, Elwyn E. Design. New York: John Wiley & Sons, 1951.

5 Feasibility, Appraisal, and Design

Feasibility analysis, appraisal, and design, taken together, form the critical juncture in the integrated project cycle. As the culmination of preliminary studies and preliminary design, they provide a comprehensive analysis of all aspects of the proposed project. The feasibility analysis examines whether or not it is possible to implement a project given the standards and criteria set forth in the preliminary design. Appraisal, which occurs after the feasibility studies have been conducted and is based on their findings, evaluates whether or not a project should be implemented. It examines the project's overall contribution to development objectives both regionally and countrywide. This larger evaluation permits comparison of competing projects, where necessary, and is the basis for justifications supporting eventual approval. Design makes use of the inputs from the feasibility analysis and appraisal processes and uses these to modify the preliminary design documents into an updated and refined comprehensive report which will serve as the basis for final decision making in project approval.

Well-prepared feasibility analyses and appraisals examine and question every aspect of the preliminary design within the context of the actual project environment. They determine whether a project can be satisfactorily carried out with the financial, technical, human, material, and organizational resources available. Thus, together with design, feasibility and appraisal function as the interface between conception and reality. They link the planning set of project tasks – identification, formulation, and preliminary design – with the action-oriented set of tasks – selection and approval, activation, implementation, handover, and evaluation.

In providing this link, feasibility and appraisal serve several other crucial functions. First, by examining project goals and by questioning all assumptions, they provide a framework to reformulate the preliminary design into the most appropriate design. Second, feasibility and appraisal help guide the implementation of the project. Not only do they point out potential trouble spots, they also discuss the use of possible contingency plans. Finally, a complete feasibility study includes criteria and baseline measures to evaluate the project, providing the framework both to monitor the project during implementation and to evaluate its overall success and completion.

In the field of project management, the bulk of literature on feasibility, appraisal, and design deals almost exclusively with economic analysis (including market studies, which are not always applicable to development projects) and technical studies, with particular emphasis on engineering criteria. In practice, however, feasibility analysis, appraisal, and design incorporate a much wider range of factors than these – including such areas as management and personnel considerations, environmental impact, and sociopolitical repercussions – together with their often complex and overlapping relationships.

This chapter will attempt to describe six important areas – technical, administrative/managerial, environmental, social/political, economic, and financial – in which studies must be undertaken to examine a project's feasibility. It will then consider the appraisal process that integrates the findings of these studies to determine if the project, as designed, can satisfy both its own and its country's objectives. Finally, it will briefly touch on how the preliminary design, whose contents and sections have already been discussed in Chapter 4, can be refined and modified into a design for approval on the basis of the findings of feasibility analysis and appraisal.

FEASIBILITY

Although feasibility studies have, for convenience, been divided here into six major types, it is important to remember that these categories are interdependent and, in the case of closely related areas, often state the same information within different analytical frameworks. After these feasibility reports are completed, it will be the task of appraisal to provide the general overview that interprets and reconciles the specific analyses undertaken in each of these areas. The sequence in which these studies are examined here, however, does not necessarily reflect the real-life situation; often such reports are conducted simultaneously, unless (as in the case of technical studies that provide vital information for economic analyses) the data provided by one study are needed before the second study can begin.

Table 5.1 outlines the major areas of concern covered by the six types of feasibility analysis; a public works project, for example, would not always require a marketing program. A survey of table 5.1, moreover, shows that particular issues within these general guidelines are determined by the nature of individual projects. The livestock project's economic feasibility study, for example, would translate the problem of demand into an examination of beef consumption habits, both in the project's own country and in foreign markets. A social/political feasibility study for a health center project would have to consider

Table 5.1. Feasibility Matrix

SECTOR

Feasibility Study	Agriculture (a livestock project)	Industry (a geothermal electrical project)	Public Works or Infrastructure (a water improvement project)	Social (a health center project)
Technical				
a. Choice of Available Technologies	Evaluation of options for	Evaluation of options for	Evaluation of options for	Evaluation of options for
(1) Manufacturing process	cattle raising, slaughtering, and processing	converting geothermal heat into electricity	pumping and purifying water	not applicable
(2) Machinery and equipment	refrigeration units, packing facilities	generators and steam converters	pneumatic equipment	x-ray machines, cardiographs
(3) Spare parts	refrigerant coils, fencing	turbines, pipes, valves	water meters, pipes, valves	tubes, fuses
b. Design Requirements	Adequacy of	Adequacy of	Adequacy of	Adequacy of
(1) Layout	cattle pens, slaughterhouse location	reservoir existing on site	water supply system site	space for all health operations
(2) Engineering design	meat processing design	power plant design	structural and sanitation design	health center structure
(3) Construction materials	domestic & foreign supply of fencing barbed wire, refrigeration equipment	domestic & foreign supply of pipes, drills, valves	domestic & foreign supply of pipes, valves, meters, cement	domestic & foreign supply of cement, reinforcing steel, bricks
c. Manpower Requirements	Needs vs. availability of	Needs vs. availability of	Needs vs. availability of	Needs vs. availability of
(1) Professional	agronomist, engineer	geologist, reservoir engineer	construction engineer, hydrologist	construction engineer
(2) Technician	refrigeration specialist	test technicians	meter readers	health designers
(3) Labor	construction laborers	oil field workers	pipe layers	construction labor
Administrative/ Managerial				
a. Institutional Structure	Organization	Organization	Organization	
(1) Support	Ministry of Agriculture			
(2) Regulatory				
(3) Appropriations				
b. Internal organization	Evaluation of project's	Evaluation of project's	Evaluation of project's	Evaluation of project's
(1) Structure	hierarchical structure	matrix structure	hierarchical-matrix structure	matrix structure
(2) Function	flexibility	flexibility & coordination	flexibility	flexibility & responsiveness
(3) Authority	control by project director	control by section director	lines of control	lines of control
c. Personnel	Analysis of need for	Analysis of need for	Analysis of need for	Analysis of need for
(1) Needs/Capacity	cattlemen, project director	engineer, geologists	administrators, engineers	doctors, nurses, med-techs
(2) Policy	expatriates, flexibility	consultant experts	foreign advisors	rigid standards of hiring
d. Management	Evaluation of project's	Evaluation of project's	Evaluation of project's	Evaluation of project's
(1) Adequacy of supervision and control techniques	methods of monitoring and control	matrix supervision, independent controls	decentralized controls and policies	committee monitoring system
(2) Scheduling techniques	timetable for raising cattle & bringing to process	barchart for implementation of power plant	timetable for installing new pipes, water meters	timetable
Environmental				
a. Environmental suitability	Adequacy of pasture, water	Adequacy of geothermal heat	Adequacy of water supply	Adequacy of access, water
b. Resource management	Adequacy of erosion measures	Adequacy of protection for lens	Adequacy of safeguarding water	Adequacy of erosion, safety
c. Ecologic baseline	Baseline of	Baseline of	Baseline of	Baseline of
(1) Micro-analysis	flora, fauna, water, air	flora, fauna, water, air	flora, fauna, water, air	flora, fauna
(2) Macro-analysis	total ecologic system	total ecologic system	total ecologic system	total ecologic system
d. Ecologic Impact	Impact upon	Impact upon	Impact upon	Impact upon
(1) Short-term	pasture, erosion	Ghyben-Herzberg lens, air quality	fresh water species	erosion, biotic species
(2) Long-term and residual	total ecologic system	total ecologic system	total ecologic system	total ecologic system

Table 5.1 (Cont.)

Feasibility Study	Agriculture (a livestock project)	Industry (a geothermal electrical project)	Public Works or Infrastructure (a water improvement project)	Social (a health center project)
Social/Political				
a. Social impact	Impact upon beneficiaries'	Impact upon beneficiaries'	Impact upon beneficiaries'	Impact upon beneficiaries'
(1) Culture and lifestyle	diet, change, shared values	use of religions sites, rural lifestyle		traditional medical practices
(2) Demography	population size and distribution	population size, composition	population size, distribution	population size, distribution
b. Political impact	Impact upon beneficiaries'	Impact upon beneficiaries'	Impact upon beneficiaries'	Impact upon beneficiaries'
(1) Equity	distribution of income	electrical distribution	water distribution	health care equity
(2) Social justice	system of land tenure, health and safety	health & safety, religious & native rights	health and safety water rights	health & safety
(3) Political organization	traditional tribal leadership	community autonomy local leadership	local leadership	local autonomy
c. Community resistance	Potential protest-tenure rights	Potential protest-native claims	Potential protest-water use rights	Potential protest-loss of autonomy
d. Institutional resistance	Potential project barriers	Potential project barriers	Potential project barriers	Potential project barriers
(1) Legal constraints	health codes & land laws	health codes & zoning laws	zoning water laws	health codes
(2) Stability of political support	foreign government support	county, state, federal government	central government support	federal government support
Economic				
a. Demand	Consumption of beef	Electrical usage	Water usage	Health needs
(1) Domestic	locally	local residential & commercial	local needs	of community
(2) Export	regionally	regional total demand	regional needs	of region
b. Supply	Beef available	Electrical production	Water supply	Available health facilities
(1) Domestic	locally	locally	locally	community doctors, clinics
(2) Export	regionally	regionally	regionally	regional hospitals
c. Marketing program	Local market, export outlets	Residential & commercial sales	User rates	Pre-paid health plan
d. Employment effect	Meat processing employment	Geothermal power plant employed	Increased employment in water plant	Employment by health centers, medical aides
e. Raw materials	Availability of	Availability of	Availability	Availability
(1) Domestic	local stock and feed	local geothermal heat	locally of pipes, valves	locally of building materials
(2) Import	regional stock and feed	not applicable	regionally of meters, valves	regionally of building materials
f. Cost-benefit (social)	Net benefit of beef exporting	Net benefit of energy self-sufficiency	Net benefit of safe dependable supplies of water	Net benefit of improving community health
Financial				
a. Project design and implementation	Total cost of building pens & processing unit	Total cost of drilling well & building power plant	Total cost of installing & building water system	Total cost of building & equipping health center
b. Cash flow studies, Profitability	Projected 10 yr.	Projected 30 yr.	Projected 10 yr.	Projected 10 yr.
(1) External	beef sales vs. replenishment & operating cost	electrical users fees vs power plant operating costs	water users fees vs. operating plant costs	patient charges vs. operating costs
(2) Domestic				
c. Source of funding	Foreign assistance	Government energy agency	Government agency	Health agency
d. Adequacy of funds				

the ways in which sophisticated medical treatment might clash cul-
turally with traditional healing practices of the indigenous society. The
environmental impact study for a geothermal electrical project would
take up the question of the effects, both short- and long-term, of the
plant facility on surrounding air quality and other ecological factors.

With the broad guidelines of table 5.1 as a starting point, and
bearing in mind the difference between an ideal model and reality, the
six types of feasibility studies can be separately examined in greater
detail.

Technical Study

Technical feasibility studies remain the foundation of all other feasibility reports. A careful and thorough investigation of technical and
physical parameters is essential for an accurate assessment of a
project's capabilities. This is true for projects in developing countries,
where a common error of foreign consultants brought in at the planning
stage of a project is to lay down technical specifications that cannot be
met by the country's own resources. Projects in developed countries, it
should be noted, founder just as readily when technical feasibility has
not been adequately determined.

Feeding directly from the specifications of preliminary design (see
Chapter 4), a technical study establishes further design criteria, conducts engineering studies to determine physical and technological
alternatives to meet budget and sociopolitical requirements, outlines
the form that activation and implementation will take, and estimates
the scheduling of project inputs and outputs to satisfy both immediate
and long-term development goals. As the bedrock of the project, this
technical analysis must therefore anticipate the broader considerations
to be taken up in the economic feasibility study by addressing three
interrelated questions:

1. Is there an adequate choice of available technologies for alternative
   design purposes, considering physical layout, engineering design, and
   availability of raw materials?
2. What are the costs of constructing and operating project facilities
   (and services), including machinery, equipment, and spare parts as
   appropriate?
3. What are the manpower requirements, from professional to labor,
   and are they locally available?

The responses to these questions will clearly vary according to sector,
as noted in table 5.1.

Besides its primary task of blueprinting humanpower, resources, and
design, the technical study must provide design alternatives, a choice of
available technologies, and cost estimates for each alternative. In the
water improvement project shown in table 5.1, for example, the
pumping equipment would have to be selected from a wide array of
types of pumps, with the availability of spare parts for the pumps in the
project's home country being an important consideration. The results of

the technical analysis are also the basis for cost estimates and implementation schedules, necessary input for both economic and financial feasibility analysis.

Technical investigators compiling a project feasibility report must fully understand the concept of alternative ways of solving potential problems. Technical solutions may differ in their 1) technical or production process, 2) size or scale, 3) location, and 4) timing. Because these factors are interdependent, a sound knowledge of their relationships is necessary to ensure consistency in the analysis; a labor-intensive production process, for example, would be appropriate only for a certain scale of production. The degree to which these factors are interdependent, moreover, will also depend on the type of project.

The importance of this aspect of feasibility analysis can be demonstrated by a closer look at some specific factors to be considered in, for example, infrastructure projects, where technical considerations are critical. What technical feasibility factors, for example, might be relevant to transportation projects? Projects for the construction of roads or bridges would have to consider such factors as need (including the project's relationships to the existing transport network), location, nature of subsurface conditions, alignment, width (traffic capacity, present and future), drainage, earthwork (cuts and fills, including selection and availability of both local materials and equipment), pavement selection, design, and construction, and the cost-benefit to the user, which will also be analyzed in the economic feasibility study.

Suppose, alternatively, the project under consideration were a waterworks project for domestic consumption. In this case, feasibility experts might examine the relative benefits to two types of water storage: earth dams versus deep wells. Determining the feasibility of an earth dam would require analysis of such factors as demand or capacity; dam location (including quality of water, stream flow and other pertinent hydrologic data, rainfall and runoff, and water losses through seepage and evaporation); availability of local materials for construction; foundation selection, design, and construction; reservoir design and construction; and purification system. Factors determining the feasibility of a deep well, on the other hand, would likewise include demand, location, pumping system/equipment, and purification system.

As the foregoing demonstrates, the detailed data generated by the technical feasibility study will almost always result in modification of preliminary design specifications, a process that will continue throughout the project's lifetime. The technical feasibility study, however, provides the first systematic investigation of project design viability.

Administrative/Managerial Study

The administrative/managerial study evaluates the strategy of the implementing agency in carrying out project activities. Although the analysis is intended to assess the feasibility of this strategy, it should concentrate on providing information and guidelines that can be used to improve overall project administration. Since the effectiveness of the management plan depends upon experience and actual practice in applying management techniques, it is desirable to include a project manager on the investigating team. The study examines four separate components: external linkages, internal organization, personnel, and management plan.(1)

External linkages refer to the structure of government and private organizations that directly or indirectly conditions the project environment. These include the administrative funding agency, the regulating agency the project must abide by, and the numerous advisory organizations that provide political, technical, and other types of support. Although the feasibility analysis can suggest little to alter the institutional relationships of the project, it should be able to determine the kinds of barriers and support the project can expect to encounter. Especially vital is information on whether the implementing agencies are capable of providing adequate support, particularly for large and complex projects. With this knowledge, project planners can prepare for contingencies and cultivate appropriate linkages to mediate possible adverse impacts of the institutional environment. One decision about project environment that will deeply affect the organizational course of the project is the choice (if available) between building up the capability of existing institutions to implement the project or creating a new organization to operate the project.

Internal organization is the actual organization of the implementing unit. While all kinds of possibilities exist, ranging from matrix to hierarchical, the study should determine whether the proposed organization can implement the project satisfactorily. Some relevant questions to be asked about the proposed organization are: Is it comprehensive enough? Is the organization appropriate to carrying out project goals? Is it flexible enough? Are internal lines of communication well-established and lines of authority clearly defined?(2) Although the most appropriate type of internal organization depends upon the project goals and requirements, one can generally say that a project requiring individual initiative, individual flexibility, and individual accountability should be organized in matrix fashion. A project requiring a high degree of coordination, authority, and supervision should be organized in more hierarchical fashion. Thus, the feasibility study should discriminate between the advantages and disadvantages of each in evaluating the project organization necessary to accomplish the objectives.

Management is the specified management plan of the project. Basic questions the analysis should ask include: Are schedules and networks sufficiently worked out? What are the control techniques and the methods of supervision? Is the entire management plan integrated so that the project manager can control all aspects of the project? Is the management of the project well enough formulated to impart the assurance that the project will be well-coordinated and controlled? Does the plan provide for contingencies? A key issue here is whether the plans are realistic, given the actual project environment. For example, procurement of certain equipment often requires a long lead time in many countries. If adequate lead time is not scheduled, it can cripple the manager's ability to coordinate activities.

Personnel is perhaps the key issue in administrative feasibility. Without competent and appropriate personnel, a project has a difficult time in succeeding. The analysis of the proposed personnel plans should evaluate several key items. First, it should ensure that the job descriptions and qualifications are appropriate and that they are written out completely. Next, it should examine whether or not the necessary personnel are available to the project. Then, the impact on every area of a project made by the choice of foreign or local personnel – not only in activation and implementation but also in preliminary design, technical analysis, and general consulting – should be examined. Finally, the analysis should question whether there is adequate provision for hiring expert consultants in crisis situations.

The four components of administrative feasibility – external linkages, internal organization, management, and personnel – are often referred to collectively as operational feasibility.(3) Taken in this sense, operational feasibility focuses on the point in time when the project has been approved and is ready for activation and implementation. An operational feasibility study must therefore include consideration of such factors as, for example, whether or not project implementation will generate the expected budgets. The project's operational feasibility will depend on how well it meets estimates in terms of 1) political acceptability and/or legality of activities; 2) organization or administrative structure and management aspects; and 3) availability of resources and operating costs.

These considerations must also be dealt with, in varying degree, by the financial and social/political feasibility studies, demonstrating the overlapping boundaries of all these analyses. In the operational feasibility report, however, the emphasis is usually on organization and management aspects. The soundness of a project is often determined by the thoroughness of its management and organization planning. With competent management, a project may be successful even when there are inadequacies in the original concept. But it is doubtful whether any project, however well-conceived, can overcome the handicap of poor management. Equally, it is difficult for managers, no matter how competent and experienced, to succeed without the necessary personnel, equipment, materials, and other resources required for effective operation and maintenance.

In sum, major areas that must be explored in the operational feasibility study are:

1. The political acceptability and legality of project operation.
2. The organization that will manage the project and supervise its operations; to be accompanied by an organization chart, initial and projected, together with the staffing pattern and functional statements of the organizational units.
3. Experience records of available key management and technical personnel.
4. Number, qualifications, and availability of required operating employees.

5. Plans for recruiting and training of required personnel.
6. Projections for competent management and maintenance throughout the project's life.
7. Availability of necessary supplies, materials, equipment, and other logistics.

Examined in turn, these areas add up to a comprehensive picture of the organizational capacities and limitations of a proposed project, a perspective that is vital to both project planners and policy makers.

Environmental Study

The environmental study addresses two separate questions:
1. Is the environment suitable for the success of the project?
2. What will be the project's impact on the environment?

In determining environmental suitability, the feasibility study must ask whether or not a given environment can support a given project. The environmental analysis of an agricultural project, for example, must raise and answer such questions as: Is the soil quality appropriate for the proposed crops? Is there sufficient water? Is there adequate drainage? Is there adequate sunlight? Is the climate right?

Industrial and infrastructure projects pose other questions, some of which were raised earlier in the area of technical feasibility in site and location studies. In this context, there is a natural overlap between technical and environmental analyses; and, where appropriate, the studies should be combined. A separate environmental study, however, adds an extra dimension to the technical study by ensuring that the technical analysis includes two important considerations: 1) the project's present environmental needs and 2) its long-term environmental needs. Environmental suitability poses the question of whether or not the ecosystem of a region can support a project over the long term. And this introduces the concept of resource management for the project.

The practical importance of examining long-term as well as short-term environmental needs can be illustrated by a fairly common example of project short-sightedness. Suppose a pulp and paper plant is built in a heavily forested area of a country. Project planners know that the forests have a projected life expectancy of twenty years but do not take into account what might happen to the pulp and paper plant after that time. In a matter of several years, with vast tracts of the forest severely depleted, it becomes evident that the environment's long-term ability to support the paper plant has not been considered, with the result that the plant will face a shutdown in the near future with corresponding waste of manpower and material resources.

Although such obvious factors that concern the environment's impact on the project are usually taken into account, with the project's environmental needs studied and systematically examined either in feasibility studies or in the project design, the reverse is not always true, which leads us to our second main consideration. Environmental studies must also ensure that systematic assessment is made of the project's impact on the environment; for, as the previous example demonstrates, this is clearly a two-way street. The studies must therefore examine a project's likely effect upon soil erosion, water supplies, wildlife, and plants.(4) They must also examine the project's potential to deplete nonrenewable resources, to create adverse micro-climactic changes, and to pollute the water, air, or land.

Several methods can be used to assess these environmental impacts. Mapping, computer simulation, social cost-benefit, various scoring techniques, and matrix methods all provide systematic evaluation.(5) Choice of the best method in each case, however, depends upon the data available, the type of project, and the sophistication of analysis desired. All these methods begin by collecting baseline data of the environment. With this data, the project's environmental impact can be analyzed in a systematic and comprehensive manner and the estimated degree of its impact can be projected.

Probably the most practical and straightforward of these methods is the matrix, which is used in figure 5.1 to illustrate the major concerns of an environmental study (see also table 5.1).(6) The matrix begins with four rows of general categories that detail the characteristics of the environment. These four categories are interfaced with eleven columns classifying the kinds of activities the project will engage in. The blank spaces are filled in with the probable type of impact each project activity will have on each sector of the environment.

PRESENT ENVIRONMENT

	Ecological (e.g., plants)	Physical/Chemical (e.g., air quality)	Aesthetic (e.g., scenic area)	Social (e.g., health)	Ecological Relationships (e.g., food chains)
Regime Modification (river control)					
Construction					
Resource Extraction					
Processing					
Land Transformation					
Resource Renewal					
Traffic Changes					
Waste Treatment					
Chemical Treatment					
Accident					

Fig. 5.1. Environmental impact matrix: potential project activities.

The most important task in the environmental impact statement, however, remains collection of the baseline data. This includes lists of the types and numbers of plants and animals (see table 5.1) and a macroanalysis of the total ecologic system. Periodic checks of the baseline can be made as the project progresses; these checks will monitor the actual impact of the project on the environment.

Environmental impact statements are costly, and their findings have, in certain industrialized nations, delayed or even halted projects. Industrialized nations can certainly afford to make choices that safeguard the environment; other nations may have harder choices to make. Regardless of the decisions that confront each country, however, an environmental impact statement informs policy makers of the environmental consequences of their decisions. With this information, a project can be planned to meet the critical needs of a nation and also to include – where feasible and practical – adjustments to ensure future resource needs.

Social/Political Study

A social/political study is seldom undertaken when project feasibility studies are being conducted. Even when one is made, it is infrequently given adequate weight in assessing the project. Yet social and political factors can often be the primary reason a project fails to achieve its ultimate objectives. This is particularly true of projects in the social sector, where success cannot be measured in economic or directly quantifiable terms.

The social/political study attempts to answer four basic questions:
1. What is the project's likely social impact?
2. What is the project's likely political impact?
3. What social factors in the project environment will hinder or aid the project in achieving its goals?
4. What political factors in the project environment will hinder or aid the project in achieving its goals?

The first step in conducting the social/political study is to collect baseline economic and sociological data of the community for which the project is intended. This data is intended to provide a general profile of the area's residents and should include demograpic information such as population level and distribution, employment pattern, levels and distribution of income, education, and the housing and health situation. Also vital to the analysis is information about the social fabric of the area. This information focuses on variables such as the degree of community solidarity and integration, the lifestyle of the residents, important customs, the residents' recreational habits, values, and family structure.

Then the political structure must be detailed. Focusing on the decision-making process, this section of the analysis describes the area's political relationship to regional and national governments and assesses its political autonomy. This section also describes the area's informal political organizations and formal political institutions, and specifies the local ordinances, zoning requirements, and statutes that will affect the project. Finally, information must be gathered on the opinions and attitudes of residents and leaders toward the project. Particularly important is resident opinion about how the project will affect the area, about how the project can be improved, and about how the project can be made acceptable.(7) While this aspect of the study is intended to collect information for future planning, it is also intended to provide avenues for local participation in planning the project. Thus, the ideal techniques to use are open community meetings. Often, however, it is not practical to hold such meetings, and other less direct techniques such as questionnaires, interviews, panel methods, and expert judgments must be used to obtain community input.

Once the basic data are collected, they must be synthesized in a report that systematically describes the total political and social environment. This is the point where most social/political analyses end, but it is actually just where the study should begin. Still to be examined are how the project, as planned, will affect the area socially and politically; and how the area's social and political reality will affect the project.

Although various frameworks, such as scoring techniques, social assessment, social accounting, and ecologic analysis, are used to address these questions, no broadly accepted framework exists.(8) Each framework has limitations, particularly in its reduction of sensitive social and political factors to quantitive indicators. Moreover, any framework imposes the limitations set by the questions it is designed to examine.   Thus, in conducting the analysis, it is wiser to concentrate less on the use of a specific framework than to pose questions about the project that are sensitive to the social and political concerns of the area. This emphasis puts extreme importance on the individuals who are to prepare the study. Ideally, they should be intimately familiar with the social, cultural, and political aspects of the area. In many instances, residents qualified to conduct the study are the most competent persons.

Let us amplify this discussion by turning to the example of a Pacific island livestock project.(9) Most appropriately, the investigators selected to conduct the study were native Pacific islanders with experience in livestock management and production. First, they comprehensively outlined the social and political setting of the area. Once this task was completed, they examined the setting in relationship to the project and noted that two social/political factors were relevant to project plans: first, the land-tenure system was traditional, meaning that land was collectively owned by entire villages, and second, there was a lack of indigenous humanpower trained in livestock production. In analyzing the first factor, they noted that the project might be hindered because an entire village must collectively agree to let its land be used for cattle raising; they recommended that the project employ someone familiar with appropriate ways of proceeding with any negotiations. The lack of indigenous skilled humanpower meant that the project would have to rely heavily on foreign personnel and foreign techniques. Since these techniques might be inappropriate to the Pacific, it was recommended that the project establish a local training program or that the project operate first as a pilot experiment. Finally, in concluding the study, the investigators noted that the traditional lifestyle and autonomy of the villages would be disrupted by the building of roads to transport the beef, the operation of processing facilities, and the intrusion upon the tenure system. Thus, in opening the area and making it more accessible, the project would strain the governing capacities of the local villages and make them more vulnerable to disruption.

Such an example shows how a social/political study, conducted by researchers knowledgeable about local settings, can reveal a possible serious conflict of interest between project goals and the underlying social fabric of a region of a country. Failure to consider such factors can undermine the success of an otherwise well-planned and executed project. A perceptive social/political feasibility report anticipates these types of conflicts and proposes modifications or alternative procedures to avert them. In cases where the project by its intrinsic nature runs counter to the social pattern of its region of operation, its chances to achieve viability in the long-term should be reassessed.

Economic Study

An economic study examines a proposed project in terms of its net contribution to the economy and to society. The study should address three interrelated questions:

1. Is the project responsive to an urgent present or anticipated economic and social need?
2. Will the project's planned economic outputs adequately serve the intended purpose?
3. Will the services proposed to be performed through the project and the benefits produced by the project justify its cost?

To respond to these questions requires a detailed study of all the economic implications of the project, such as the demand for and supply of all project outputs, the project's ability to earn foreign exchange, its effect on employment, and its use of natural resources. Once these studies are completed, the project's overall economic impact can be assessed by means of a cost-benefit (c-b) analysis. This analysis can be used for both private and public projects. In a private investment project, the c-b analysis examines private profitability – that is, the project's ability to earn a net profit for its investors. In a public project, social cost-benefit analysis is used. This analysis examines the project's social profitability – its contribution to the national economy and to achieving specified national goals such as economic growth, social growth, and income redistribution. The remaining discussion focuses on the latter type of assessment.

There are various techniques of social cost-benefit analysis. However, the three most commonly used are the net present value (npv), the cost-benefit ratio (c/b), and the internal rate of return (irr).(10) Each of the techniques, and in fact the entire concept of c-b analysis, has basic limitations.(11) Before addressing these limitations, however, it is necessary to describe techniques with a specific example.

Let us consider the Ratnigiri fisheries project,(12) a development project in which the Maharashtra government intends to promote the well-being of individuals in the Ratnigiri District by:
1. Building thirty fishing trawlers and financing their sale
2. Building a freezing plant to package the catch of shrimp and fish
3. Constructing an ice plant
4. Constructing a service station for the trawlers
The Ratnigiri District Fisheries Federation is to be the implementing group, and it will be responsible for selling the trawlers to local fishermen and for operating the plant and service station. Operations based on the project are expected to continue for twenty-two years with 1970 as the base year. Social cost-benefit analysis will be used to determine the project's net economic contribution to society.

To prepare the analysis, the first step is to estimate the project costs for each of its twenty-two years. These estimates should include all capital costs such as the price of trawlers, freezers, and plant construction; they should also include all operating costs such as wages and salaries, taxes, and loan repayments.

The next step is to estimate the benefits generated by the project. In this instance, the benefits would include revenue from the sale of frozen fish and shrimp, money earned from the sale of ice, and, in the final years, money from the sale of scrap machinery. The costs and benefits are then listed year by year. Columns 1 and 2 of table 5.2 illustrate five of the project's twenty-two years.

Table 5.2. A Partial List of Project Costs and Benefits

For Year	To Project Sponsors		To Society	
	Benefits	Costs	Benefits	Costs
1	289	2273	289	1742
5	2388	3105	3051	1503
10	2585	2862	3327	1503
15	2470	2544	3182	1479
22	1464	818	1678	536
Total all years*	47258	58972	59601	36340

*Includes also those yearly costs and benefits not listed

These figures, however, simply represent the project's financial ledger. They reflect the costs and benefits to the project sponsor, not the project's actual contribution to society. To determine contribution to society, changes must be made in calculating the costs and benefits. First, in determining costs, only those payments that reflect the actual use of a societal resource must be charged against the project. Payments that simply represent the transfer of control over resources from one segment of society to another should be deducted. These economic transfers include project costs such as taxes, loan repayments, and interest payments on loans.

Second, since the project contributes to society above and beyond earning a profit, this contribution should be added into the calculation of benefits. In this respect, the project will contribute to society by 1) promoting India's self-sufficiency through the import earning of foreign exchange, and 2) promoting development by employing unskilled workers in the Ratnigiri District, which is classified by the Indian government as "backward." To reflect these social contributions, the project's net earnings of foreign exchange and its wage payments to unskilled laborers must be weighed more heavily than their actual market value. This would signify in economic terms the project's contribution to society.

In this case, the foreign exchange is valued forty percent more highly than the official market price. This percentage is based on several studies and reflects the scarcity of foreign exchange in India, as well as its value in promoting self-sufficiency. The project's wages to unskilled workers are valued twenty percent more highly than their actual price. Again, this percentage is based on several studies; basically, it weights the project's contribution to the national development goal of employing low-status groups. It must be noted that wages are counted as project costs. Therefore, in charging costs to the project, the wages paid to unskilled laborers are reduced by twenty percent. Table 5.2 demonstrates how the stream of costs and benefits is altered by evaluating the project's contribution to society.

Using the costs and benefits to society shown in table 5.2, we can now calculate 1) the net present value (npv), 2) the benefit-to-cost ratio (b/c), and 3) the internal rate of return (irr). It should be noted that if this were a formal analysis, estimates of all project expenditures and receipts would have to be itemized for each of the project's years. However, for this illustrative example we need only be concerned with the total costs and benefits listed in table 5.2. Calculation of the npv can now be demonstrated.

The net present value (npv) is, quite simply, the amount remaining after subtracting the present value of all project costs from the present value of all project benefits. The key terms are present value. This concept can be explained as follows: Since the project's operations occur in the future, the project will incur costs and produce benefits at different points in time. Hence, it is necessary to express future costs and benefits in terms of their present worth (the present in this case is the base year of 1970). For this project, all future costs and benefits must be translated into 1970 rupees. This can be accomplished by using a social rate of discount, which is a specified percentage at which to devalue future project costs and benefits. In essence, a discount rate assumes that the exact same benefits produced by the project decline in value each succeeding year. For example, if the project earns 100 rupees in 1990, this amount – when expressed in 1970 rupees – is much less. It is less because inflation, constantly rising incomes, and interest rates mean that the purchasing power of the 100 rupees declines in the future. This is the rationale for a financial discount rate. However, we must calculate a social rate of discount.

In calculating the social discount rate, one must also weigh the decline in social value of future benefits. For example, fish for the local market are one of the Ratnigiri project's outputs. The social utility of one ton of fish in 1970 is much greater than its social utility in 1990. This is because the people need the fish now to supplement their diet. Therefore one ton of fish in the present is much more useful than one ton of fish in the future. Economists refer to this concept as a social preference rate, or a preference for the present. In this case, it assumes that individuals and social groups would consider one ton of fish today much more valuable than one ton of fish in 1990. The key question is how much more valuable. And this question is answered by the social rate of discount, since this rate is the specified percentage by which to devalue future project benefits, such as fish.

The social rate of discount is critical because it reduces future costs and benefits sequentially, in an annual time series. Thus, if a ten percent discount rate is used, then one year from now 100 rupees of project benefits will be devalued to ninety rupees. But two years from now, 100 rupees of benefits are devalued by the ten rupees lost during the first year plus an additional ten percent lost during the second year. This means that two years from now 100 rupees of project benefits will be valued at only eighty-one rupees. The discount rate thus drastically reduces a project's social profitability. Moreover, the higher the discount rate, the greater the magnitude of reduction. Table 5.3 demonstrates what happens to the Ratnigiri project's costs and benefits when discounted at 200 percent, ten percent, and thirty percent.

Needless to say, an appropriate rate of discount must be chosen to make the npv meaningful. In this instance the discount rate is ten percent; it was chosen because it reflected the Indian level of consumption, population growth, time preference for consumption, and several other variables. Given the discount rate, npv can now be calculated. The formula is:

$$\text{Npv} = \sum_{t=0}^{T} \frac{B_t}{(1+r)\,t} - \frac{C_t}{(1+r)\,t}$$

Where T = the project life in years from the base year
B = project benefits in the tth year
C = project in the tth year
r = the social rate of discount

Table 5.3. Ratnigiri Project – Discounted Project
Costs and Benefits
(Selected Years)

Year	Discounted at 0%		Discounted 10%		Discounted 30%	
	Costs	Benefits	Costs	Benefits	Costs	Benefits
1	1716	406	1583	263	1340	222
5	1399	2798	933	1895	404	820
10	1399	2798	579	1281	108	239
15	1399	2798	353	760	28	60
22	515	1477	66	206	2	5
Total* all years	34179	54642	15277	20979	6673	6661

*Includes totals from all 22 years

The formula reflects the time series necessary to calculate the discounted project totals. But in this case, we simply take the discounted total net benefits and costs from table 5.3:

$\underline{b}$ = 20,979,000

$\underline{c}$ = 15,277,000

$\underline{b} - \underline{c}$ = 5,702,000

Thus, 5,702,000 rupees is the npv.

The benefit-to-cost (b/c) ratio is the discounted sum of all project costs divided by the discounted sum of all project benefits. The formula is simply b/c or in this case, 2097000/15277000 = 1.37. The decision rule is simply that a project contributes to society if b/c is greater than 1.

The internal rate of return (irr) is the discount rate that will make the project's net present benefits equal to its net present costs over a given period of time. Unlike the b/c ratio or the npv, the internal rate of return does not rely upon a specified discount rate. Instead, the irr determines the discount rate at which the project will neither benefit nor cost society. To calculate the irr, different rates are used until the rate is found that will make the net present value equal to zero. In this case, the irr is twenty-six percent. This percentage does not automatically indicate whether the project is justified based on its contribution to society. It requires someone to set an evaluative standard, that is, a desired social discount rate. If the project's irr exceeds this standard, then it is deemed to benefit society.

Each of these three techniques arrived at a single figure, which may be considered the measure of the project's economic benefits to society. The three figures arrived at for this project were:

Net Present Value	Benefit-Cost Ratio	Internal Rate of Return
5,702,000	1.37	26%

These figures can be used to compare competing projects or competing alternatives of the same project in a systematic and somewhat objective fashion. As this example demonstrated, however, there are limits to cost-benefit analysis.(13) First, only those project impacts that can be quantified in economic terms can be incorporated into the analysis. Thus, social projects, which may produce benefits such as teaching a village how to organize or instilling in the villagers a sense of pride and self-worth, cannot be adequately assessed by using cost-benefit analysis. Second, the definition of certain benefits must be conceived very narrowly. For example, in this case self-sufficiency was defined as earning foreign exchange, and this is an extremely narrow definition. Finally, in determining weights by which to value a project's contribution to society or in determining the social rate of discount, there is too much room for discretion and arbitrariness. Given this flexibility, a cost-benefit analysis can be manipulated to show a social profit.

Put in perspective, then, cost-benefit analysis allows one to compare competing projects and alternative approaches to the same project. But it is not a precise measure of the project's actual value to society. The term "social" cost-benefit is misleading; it creates the illusion that the analysis has considered the social consequences, when in fact, as the example demonstrated, very few social implications can be considered and even these are defined too narrowly. In most instances, therefore, it is necessary for the decision maker to take the calculations of cost-benefit as an approximate magnitude of the project's actual worth.

Financial Study

The financial study addresses five basic questions:
1. What are the magnitudes of the capital and operating costs of the project?
2. What are the sources of funds and draw-down schedules, and are they sufficient to cover costs of activities and implementation? What are the alternative financing schemes from other funding sources?
3. What is the projected cash flow of the project? To what extent are necessary borrowings scheduled to meet running deficits at activation? How soon do initial revenues come in to take up part or all of operating costs?

4. Is there an adequate accounting system to regularly provide balance sheets, cash flow statements, debt servicing schedules, and other financial reports?
5. What are the provisions for project-completion investment and other means of recovery investment and operating costs?

An important feature of the financial study is that it totals up the cost of project implementation and design that was broken down separately in the other feasibility studies. In many projects, therefore, economic and financial feasibility considerations overlap, and in some cases there might be good cause to conduct these two analyses simultaneously.

The two factors to be distinguished in financial analysis are 1) whether the project can succeed with the amount of money projected in the project proposal, and 2) whether the project is expected, if it is in the private sector, to show a profit. In private sector projects, financial analysis will also determine the rate of return on the investment.

Assessing financial profitability and debt service capacity during the project's lifetime involves a projection of all revenues and expenses, receipts and expenditures, defined as follows:

1. Revenues: transactions that generate income, whether or not cash inflows are involved.
2. Expenses: transactions that reduce income, also irrespective of cash flows.
3. Receipts: transactions that involve cash inflows, whether or not income is generated.
4. Expenditures: transactions that involve cash outflows, whether or not income is reduced.

Simply stated, revenues and expenses affect project income, and receipts and expenditures affect cash position. Thus, revenues and expenses determine the project's profitability, and receipts and expenditures determine debt-servicing capacity, which is more directly dependent on cash position.

To determine the project's profitability and debt-servicing capacity, projections of the following financial statements are made:

1. Profit and loss statement (income statement)
2. Balance sheet
3. Cash flow statement

The periods covered by the project statements may vary from the first few years of normal operation to the entire project lifetime, depending on the purpose for which the statements will be used, and the reliability of estimates for later years.

Many projects, it should be noted, are financed through loans from development banks such as the World Bank, the Asian Development Bank, and others. The World Bank normally follows a policy to create a balance among the need to use scarce resources efficiently, considerations of equity, and the need to generate additional funds to replicate the project to reach the largest numbers of potential beneficiaries. The Bank also scrutinizes each project to ensure that the fund requested will be sufficient to implement the project. In the long run, this examination helps to assure a successful project, which in turn helps to ensure the Bank that its loans will be repaid.

Completing the Feasibility Studies

Once the feasibility studies have been completed, they must be packaged together as a single document. The individual studies form the heart of the document, while an introductory and concluding chapter provide organization and coherence. The introductory chapter summarizes the major findings of the studies. Since these findings are intended for the decision maker who may not have time to read the entire volume, each finding should be brief and precise and should reference the page numbers where the detailed information can be found. The introductory chapter should also include a description of the project as well as its relationship to a larger program and to other related projects. Finally, the introductory chapter should clearly and explicitly list the goals and objectives of the project.

The feasibility study should conclude with a final chapter on the evaluation of the project. Included in this chapter should be a discussion that specifies the data required for the evaluation. Generally, these data should measure the extent to which the project has achieved the goals and objectives specified in the introductory chapter. For example, if one takes the Ratnigiri Fisheries project discussed earlier, the project goals and objectives included increasing self-sufficiency and promoting the development of low-status groups. Relevant measures of the project's achieving these goals could include the amount of foreign exchange earned by the project, the extent to which the project generated income to the Ratnigiri District, an assessment of the project's impact in generating new subsidiary business enterprises, the number of unskilled laborers employed, the numbers of these people advancing to skilled-labor positions, and the number of people learning a new trade or skill. Usually, project goals also specify that the project have acceptable environmental and social impacts. Thus, in the case of the fisheries project, the concluding chapter would also stipulate the collection of environmental baseline measures, such as the number of fish and shrimp in the fishing ground. Periodic checks against the baseline would monitor the depletion of the resource. As a final issue, the concluding chapter should discuss who is to collect the data, when the data should be collected, and who should conduct the evaluation.

APPRAISAL

After the individual feasibility studies have been assembled, an appraisal report must tie together these diverse findings, attempting to reconcile conflicting results and providing an overall assessment of the project's likelihood for success.

Project appraisal must address two questions:

1. Will the project as designed meet its own objectives as well as the larger needs of its location and country?
2. How does the project compare with other projects it may be competing with for funding?

Although the competitive factor is not always present in project selection, it can be an important dimension in situations where a number of project proposals have been put forward to fill a particular need, or where there is not enough funding to cover all areas of development. In such cases, comparing of projects to assess which one provides the most jobs, for example, becomes an important task.

The primary function of appraisal, however, remains to evaluate a project's potential to meet its own stated objectives and to provide for long-term economic growth in the larger framework of local and national needs. It should be noted that some debate has been focused on the scope of the appraisal function – whether it consists merely of a social cost-benefit analysis within a larger country framework or whether, in fact, some of the issues involved at this level of decision making – disruption or strengthening of cultural values, for example, or increase or decrease of life expectancies of citizens – can even be quantifiable.(14) While social cost benefit at this level is interpreted in strictly economic terms, such as benefits to the country's economy, consumer surplus, and income, social cost also includes intangible factors such as equity and social justice.

No matter how these larger issues are approached, there is no substitute for sound, thoroughly researched feasibility studies as the groundwork for decision making. In this respect, all aspects of feasibility must be examined, from technical to social-political. All too often, a project fails to achieve its ultimate goals because the social and political impacts were not addressed. And equally all too often, an ambitious project design proves too sophisticated to implement in an environment with limited resources, making the project impossible to sustain without continued reliance on outside aid. Such mismatings of plan with reality would be less likely to occur if all feasibility studies had been both thoroughly executed and intelligently appraised. If a project is to be feasible in the true sense of the term, it must be viable within the environment it has been designed to improve; all long-term projections of benefit are undermined if the most basic capabilities and limitations of site and country have not been carefully considered.

Assessment Factors

How is the integration of feasibility studies and outside policy factors into a comprehensive appraisal to be accomplished? As mentioned earlier, all data provided by the feasibility reports, including conflicting findings, must be taken into account without compromising the main factors involved. Thus, the process of appraisal involves more than simply adding up projected gains and losses as quantified in the feasibility studies. If, for example, a highway project between two market towns will provide employment for unskilled labor and will bolster small-farm economy, how should these two pluses be weighed against the minus that the highway may produce more rapid center growth, disrupting the rural social structure?

Such decisions frequently have a political dimension that varies widely with the situation, and this political aspect is crucial because it goes beyond feasibility. It addresses the question of whether or not a project should be undertaken. It also defines alternatives, providing a basis for making a decision to identify and select a design for final approval.

To illustrate appraisal, let us take an infrastructure project to build a highway. The first step in writing the appraisal report might be to provide an overview of this highway project as its fits within the larger transport system of the country. Such an overview would include a description of the existing highway system, a description of existing transport systems other than highways, an assessment of ways in which lack of highway transport has been slowing the country's economic growth; a description of any national program for highway development together with this project's priority in the program and reasons for assigning it this priority; and, finally, the development plan for the region this highway project will tranverse and how the project fits into this plan.

Next, an appraisal would compare the project to other transport systems currently in use. It would describe existing distribution of traffic among the various types of transport in the project area; it would estimate the effect the highway project would have on present distribution and on the economics of the other transport systems. It would list the comparative availability of types of vehicles, operating personnel, and other components among the various types of transport systems, together with their relative costs of operation.

From this overview, the appraisal would move into analysis of specific components based on information provided by the various feasibility studies. Under technical analysis, the appraisal would summarize findings of the technical feasibility report, including such engineering aspects as existing road conditions, alternative technical solutions, preliminary surveys and plans, construction standards, availability of local resources, anticipation of special construction problems, and preliminary design for project implementation.

The appraisal's administrative/managerial section would outline the important features of construction organization, as provided by the administrative/managerial feasibility study, and − a second important factor − the organization of maintenance and operation of the highway after it has been completed. Turning to environmental impact, the appraisal would note what effect, if any, alignment or location of the highway would have on natural resources. If the effect appears detrimental, the appraisal would select the best alternative route from among the choices given in either the technical or the environmental feasibility study. It should be noted, however, that even if the original route is shown to have an adverse impact, this negative factor must still be weighed against all the other positive factors the project may possess, with final selection of the route to be used determined in the wrap-up of the appraisal report, after all pros and cons have been carefully weighed. Similarly, in assessing the social/political impact of

the highway, the appraisal would pinpoint its benefits to users, providing them ready access to work and recreation, and whether or not
the local community would be likely to resist or support such a highway.
Finally, since political considerations can often override technical and
any other feasibility studies, the appraisal should take note of the
political climate as it bears on construction of the highway.

In assessing economic feasibility, the appraisal would first summarize findings for each technical alternative listed in the technical
feasibility report, listing such benefits as savings in transport costs
provided by the project, savings in time costs, stimulation of economic
development of the location and the country, other miscellaneous
project benefits, such as reductions in accidents, and, finally, overall
economic feasibility – the summary of project costs and benefits as
given in the economic study, using such accepted indicators as net
present value, cost-benefit ratio, internal rate of return, and other
methods.

In tying the financial analysis to the economic analysis, the appraisal would again summarize costs for each alternative listed in the
technical feasibility study. In each case, total costs would include
construction cost, cost of maintenance and operation, revenues (if any),
and financial profitability (if any).

Last and most important, on the basis of all information previously
encapsuled, the appraisal would present its choice of, and reasons for
choosing, the most feasible alternative. All the pluses and minuses of
the different feasibility sectors must be weighed, both against each
other and against the larger economic and political concerns that are
frequently outside the scope of any of these reports. Since both the
individual factors involved and the policy-making climate vary so
widely from situation to situation and country to country, guidelines are
difficult to set for this delicate final task. But if it has conscientiously
absorbed and integrated the contents of all the feasibility studies, the
appraisal should not contain any startlingly new information; rather, it
should simply represent the next logical step, based on the feasibility
studies.

FINAL DESIGN

After the feasibility studies have been conducted and the appraisal
written, and before the project is formally selected and approved, some
design modification may occur – that is, the project's preliminary
design must almost always be modified to a greater or lesser degree,
based on the findings of the feasibility studies. This modification, it
should be emphasized, is an ongoing process that continues past
appraisal through approval and activation, though for convenience we
distinguish preliminary design occurring before feasibility studies have
been conducted from final design, the cumulative result of the modification process that has been taking place throughout the feasibility
and appraisal processes. (It must be noted that before work can begin on

the detailed final design, initial approval must be given to the project. This approval must be obtained because the costs of completing the final design are approximately ten percent of the total project budget.)

This modified design becomes the basis of final specifications, contract drawings, and all the myriad details of the technical design framework that must be finalized to some point before project activation and implementation begin, though design modifications will continue to be made all the way through the project's life cycle. Such detailed specifications include not only technical design but also the blueprint of tasks and activities required in the next phase of the project cycle. Design is therefore not an isolated task occurring at one point in time but rather an ongoing process that tends to overlap and merge with many of the other tasks in the integrated project cycle. In this respect it serves to remind us that the framework of the integrated project planning and management cycle is intended to be a conceptual tool and not a rigid representation of reality. In real life, the sequence of tasks presented schematically in the IPPMC often occur reversed, simultaneously, or not at all. In some cases, a project is selected and approved before a single design has been drawn; in others, tasks or even whole phases of projects are dropped as not applicable. As a generalized sequence of events, then, the IPPMC model itself resembles the specific task of project design; meant to be a comprehensive framework within which to organize all project contingencies, it is subject to continuous modification according to the demands of the individual situation.

NOTES

(1) Vincente Muro, Preparing Feasibility Studies (Systems Publishing: 1975, Manila, Philippines), pp. 85-116.

(2) Many of these questions are taken from: In-Joung Whang, "Administrative Feasibility Analysis for Development Projects: Concept and Approach," (Asian and Pacific Development Administration Centre; Occasional Papers Series No. 4, 1978, Kuala Lumpur, Malaysia), pp. 8-11.

(3) A Guide to Project Development (Republic of the Philippines National Economic and Development Authority: Manila, 1978), pp. 129-33.

(4) A complete list of all environmental factors is included in: Paul N. Chermisinoff and Angelo C. Morresi, Environmental Assessment and Impact Statement Handbook (Ann Arbor Publishers: 1977, Ann Arbor).

(5) David Seader, "Evaluation and Planning Techniques," in David Hendricks, et al., eds., Environmental Design for Public Projects (Water Resources Publications: 1975, Fort Collins, Colorado), pp. 521-71.

(6) Adapted from Chermisinoff, Environmental Assessment and Impact Statement Handbook, pp. 90-91.

(7) Desmond M. Connor, "Public Participation," in Hendricks, Environmental Design, pp. 575-605.

(8) Bruce Koppel and Charles Schlegel, "Sociological Perspectives on Energy and Rural Development: A Review of Major Frameworks for Research on Developing Countries" (Paper presented to the Annual Meeting of the Rural Sociological Society, August 24-26, 1979, Burlington, Vermont).

(9) John E. Walsh, Preparing Feasibility Studies in Asia, (Asian Productivity Organization: 1971, Tokyo), p. 78.

(10) William Ward, "Competing Evaluation Systems: A Survey of Project Appraisal Methods," Xerox copy from Economic Development Institute, 8/29/75; Andar Andarup Ray and Herman G. van der Tak, "A New Approach to the Economic Analysis of Projects," Finance and Development, March 1979, pp. 28-32.

(11) This example is based upon: S.N. Mishra and John Beyer, Cost-Benefit Analysis: A Case Study of the Ratnigiri Fisheries Project, (Hindustan Publishing Company: 1976, Delhi, India).

(12) Ibid.

(13) Warren C. Baum, "The World Bank Project Cycle," Finance and Development, December 1978, pp. 14-16; E.J. Mishan, Economics for Social Decisions: Elements of Cost-Benefit Analysis, (Praeger Publishers: 1975, New York); United Nations Industrial Development Organization, Guidelines for Project Evaluation (New York: United Nations, 1972).

(14) See, for example, Dennis A. Rondinelli, "International Requirements for Project Preparation: Aids or Obstacles to Development Planning?" Journal of the American Institute of Planners 42, no. 3 (July 1976); Warren C. Baum, "The World Bank Project Cycle," Finance and Development (December 1978).

SELECTED BIBLIOGRAPHY

Finsterbusch, Kurt and C.P. Wolf, Methodology of Social Impact Assessment. Stroudsburg, Penn.: Hutchinson and Ross, 1977.
Guidelines for Project Evaluation. New York: UNIDO, 1972.
Hendricks, David, ed. Environmental Design for Public Projects. Fort Collins, Colo.: Water Resources Publications, 1975.

Little, I.M.D. and J.A. Mirrlees. Project Appraisal and Planning for Developing Countries. New York: Basic Books, 1974.

Nader, Laura and Stephen Beckerman. "Energy as It Relates to the Quality of Life." Annual Review of Energy 1 (1978): 1-23.

Packard, Philip C. Project Appraisal for Development Administration. Paris: Mouton, 1974.

Schneider, Hartmut. National Objectives and Project Appraisal in Developing Countries. Paris: Organization for Economic Cooperation and Development, 1975.

Phase 2 –
Selection, Approval,
and Activation

6 Selection and Approval

Selection and approval is the task that follows project identification and formulation, preparation and feasibility analysis, and project design. On some occasions, the selection and approval process precedes that of final project design. The task involves an appraisal process which, if favorable, leads to selection and formal approval of the project so it may be funded and implemented. The selection and approval task, although depending on activities accomplished during the preceding stages, may in practice be influenced by personal preferences of the decision makers. Sound information and thorough analysis will, however, lead to a better selection between competing alternatives.

In actual practice, selection and approval forms an integral part in the project planning stage. Project identification, feasibility, appraisal, selection and approval are a continuous process of planning, formulation, replanning, and reformulation.

THE STEPS OF SELECTION AND APPROVAL

Selection and approval, which does not usually occur until the complete and formal design function has been completed, generally involves the following steps, though not necessarily in this order:
1. Review appraisal report of the short list of competing approved projects including proposed conditions, etc.
2. Select most appropriate project.
3. Select and prepare negotiating team.
4. Prepare negotiation position, agree on acceptable conditions.
5. Obtain formal government approval of loan agreements, funding authorizations, counterpart financial commitments and other necessary authorizations.
6. Prepare loan documents.
7. Prepare formal implementation or operations plan.

111

8. Secure legislative, administrative, legal, and other requirements necessary to meet conditions for loan and implementation effectiveness.(1)

The selection and approval of projects, especially for those in the public sector, depends a great deal upon development objectives and policies that emanate from the political process. For example, development policies may place emphasis on equity, employment, basic needs, regional and rural development, population planning, education, and growth as desirable outcomes of the development process. In general, then, projects to gain selection and approval will need to be seen by decision makers as meeting these objectives. In many countries, development policies and programs will be depicted in a development plan. Based on defined development policy criteria, the development process at all levels will require social benefits to exceed social cost. In spite of clearly defined development goals, from time to time political and social considerations within a country, or wishes of political leaders or powerful pressure groups, will exert influence upon the development process and favorite projects may be approved for political reasons.

In the private sector – although even here the task is not entirely free from the influences of development policies of governments – selection and approval is made with more consideration of costs and benefits and return on investment through price mechanism and competitive bidding.

MECHANISMS FOR PROJECT SELECTION AND APPROVAL

In countries that have development plans, selection and approval for government projects forms part of the formulation of the annual operation plan, which applies to national projects as well as to local projects managed by regional governments. The mechanism of giving approval to projects, whether from the national public sector or from the local government, is normally carried out within the planning and budgeting system, or by some other central authority. Here the role of the central and regional planning bodies as well as the budget offices is crucial. Although project proposals generally originate from operational departments, the selection process for a project usually involves other bodies. A budget committee or a planning committee is usually formed to select and approve projects. Criteria and procedures on project approval are often planned and developed from the experience gained from activation and implementation of similar projects.

Countries without development plans establish decision-making mechanisms within government departments for project selection and approval. Key government departments and agencies, such as the Treasury, or central planning agencies may integrate or coordinate the decision-making process.

In many cases, regardless of whether or not the country has formal development plans, project selection and approval will require cabinet or parliament to approve a particular project. This action is normally for projects of strategic importance, projects entailing large amounts of capital provided by the national resources, or projects of a controversial nature, perhaps involving a conflict of interest. In a large number of countries, the involvement of the legislature is fairly high in selection and approval, as project selection often has a political impact and its approval involves complex political deliberation.

According to the experience of the National Economic and Development Authority (NEDA) in the Philippines, government projects will be included in both the operating funds program and the capital development program of the government's budget after the prospective sources of funds have been identified. Several requirements must be satisfied to qualify projects in these annual programs:(2)

1. The feasibility study, including preliminary engineering design, must be completed in all respects.
2. The project should indicate a higher feasibility rating than that of the marginal projects in the program.
3. The amounts and proposed sources of funds must be positively identified, clearly presented and justified.
4. The source of funds should be duly authorized.

The selection and approval processes in the Philippines are based on an adjustment procedure, and must be obtained from the Ministry or Department concerned with the subject matter areas in which the project falls (Ministry of Industry, Ministry of Agriculture, National Economic and Development Authority, Batasan Bayan, etc.) and then from the Budget Commission and the Office of the President. Once selection and approval of projects has been done, steps are taken to formulate financial plans or budgets. Normally the financial planning has major steps such as preparation, authorization or appropriation execution, and reporting (see figure 6.1 as an example).

Besides those projects within the public sector, some projects are financed through private capital investment and loans as the major component of their financial resources. In this case, the private sector has its own procedures in selecting and approving projects, which are often carried out through the use of market mechanisms or competitive bidding.

There are also projects funded by foreign aid, either from government to government or from international agencies. In these cases, the selection and approval procedures are different because they are determined by the donor country or international agency concerned. In recent years, these procedures have undergone changes due to considerations in the interest of the recipient countries, such as on matters of terms and conditions, and especially on whether the aid is tied to the use of the aid donor's products or consultants or is available to use on an open system.

In World Bank projects, for example, the scope of project appraisal has a broader operational framework than traditional cost-benefit analysis. The individual project is evaluated not only in terms of financial and technical viability but also in terms of its political contribution to development goals, such as sectoral, spatial, and environmental effects.

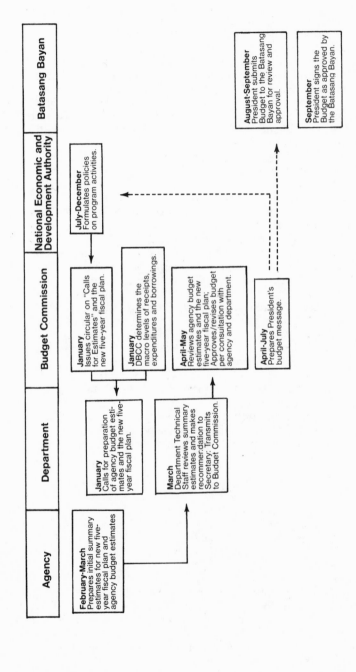

Fig. 6.1. Major steps in the preparation of the national budget.

Source: Republic of the Philippines National Economic and Development Authority.

In many cases, the criteria for project selection and approval are considered according to the priority scale set by policies of the higher government authorities, especially in countries where the public sector has much influence on the development of the private sector. Various loan and capital investment incentives serve as instruments toward the submission of project proposals, which are more relevant to support the accomplishment of development objectives as defined in the political process.

The mechanism of approval of projects financed through loans and private capital investments is executed under its own procedures. In these cases, the bank or investment board of the finance agency funding the project may take an active role in this field.

In most countries, the type of funding source determines the required legal/administrative authority for financing. In principle, the procedures of and regulation on the selection and approval mainly depend upon the source of finance, and whether it originates from the planned public sector, local government, overseas or international aid, or a private unit.

The process of selection and approval is linked to the preceding work of feasibility design and appraisal. The mechanism of appraisal is based on the criteria of sound project feasibility, such as the use of appraisal techniques, that is, cost-benefit analysis, discounted net benefit flows for relatively simple projects, cost effectiveness and the cross-over discount rate, etc. The appraisal process involves use of skills in administration, economics, engineering and other related fields.

In practice, many problems and difficulties arise when applying systematic procedures. This is especially the case in developing countries, where data are often lacking or inaccurate, and there is a shortage of trained specialist staff. Problems and difficulties may also appear that are social and political in origin, such as corruption, unstable political conditions, and so on.

FACTORS FOR CONSIDERATION IN SELECTION AND APPROVAL

Rondinelli points out that "the tenuous relationship between project proposal and priority need of developing countries is often reflected in the promotion of pet projects by individuals, groups, government agencies and by units within the international assistance organizations themselves, leading to biased appraisal and selection."(3)

From the economic point of view, projects are often selected on the basis of the expected net social return, which is determined by utilizing some investment criteria. Financial decisions are based on the availability of a particular technology. Consideration of the location and resources required for a project may determine the priority ranking of a project in the selection and appraisal process. The question of management and organization feasibility is also applied in the selection process, particularly in the selection and approval of large and highly technical investment projects. Relative difficulties are often faced by policy makers in appraising social development projects, as exact economic criteria cannot be used as a basis for measurement. Recently new concepts have been developed to face the requirement of having social projects assume equal importance with economic ones. The criterion of social benefit and the criterion of least cost have been applied to this type of project.

The selection and approval of projects, especially development projects comprised in the public sector, mostly depends upon the development policies and priorities that emanate from the political process. Cases in point are policies on equity, employment, basic needs, regional and rural development, population planning, education, growth, and relative degree of stability in the process of development, all of which are intended to promote equity through growth and stability, the triple objectives of development effort. In a planned public sector, development policies and programs will be depicted in a development plan. Based on development policy criteria, social benefit should exceed social cost. In spite of the aforementioned, though, from time to time political and social consideration or wishes of political leaders or certain groups exert influence upon the process or the plan.

The process of project selection and approval should also be analyzed within the frame of a certain development program, as projects usually form a conceptually discrete activity which is part of a program.   Consistency and the inner supportive aspects of several projects are one important consideration. All of them should be responsive to policies that have been adopted by a political or specific business decisions. Within this framework, the procedural aspects for interagency cooperation become conspicuous. This might be the important problem in project feasibility and an important criterion for project selection and approval. In practice, this aspect of cooperation has been much neglected and will be more difficult to achieve if program coordination involves different operational departments or institutions.

Approving projects of the public sector means authorizing to implement them. But sometimes it is necessary for implementation to be authorized by another decision, such as an executive order, and sometimes, in fact, through legislation.

It is also possible that projects in one budget year are approved "en bloc" as appendices of the budget documents. In general, this is done at the time with the appointment of project managers and the formulation of the organizational setup. For the private sector, project approval is given in the frame of a financial agreement through an institution representing the shareholders, credit and capital investment institutes. The approval often takes the form of a contract specifying the terms and conditions in the implementation of the project.

In many instances, the smooth implementation of a project requires not only one but several authorities of approval.

Project proposal is presented to those concerned with making decisions to implement and finance the project. No matter how feasible a project may appear, it cannot get off the ground without the necessary financing. Negotiation for financing the project constitutes the critical link between a project's feasibility study and its implementation.

Generally, sponsor institutions, international funding agencies and domestic financial bankers concerned with the project are involved in the negotiation process.

When the project is funded by international funding agencies or foreign financing, certain procedures are followed:
1. Preparation of the loan proposal
2. Loan negotiations
3. Loan execution
4. Loan availment(4)

A complicating factor is if the negotiations occur between different countries or between a country and an international agency who impose the fulfillment of their own conditions. In the selection and approval of projects financed by budget, loan, or private capital investment, "bargaining" is frequently experienced in the negotiations to reach a settlement that will satisfy the needs of both sides.

TENDERING

After the approval of loan agreements, funding authorization and counterpart financial commitments, tender documents are then negotiated and prepared. Detail engineering design has already taken place in the first phase of the integrated project planning and management cycle. More detailed estimates involving quantities and unit costs are necessary for inclusion in feasibility reports supporting authorization or approval for construction.

Estimates will also be needed for annual costs for financing and for operation, maintenance, and replacement. The feasibility estimate may not be given in full detail, but in overall amount it should represent a ceiling within which the project features can be built, barring significant advances in unit prices.

Because of widely varying economic and labor conditions in different localities, the estimator should become familiar with local conditions, probable sources of material and labor supply, cost of similar work in the locality, and probable changes in costs of materials and labor that may occur before actual construction due to economic adjustment.

The final estimate will be based on the subsequent detailed studies made in connection with the preparation of specifications and should be in sufficient detail to serve as a guide in securing bids and awarding a contract for construction. Although the actual details required will vary from country to country and agency to agency, the type of content for detailed engineering work could include the following:
a. Final technical design
b. Formulation of specifications and cost estimation
c. Preparation of contract documents

d. Bidding operations.

The negotiations are often followed by tendering and contracting activities. The United Nations manual Contract Planning and Organization divides projects into two contracts, one for the plant and one for the civil engineering and building works. Tendering and contracting activities normally have the following processes:(5)

1. Plant
   1.1   Preparation of inquiry documents for plant
   1.2   Selection of vendor (manufacturers) to whom inquiry is to be sent
   1.3   Preparation of tenders by vendors
   1.4   Appraisal of tenders by purchaser
   1.5   Contract negotiation with selected vendor
   1.6   Obtaining approval of Board to place contract and obtain contract signature
2. Civil Engineering and Building Works
   2.1   Preliminary preparation of inquiry documents
   2.2   Selection of local firms to tender
   2.3   Finalization of inquiry documents after receipt of data from equipment vendor
   2.4   Preparation of tenders by local firms
   2.5   Appraisal of tenders by purchasers
   2.6   Contract negotiation with selected contractor
   2.7   Obtaining Board approval and placing contract

Tendering is a formal procedure by which competing bids for a particular contract are invited, received and evaluated. Tendering can be either open or selective. When the tenders are invited through advertisements or other forms of public notice it is called "open tenders" and the procedure is called "selective tender" when only selective contractors are invited to tender.

The purchaser can select the tenders through prequalification procedures, in which eligible firms are invited to provide evidence of their ability to perform the services desired by the purchaser.

The criteria for prequalification include:

1. The experience of the bidder in the work involved.
2. The technical capabilities of the bidder's organization to handle the job, particularly the key person and equipment.
3. The financial soundness of the bidder's organization.(6)

The purpose of inviting tenders for a certain contract is to induce those firms able to provide the desired services into offering their lowest prices; this process is called bidding.

THE BIDDING PROCESS

The specifications of a project, the contractual conditions and the instructions to the bidders are contained in the tender document. The volume of the tender documents varies with the type and size of the project. The bidders have to ensure that the specifications of the project are described with sufficient clarity and in sufficient detail to form the basis for competitive bids. Specifications of projects consist of a definitive description of the object to be tendered, and normally include the following:

1. Specifications describing the project, the prevailing geographic and climatic conditions, relationship with other construction works, the units of construction according to location and nature of works, the quality of materials and workmanship to be used, etc.
2. A bill of quantities setting out the expected quantities of different parts of the works as calculated from the drawing, classified according to trade or location.
3. A set of drawings.

General instructions to bidders include a complete set of rules and procedures to be followed in preparing and submitting bids. Usually projects financed by local institutions have different arrangements compared to projects financed by international institutions. International bidding, though slow to open to local bids, is often arranged if projects are financed by foreign institutions. Recently major national projects funded internally have sometimes been open to international bidding.

The general instructions to bidders usually consist of the following but may not be limited to these: a) when and where bids have to be made; b) eligible bidders; c) date, hour, and place of bid opening; d) validity period of bids; e) requirements; f) the names and addresses of officials to be contacted for supplementary information; and g) bid opening procedures.

Contractual conditions will vary in accordance with the nature of the projects and the prevailing practice in the Borrower's country. Conditions may not be limited to provisions for: 1) performance bond, 2) penalty condition and amounts, 3) contractor's warranty or guarantee, 4) price adjustment clause, 5) mode of payment, 6) currency of payment, 7) right of the government to reject bids, 8) evaluation and comparison of bids and award of contracts, 9) language interpretation, 10) insurance, 11) force majeure, and 12) post qualification of bidders. The bidding process for project implementation has the following steps:

1. Advertisement for bid

In the open tenders, the tenders are invited through advertisements or other forms of public notice. Usually pre-tender advertisements (prequalification notice) have been made before invitation bid. If firms capable of submitting competitive bids are thus given advance warning of the upcoming invitations to tender, they can do some preliminary work in preparing their bids already before the invitation to tender reaches them.

The information contained in an invitation to bid normally includes:

a. An appropriate reference to bank or international development agency assistance to the project.
b. A brief description of the project types, and number of institutions.
c. Financing institution.
d. A description of subject areas and type of projects

e. Duration of the projects
f. The name and address of the agency or office from which tender documents or further information can be obtained.
g. The fee required for receipt of tender documents and the dates and period during which these documents can be obtained.
h. The time, date and exact location for submission of bids and the time, date and exact location for opening of bids.
i. A statement that the government/purchaser has the right to reject any or all bids.
2. Prequalification of bidders
3. Evaluation of bids

The purpose of evaluation is to determine "the lowest evaluated bid," but different countries have different regulations. In Indonesia, for example, normally the contract is awarded to the bidder with "the lowest satisfactory tender." This expression serves to indicate that the contract should be awarded to the bidder who has submitted a bid which is not only low in terms of price but also advantageous with respect to other criteria stated in the bidding documents.

A technical analysis should then be made to evaluate each respective bid and to enable a bid comparison and award recommendation to be prepared for consideration by government's tender board or other appropriate authority.

4. Award of contract

After making the awards, contracts are entered into. Contracts can be integrated contracts, so-called "package-deal" or "turn-key" project, with one main contractor responsible for engineering, equipment, supply, and construction or divided/separated contracts with more than one contractor involved in the project. A "package deal" or "turn-key" project can be divided into several contracts. Only one contractor is responsible to the purchaser and subcontractors are only responsible to the main contractor. If a foreign firm is appointed to the entire project, usually local firms will be appointed as subcontractors and suppliers for certain local works and services.

An example of such subdivision is:

Small-Scale Process Plant(7)

Product or Service	Supplier
Equipment supply	Overseas manufacturer
Equipment installation	Local contractor under supervision of overseas manufacturer
Supporting steelwork Supply and erection	Local contractor
Civil-engineering and building work including site facilities	Local contractor

Plant commissioning   Overseas manufacturer assisted by
                                           local installation contractor

Project design: steel work,
    building and civil engineering
    design, project coordinator   Purchaser through overseas
                                           consulting engineer

In some developing countries lacking in specialists, this process becomes a problem. Normally, foreign firms do not have any information about local firms; they depend on the purchaser to appoint local firms. "Vested interests" of individuals, groups, government agencies, especially in government projects, lead to biased selection of local firms.

To avoid this problem, consultants are often assigned to assist the government in selection of contractors, and they undertake the following tasks:

1. Assessment of availability and capacity of local and foreign contractors.
2. Decision on the form and diffusion of the announcement.
3. Evaluation of the prequalification documents.
4. Analysis and evaluation of bids.

In contracts, the technical specification, funding requirements, implementation schedules and managerial or organizational arrangements should clearly be formulated. In addition, a project design refinement is also needed. A form of contract is, at the same time, often a form of project approval.

SUMMARY

The selection and approval task thus takes place in different ways. The actual process followed will depend on a number of interrelated variables, such as the degree of formal development planning in the sector concerned, the extent of public and political support for the project, whether or not the project is private or public, and the type of funding used for the project.

When the selection and approval process has been completed, the project is on the threshold of becoming a reality. Steps can now be taken to activate the various resources required to begin the project.

NOTES

(1) Dennis A. Rondinelli, "International Assistance Policy and Development Project Administration: The Impact of Imperious Rationality," International Organization 30, no. 4 (Autumn 1976): 603.

(2) Philippines National Economic and Development Authority, A Guide to Project Development, December 1977, p. 144.

(3) Dennis A. Rondinelli, "International Assistance Policy," p. 586.

(4) Philippines National Economic and Development Authority, Guide, p. 150.

(5) United Nations Industrial Development Organization, Content Planning and Organization (New York: UNIDO, 1974).

(6) Philippines National Economic and Development Authority, Guide, p. 155.

(7) P.D.V. March, "Initiation and Planning of Contracts," Contract Planning and Organization (New York: United Nations, 1974), p. 25.

SELECTED BIBLIOGRAPHY

Alba, Manuel S. "Guide to Project Development." Manila: National Economic and Development Authority, 1977.

Clifton, David and David Fyeff. Project Feasibility Analysis. New York: John Wiley & Sons, 1977.

Cracknell, B.F. "Some Problems in the Application of Project Appraisal Techniques." Journal of Agricultural Economics 22, no. 3 (September 1971): 267-73.

King, John A., Jr. "Appraising a Project," In Economic Development Projects and Their Appraisal: Cases and Principles from the Experience of the World Bank. Baltimore: Johns Hopkins Press, pp. 3-15.

Lab, Deepak. Method of Project Analysis: A Review. Baltimore: Johns Hopkins Press, 1977.

McColl, G.D. and C.D. Throsby. "Multiple Objective Benefit-Cost Analysis and Regional Development." The Economic Record 48, no. 122 (June 1972): 201-219.

Merret, A.J. and Allen Sykes. The Finance and Analysis of Capital Projects. 2nd ed. New York: Halsted Press, 1977.

Walsh, John E. Preparing Feasibility Studies in Asia, Tokyo: Asian Productivity Organization, 1971.

7 Activation

The second task in Phase 2 of the integrated project cycle, activation, involves the coordination and allocation of resources that serve to make the project operational. At the project level, this means setting up the management and organizational structure to enable the project to become operational. The procedures necessary for particular projects will vary but will need to include such factors as personnel, resource procurement, and management information systems. Linkages with policy makers, various authorities, and subcontractors must also be established.

The implementation of projects depends also on the macro-infrastructure within which the project must be implemented. Work and procedures must conform to labor laws, environmental regulations, and other standards set by the sponsoring government or other organizations. The funding terms of the project may mean that its implementation must be directed through a specific format. Projects in the private sector may plan their own budget, and will have their own financial and personnel system based on the result of negotiations and on the contract. Private projects must also give attention to coordination patterns and external linkages for smooth implementation.

ELEMENTS OF AN ACTIVATION PROGRAM

Effective activation of the project demands the following steps:
1. Establishment of a specified work program for the project. This will include detailed and definitive plans for the preliminary design.
2. Establishment of a financial program or plan and accounting procedures for public investment projects based on the financial procedures of the budget system.
3. Recruitment and assignment of core staff, and procurement of other resources.

4. Improvement of several standard operating procedures.

Since planning and controlling the implementation of projects are the primary purposes of activation, the specified work program of the project must include not only actions related to the physical work but also planning and administration. Each specific work program could be divided into design and construction. In building, for example, projects could be divided into foundations, steel framework, roofing and cladding, and site services.

According to Marsh, the specific work program is influenced by three major factors: 1) the type of skill to execute the work, 2) geographical considerations, and 3) use of local resources.(1) Marsh also points out that the main functions of the specific work program are to:

1. List all the major activities necessary to complete the project, ensuring that none are overlooked.
2. Clearly define the work for the whole project and for each individual work program.
3. Enable a schedule establishing the time required for the completion of each work program to be prepared; also enable the preparation of a schedule identifying the resources required for the completion of each work program.
4. Prepare from these schedules estimates of cost, and subsequently monitor these estimates against the actual cost incurred.
5. Allocate responsibility for the completion of each work program regarding specification, time, and cost.

Attention should be given in project implementation to provisions concerning standardization and normalization. Standardization possibly covers price, cost, quality, and so forth, of various products or construction and also services. Provisions on standardization can be issued by the government, but can also be made by private institutions. In many cases unit cost, unit price, and quality become an essential part of the approval document or contract. In many developing countries, where standardization and normalization have not yet been established, designing an appropriate scheduling technique becomes a problem.

FINANCIAL ACTIVATION

One important element of project control is cost control. The responsibilities of the cost function should include:

1. Conducting project audit.
2. Preparing periodic comparisons of actual versus programmed cost.
3. Preparing comparisons of actual versus programmed humanpower allocation.
4. Updating the cost of complete projection reports and funding schedules.
5. Facilitating the flow of funds from the customers and to and between the subcontractors.
6. Providing a comparison of costs sustained by activity to the established cost standards.

7. Sponsoring a cost-improvement program.

Procedures of authorization, disbursements application, transaction and contracting, and accountability should be clear. In many cases, the forms of financing differ according to the type of projects.

Provisions of budget implementation form the main basis on which the implementation of projects of the public sector are executed and monitored. The provisions are aimed at facilitating control as well as ensuring flexibility of implementation. The balancing between preaudit and postaudit should be resolved. Loans and capital investment projects of the private sector also have their own disbursement procedures and schedules, accounting standards, and other terms of implementation. Periodic adjustments of policies and procedures in the implementation of projects, especially in the private sector, depend on policies and priorities in incentives for capital investment.

Regarding the implementation of the financial aspects of the project at the activation stage, clarity (in the general and special stipulation) concerning the provision of tender bids and contracts as well as procurement procedures is needed. In most developing countries, foreign tenders and contracts pose a problem of diminished capacity in the bargaining process. Problems of open tender, limited tender, prequalification, claim, and so on, require clear and easily understood criteria and stipulations.

Good financial administrative procedures are necessary to activate the financial plan, and authority for provisions should be ensured to implement the budget. Guidelines of cash-flow formulation are useful, as they allow the financial soundness of the project to be perceived. This is of great importance, especially with economic projects.

PROJECT ORGANIZATION

Project organization is an important task in project implementation. Organizations are the "engine" of management. To achieve goals and objectives, people, skill/knowledge, and resources must be joined together and interact in appropriate ways. Establishing and defining a proper organization during the activation stage can save a great deal of time and resources during project implementation.

Organization relationships between all resources, that is, people, money, material, knowledge, etc., have to be developed through final organization. Various standard operating procedures or internal administrative/operative rules/procedures should be formulated at this stage: for example, written policy statements, information system procedures manuals, job description/delegation and division of authority, work shift and schedules.

The size of the project determines the formulation of the hierarchy of the project organization. In large projects, more formal hierarchical levels are established, specialization becomes more important and is developed in separate organizational units. But in small projects, sophisticated formal hierarchy can be ignored. In either case, project organization should be action-oriented and non-bureaucratic; too much formality can reduce flexibility and creativity.

A project is a dynamic process and not a static system. During some phases of a project, responsibilities of individuals and systems will be constantly changing. The operation of project systems needs flexibility to facilitate systems' adaptations to the changes of project objectives, individual responsibilities, and project phases. Top project managers have to give more authority and policy decisions to lower organization, who are closer to the sources of problems. This allows them to devote more time to the vital decisions concerning project strategies and operations.

Thus, project organization requires greater coordination and integration of all resources than hierarchical organization.

In some developing countries where government employees are involved in projects, formal hierarchy in traditional government structure influences the formal hierarchy of the project organization. In such cases, organization becomes rigid and strict decision models are used.

TYPES OF PROJECT ORGANIZATION STRUCTURES

Normally, project organization has different types of organizational structures, such as functional organization, task organization, and matrix organization.

A functional organization is an organizational structure broken down into different functional units such as accounting, research, engineering, and administration. The base of this hierarchical structure is formed by management theories such as line and staff relation, authority and responsibility, and other (see figure 7.1).

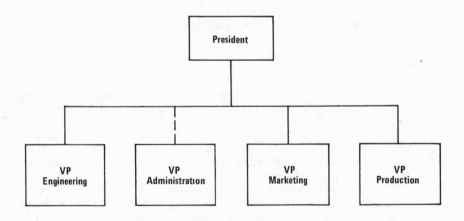

Fig. 7.1. Functional organization.

The strength of this structure is in its centralization of similar resources, its weakness is the opposite of its strengths. In multiprojects, conflicts invariably arise over the priorities of different projects in the competition for resources.

In task organizations, all the resources necessary for the accomplishment of a project are separated from the regular function structure (see figure 7.2). The project organization becomes an autonomous organization headed by the project manager. For its duration, all the personnel on the project are under the direct authority of the project manager.

The strength of the project organization structure is in its single objective. Communication is effective in a closed organization and the project manager can control all resources directly. Duplication of facilities, inefficient use of resources, and job security, however, all become problems in project organization.

The matrix organization structure tries to maximize the strengths and minimize the weaknesses of both the project and the functional structures (see figure 7.3). The strengths of this structure are the balancing of objectives, the coordination across functional department lines, and the visibility of the project objectives through the project coordinator. The weakness is that the individual in the middle is working for two bosses. Vertically, this person reports to the functional department head; horizontally, the individual reports to the project coordinator.   To avoid this problem, the roles, responsibility, and authority of each of the positions must be clearly defined. Figure 7.4 illustrates the project coordinator's functions and responsibilities.

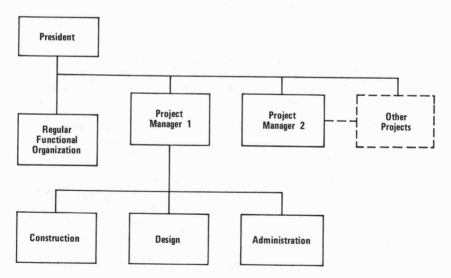

Fig. 7.2. Project organization.

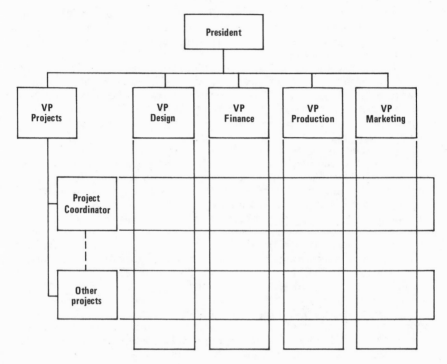

Fig. 7.3. Matrix organization.

SELECTING A STRUCTURE

Selecting an appropriate project organization structure is not an easy task. Among other factors, the project management must also be aware of the relationship between the formal system and the informal structure. The following factors have to be considered in selecting an appropriate structure.(2)

1. The relationship between organizational design, the skill of the project manager, and the project planning and reporting system.
2. The key factors that will influence the organizational design decision, such as

	FUNCTIONAL	MATRIX	PROJECT
Uncertainty	Low	High	High
Technology	Standard	Complicated	New
Complexity	Low	Medium	High
Duration	Short	Medium	Long
Size	Small	Medium	Large
Importance	Low	Medium	High
Customer	Diverse	Medium	One

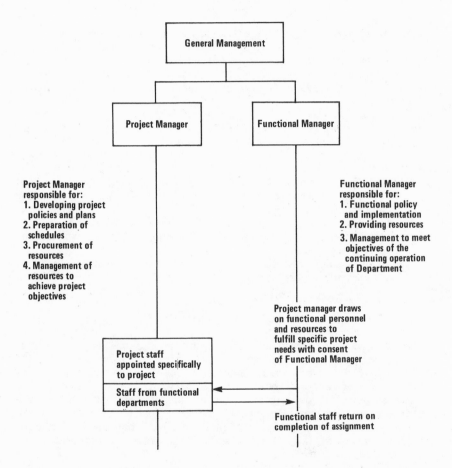

Fig. 7.4. Relationship of project and functional management.

	FUNCTIONAL	MATRIX	PROJECT
Interdependency (within)	Low	Medium	High
Interdependency (between)	High	Medium	Low
Time criticality	Low	Medium	High
Differentiation	Low	High	Medium
Resource criticality	Depends	Depends	Depends

3. Advantages and disadvantages of each organizational structure.

In practice, there is no single perfect organizational structure for managing projects. Each structure has its relative strengths and weaknesses. The final decision depends on various factors, such as the nature of the task, the needs of the organization, and the environment of the project.

According to Rensis Likert, organizations will be most effective when the following conditions exist:(3)

1. There is a supportive atmosphere of mutual trust and confidence with a high degree of mutual assistance and interest in the welfare of others.
2. There is group decision making at each level through the creation of work groups consisting of a supervisor and all subordinates, and overlapping work groups.
3. Performance goals are high at all levels of the organization.
4. Uniformity of goals is determined by a supportive atmosphere and group decision making.
5. There is a high degree of mutual influence and trust between supervisors and subordinates.

SELECTING A MANAGER

Selection and appointment of a competent and capable project manager is vital for project implementation. Criteria of procedure for the manager's selection and appointment should be formulated. The decision concerning the appointment forms a part of the decision on the implementation of the project, and stipulations are provided on the delineation of the project manager's authority and responsibility. There is also an important position beside the project manager, namely the project treasurer. Quality staff or sometimes strategic personnel should be given due consideration.

Paul O. Gaddis points out some of the qualifications for a successful project manager as the following:(4)

1. His career must have been molded in the advanced-technology environment.
2. She must have a working knowledge of many fields of science, the fundamental kind of knowledge she can augment when necessary to delve into the intricacies of a specific technology.
3. He must have a good understanding of general management problems, especially marketing, control, contract work, purchasing, law,

and personnel administration. The concept of profitability should be familiar to him.

4. She must ·have a strong, continuous, active interest in teaching, training, and developing her supervisors.

These qualifications indicate that a project manager should be not only a technical person but also an administrator, a leader, and a manager.

The project manager must usually combine technical knowledge of the subject matter with management abilities for leadership of the entire project team. (Sometimes, a narrowly trained engineer or technician lacks the administrative and managerial capacity.) Training in administration and managerial skills for all project managers, therefore, is most desirable.

DEVELOPING AN OPERATIONS PLAN

Another important process during activation is to develop a detailed plan of organization and administration. Administrative support is not self-generating; rather, it must be concurrently planned with formulation of development policies and projects.

The activities of the different administrative units and participatory organizations concerned with project implementation should be effectively coordinated. The effective monitoring systems and the availability of management information systems to support such monitoring must also be developed within the administrative system. Inadequate organization and administration planning lead to ineffective project implementation.

Skilled workers should be available to undertake the implementation stages. Recruitment programs have to be established to ensure that humanpower requirements of the project are met on schedule. Regulations, including the conditions, of personnel administration will influence to what extent the project succeeds in recruiting workers. In some developing countries, the unavailability of skilled workers is a major critical factor. In this case, adequate training of the project staff must be initiated.

When activation is completed, the project manager will need to develop techniques and procedures for implementing the project once it becomes operational. A variety of implementation techniques is available to the project manager, and the manager's choice will depend on the needs and complexities of the project, as well as personal preference.   The next chapter considers this broad range of alternative implementation and scheduling systems.

NOTES

(1) P.D.V. Marsh, "Initiation and Planning of Contracts," in Contract Planning and Organization (New York: UNIDO, 1974), p. 6.

(2) Robert B. Youker, "Organizational Alternatives for Project Management and Overview," Project Management Quarterly 8, no. 1 (March 1977), p. 21.

(3) Quoted in Michael Berger et al., "Project Organization," Graduate School of Management, Vanderbilt University, March 1974, p. 24.

(4) Paul O. Gaddis, "The Project Manager – His Role in Modern Industry," Harvard Business Review 37, no. 3 (May/June 1959), p. 95.

SELECTED BIBLIOGRAPHY

Berger, Michael, Johnson, R.A., Lowenthal, James, and Raymond Radosevich. "Developing Project Organizational Systems." Graduate School of Management, Vanderbilt, March 1979.
Berger, Michael, Johnson, R.A., Lowenthal, James, and Raymond Radosevich. "Project Organization." Graduate School of Management, Vanderbilt University, March 1974.
Gaddis, Paul O. "The Project Manager – His Role in Modern Industry." Harvard Business Review 37, no. 3 (May/June 1959): 89-97.
Lewis, David H. "Project Implementation: Organization and Staffing." Economic Development Institute, 1976.
The Philippines National Economic and Development Authority. A Guide to Project Development. Manila, 1978.
Taylor, W.J. and T.F. Watling. Practical Project Management. New York: John Wiley & Sons, 1973.
Youker, Robert B. "Organizational Alternatives for Project Management and Overview," Project Management Quarterly 8, no. 1 (March 1977): 21.

Phase 3 –
Operation, Control,
and Handover

8 Implementation

The first step in the third phase of the integrated project planning and management cycle is the <u>implementation</u> of the project. It involves: 1) programming the implementation of the project by breaking it down into various component tasks, operations and project activities, 2) establishing an organization and staff to implement the project, 3) directing the execution of the project by assigning various project tasks and activities to responsible groups within the project organization, and by procurement and allocation of necessary resources such as worker-power, money, material, machinery, time, space, etc., to each project activity, 4) coordinating, monitoring, and control of the performance of various groups and the use of project resources in such a way that all project activities are completed in an orderly and optimal fashion within the constraints of time and resources available.

The technical aspects of the implementation phase will depend upon the type of project and are specified according to project specification, standards and documents in the planning and design phase. The managerial aspects of the implementation phase are dependent upon the type of project, type of contract, and so forth and are based on the rules and procedures established during the two earlier phases.

Some of the prerequisites of successful project implementation are discussed earlier in Chapters 2 and 7 of this book, where the general problems of project management, activation of projects, qualities of project managers, project organization, budget and personnel systems were described. The focus of this chapter is on the tools and techniques for project implementation where methods for planning, programming, scheduling, monitoring and control of the project implementation phase using traditional and network approaches are discussed in detail.

INTRODUCTION TO PLANNING, SCHEDULING, AND CONTROL TECHNIQUES

The enormous size and complexity of numerous projects in military, public works, and the private domain during and after World War II in developed and developing countries, and the speed with which projects have to be planned and implemented in a rapidly changing environment, have created a need for new and sophisticated project management techniques. Implementation of numerous complex projects in the development of weapons and aerospace systems, some of which involved the coordination of the work of many thousands of contractors and agencies under very tight schedules, forced their project managers to view the management of these projects as a serious, scientific discipline. Thus, project management in the last thirty years has become more a science than an art. A correspondingly rapid progress in the fields of applied mathematics, network analysis, optimization techniques, operations research, as well as the availability of high-speed digital computers, has facilitated the implementation of these new scientific techniques in project management. This series of advances led in turn to the development and rapid growth of the family of network techniques for project management.

This chapter will first discuss the traditional techniques for planning, scheduling, and control of projects; network techniques and their applications in project scheduling, monitoring, and time-cost; and resource control.

TRADITIONAL TECHNIQUES

Four techniques often used for planning, scheduling, and control of development, construction, and engineering projects will be briefly discussed. These methods are: Project Breakdown Structure (PBS), Gantt or bar charts, Milestone charts, and the Line of Balance method (LOB).

Project Breakdown Structure (PBS)

PBS is a modification of the traditional industrial engineering technique known as the Work Breakdown Structure (WBS).(1) PBS has been used mostly in projects dealing with design and development or production,(2) but it also applies to projects dealing with development and construction.

PBS is a systematic and disciplined approach for breaking down a project into its many components and subcomponents. PBS lists all the activities that must be carried out to complete the project in a systematic, hierarchical, and structured way, enabling the manager to visualize the whole project, together with all its major subprojects and minor activities and their interrelationships, in a single diagram.

A PBS diagram resembles an organizational chart for completion of the project. It relates various project activities to the organizational structure of the project, exploding the project in a hierarchy of levels from subprojects and important operations down to the level of manageable tasks and activities.

To prepare a PBS diagram for a project, the main project is identified on the top center box. The next lower level contains major project elements such as main subprojects, operations, facilities, systems, end products, etc. On the next lower level, each of these main elements is subdivided into its major components. The level-by-level breakdown continues in this manner until the end items or operations are all identified. The end items are subdivided into another hierarchy of levels of functional activities that must be carried out. The breakdown into lower-level tasks is continued to the level wherein each element or activity identified is a self-contained, manageable unit which can be carried out under the jurisdiction of a definite functional manager or task group. The end elements or activities can be called the Project Activity Package (PAP). A PAP may be a design, document, project, hardware item, service part, or anything that is necessary for the completion of the project and takes time or resources. The responsibility for executing, budgeting, planning, scheduling and control of each PAP must be well defined.

Breaking down projects into activity packages (PAP) can be easily carried out if the person responsible for the task has familiarity and experience with the project and if various other people and groups involved in carrying out the project are consulted. The problem can be simplified by classification of jobs and activities on the basis of physical and geographical location and division of project, organizational and departmental responsibility, type of expertise, craft or trade, type of material, equipment and methods used, the established reporting and controlling format within the organization, resources used, and so on. Figure 8.1 shows a simplified PBS diagram for a construction project.

The process of drawing the PBS diagram is itself a beneficial experience, because it forces the project manager, the supporting staff, and the personnel in charge of various, related operations to study the entire project and to think through all its details, components, and elements. Such thinking prior to acting will clear the scope of the work to be done by various groups, prevent future conflicts and omissions, reveal the dependence of tasks and activities of various groups to each other, and create important insights into and understanding of the entire project. It is a systemic way to look at the project and see the forest despite the trees.

PBS can be used as a framework for the project's information system as far as planning, budgeting, accounting, and control are concerned. Only after determination of the PBS, in fact, can a sound basis for project planning, scheduling, and control be established. PBS diagrams are used as a first step in the preparation of Gantt and milestone charts and networks for projects.

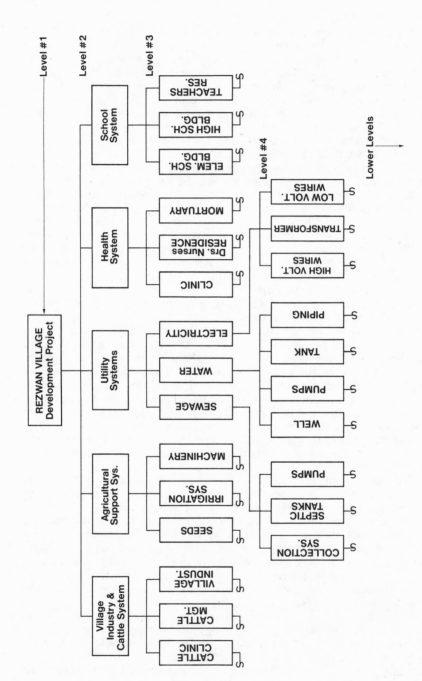

Fig. 8.1. Typical PBS diagram for a village development project.

Gantt or Bar Charts

One of the most popular techniques of project planning, scheduling, reporting, and control used for simple projects is the Gantt or bar chart. This technique, introduced as a production tool at the beginning of this century by Henry L. Gantt, a scientific management pioneer, graphically represents the progress of a project versus the time-frame it must be completed in. Gantt charts are excellent graphical representations for scheduling the execution of various project activities. They can be used as simple and easily understood models for communicating information to all levels of project management and supervision.

Preparation of Gantt charts: project planning and scheduling

To prepare a Gantt chart, the following steps must first be taken: 1) each project has to be broken down into discrete component activities, 2) the sequence of execution of these activities must be established, and 3) the duration of these activities must be estimated. The project cannot be broken down into component activities unless it is analyzed thoroughly and the time estimate for carrying out each activity is determined. The job analysis must be conducted in cooperation with the people responsible for carrying out these activities. This cooperation must be obtained so that their experiences, views, and know-how are used in preparation of the schedule, and their future commitment to keep with the schedule is ensured. When PBS for a project is available, it can be used as a basis for construction of the Gantt chart.

Step 4 in the preparation of the Gantt chart, then, is to list all the activities in sequence of time and determine those that can be carried out simultaneously and those that must be carried out sequentially.

In the Gantt chart, the horizontal axis represents the time scale for completing the project. The unit of time scale used can be day, week, or month, depending upon the total length of the project. The listing of the project tasks or activities is shown in the first lefthand column. The schedule of each activity, graphically showing its starting, duration and completion times, is rendered by horizontal bars drawn on the row representing that activity. For this reason, Gantt charts are also called bar charts or bar diagrams. The bars are drawn according to a time scale laid out across the top of the chart; the length of each bar represents the estimated time needed for carrying out the corresponding activity.

Figure 8.2 shows a typical bar chart for a construction project. The projected schedule of each activity is shown by horizontal bars with light shading in the upper part of the row representing that activity. The scheduled starting and completion times of each activity are distinctly marked. The actual progress of the activity showing the period when the work is being done is represented by horizontal bars with dark or red shading in the lower part of the row corresponding to that activity. At any given time, the actual progress of project

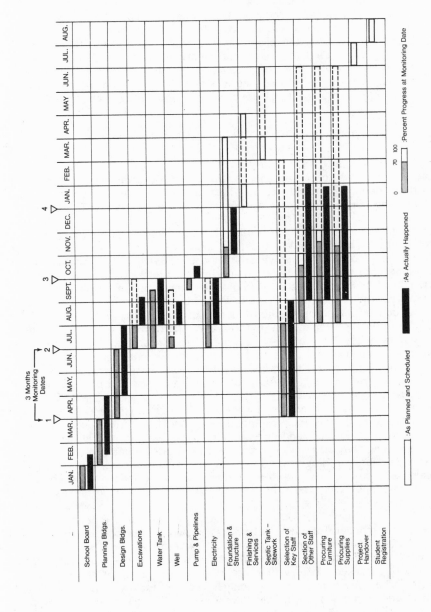

Fig. 8.2. Gantt chart for a rural elementary school project.

activities can be measured against the planned schedule as project progress is directly recorded on the chart. The lower bar shows the time that work on each activity has been in progress; it does not show the percentage of work accomplished and the percentage remaining. This information is usually shown by darkening or coloring the upper bars, which represent the planned schedule proportional to the percentage of progress in that activity. At each reporting interval, the percentage of the progress of each activity is estimated and the corresponding bar is darkened up to that percentage.

Project monitoring and control using bar charts

Project progress is usually monitored in uniform biweekly or monthly intervals. Monitoring reports describe the status of various activities and note the completion dates. For activities in progress, the actual versus scheduled starting dates, the percentage of progress at the monitoring time, and the expected versus scheduled completion dates are recorded. An explanation for the delays or other abnormalities in the project progress and the expected change in the scheduled completion date of the project are reported.

Advantages of bar charts

The bar chart's most important advantage is that the planning, scheduling, and actual progress of a project are all graphically recorded on a single sheet of paper. It is a very simple and effective tool for showing the status of the project and its component activities to all levels of management and people concerned. It singles out the activities that are either behind or are ahead of schedule so that extra resources can be committed or withdrawn accordingly, thereby focusing the attention of top-level management only on problem spots, a technique that leads to management by exception.

Disadvantages of bar charts

As a project management tool, however, the bar chart also has certain disadvantages. The most important one is that it cannot show interrelationships among various activities. Therefore, the impact of speed or delay in carrying out an activity on other activities, or on the whole project, cannot be carefully assessed. Bar charts do not single out those critical activities in which any delay in completion may delay the entire project. When some noncritical activities fall behind schedule, the chart can trigger a false alarm by signaling that the whole project is behind schedule. Bar charts do not show the float in the noncritical activities; this information is needed to know the degree of flexibility in scheduling the resource-consuming activities. The effect of a slip from schedule for an activity cannot be easily assessed in the schedule of the other activities. Therefore, and often at some later date, the schedules can become outdated and inaccurate.

Updating of bar charts is carried out manually, a task not as quickly accomplished as computerized methods. This also adds another factor toward making the charts outdated a few months after the start of the project. Because bar charts cannot show many activities, they cannot include sufficient planning and scheduling details. This lack of detail makes the early detection of slippage in scheduling almost impossible. Therefore, preventive control measures cannot be applied as easily as with network methods. The planning and scheduling of a project are carried out at the same time in the preparation of bar charts. Therefore, the time schedule of each plan has to be prepared when the original charts are drawn. This reduces planning flexibility considerably and does not provide sufficient opportunity for considering alternative plans with different schedules.

In preparing the bar charts for most projects, a desired completion date is usually assumed and the schedules are worked backward from the completion dates. Thus the entire schedule can break down when the completion date of the project is changed or brought forward.

Bar charts, in sum, are efficient and simple planning, scheduling, reporting, and control tools for small projects with a limited amount of activities. They are not suitable, however, for large and complex projects. Bar charts serve to communicate the overall status of project progress to higher levels of management. Many project managers in operation or field levels are so fond of using bar charts that they request scheduling information in the form of CPM, PERT, or Precedence Networks to be presented to them in bar-chart forms. This practice has led to the creation of network-based bar charts, discussed later in this chapter.

Milestone Charts

Milestone charts are obtained by modifying and refining the Gantt charts to provide a better tool for monitoring and control of project status and progress. For this purpose, project milestones or progress measurement checkpoints are introduced on the bar charts. These milestones represent significant events or important points of time in the life of the project or each activity. Progress reporting using milestone charts is more meaningful because the milestones can be checked off as they are reached.

Introduction of milestone charts was an attempt to establish interrelationships among various project activities. Figure 8.3a shows a Gantt chart for a simple project; figure 8.3b shows a milestone chart for the same Gantt chart where milestones have been introduced. Introductions of milestones transforms the bars into related events and activities and shows a relationship between the starting and finishing times of various activities. Without using milestones, the dependency of activities on one another cannot be shown except by breaking each bar into smaller bars and activities. Milestone charts, it should be noted, do not indicate the true logical interrelationship between various activ-

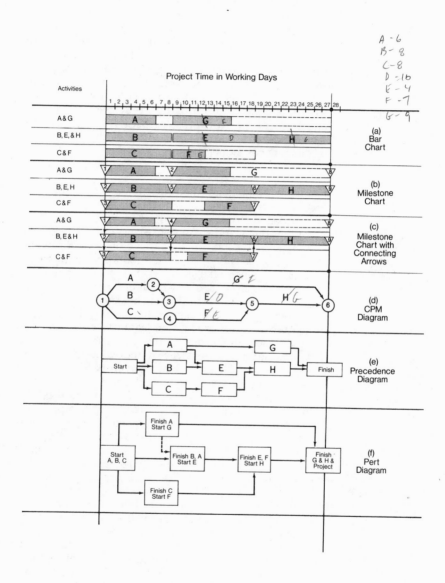

Fig. 8.3. Evolution of a bar chart to a milestone
chart and to network diagrams.

ities. Therefore, if significant changes should occur in the scheduling of projects with numerous activities, confusion will arise and milestone charts will soon lose their usefulness and become outdated.

To overcome this difficulty, milestone charts were further modified by the introduction of dependency arrows to indicate logical relationships between milestones. These arrows show the interdependence of milestones on each other, as shown in figure 8.3c. The addition of these arrows was a significant development which transformed the milestone charts into the forerunner of the network systems. This transformation is seen in figure 8.3d, e, and f, where by introduction of rectangles and connecting arrows the milestone diagram of figure 8.3c is transformed into CPM, PERT, and Precedence Networks, respectively. Comparison of these figures shows how the various networks evolved from bar charts and the major differences among them.

Line of Balance Method (LOB)

The Line of Balance method (LOB) was developed in 1941 as a tool for monitoring and controlling the war production plant of the Goodyear Tire and Rubber Company. It was further developed and applied successfully in the United States Navy production mobilization program during World War II. Ever since the war, it has been applied to monitoring and control of research and development projects, design and construction of defense systems, and other such uses.

LOB is a graphic technique for programming, scheduling, monitoring, and controlling projects or production against an established plan. It shows the status of the project, the condition of various activities, and whether or not the objectives of the whole project are being met. It also shows the activities that are not in balance (behind schedule) with the rest of the activities. LOB focuses the attention of management on potential problems and delays and is thus based on the concept of management by exception. LOB enables the project or production manager to compare the actual and planned progress against each other, to pinpoint activities deviating from the plan, to determine the severity of these deviations, to assess their effect on the overall project status, to obtain early warning on the troubled activities, and to determine the magnitude of the corrective actions needed to put the project back on schedule.

LOB has been applied along two separate lines: 1) in quantity production of products where many repetitive operations or units are involved, such as factory operations or housing projects consisting of construction of many similar units or stories, and 2) in monitoring and control of projects consisting of many one-time activities or operations. As both of these lines have application in development projects, the two approaches will be briefly discussed in this chapter.

Application of LOB in multiple-unit production projects

Monitoring and control of production plans and schedules of these types of projects are accomplished by means of the following diagrams:

1. The Objective Chart shows the cumulative delivery of the units as a function of time from the beginning of the project. As an example, for a housing project consisting of the delivery of 350 units within two years, the delivery plan or the objective chart is as shown in figure 8.4a.

2. The Unit Plan Diagram represents the plan or program for construction or production of each unit, hence its name. It shows the important stages, items, or milestones in the construction or manufacturing process representing the accomplishment of key activities and operations. It shows how and when various components must fit into the assembly process, and exactly when each component must be available. The plan is arranged as a diagram similar to a milestone chart. A typical unit plan for construction of the housing project is shown in figure 8.4b. Only key events and milestones representing the start or completion of critical operations, parts, subassemblies, and activities requiring considerable lead time should be shown in the unit plan diagram. All the milestones are represented in ascending order of their lead time. The horizontal axis shows the time (number of working days, weeks, etc.), counting backward from the final completion date of the unit, when various milestones must have happened.

Various symbols are used to show different types of activities, stages, or milestones in the chart. Milestones are numbered sequentially, first from left to right, and second from top to bottom, as shown in figure 8.4b.

3. The Progress Chart represents the actual status of the project milestones in the form of shaded bars at a given monitoring time. A typical progress chart is shown in figure 8.4c. On this chart there is a step-shaded Line of Balance, which represents the scheduled project progress according to the plan and objective. The horizontal axis represents the unit plan milestones of figure 8.4, where each milestone is shown by one space. The vertical axis represents the number of units and has the same scale as the objective chart. The shaded verticle bars at each position represent the number of times the milestone represented by that position has been reached from the start of the project up to monitoring time. The Line of Balance shows where various items represented by the milestones should be on the monitoring date.

Construction of line of balance

For construction of the LOB for a given monitoring date, such as December 1, 1978, the following steps must be taken:

1. From the objective chart, according to the contract, 100 housing units should have been completed and delivered by this date.
2. Consider milestones 1 and 2 (construction of the foundation and ordering panels and structural elements): from the unit plan diagram

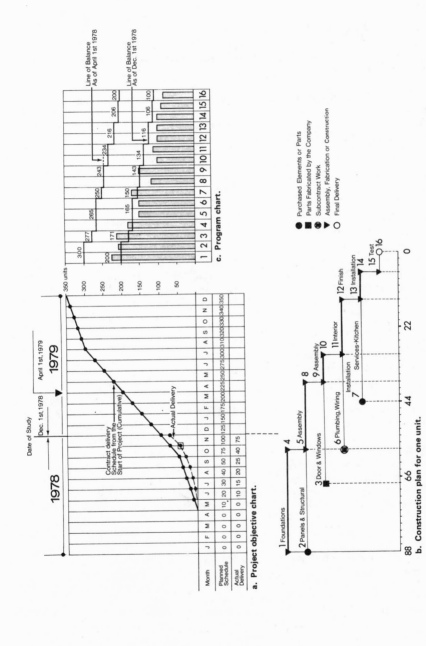

Figures 8.4 (a,b,c). Line of balance diagram for a housing project consisting of the construction of 350 similar units.

146

it is seen that 88 days lead-time is required from the start of these activities to the end of completion of the construction of one housing unit.

3. If milestones 1 and 2 happen on this date (December 1, 1978) for a housing unit, that unit will be completed and ready for delivery four months later, that is, on April 1, 1979 (each 22 working days is equal to one month). By that time, according to the objective chart, 200 housing units should be ready for delivery. Therefore, on the monitoring date we should have started construction of the foundation and ordering panels and structural elements (milestones 1 and 2) for at least 200 units.

4. For milestones 1 and 2, the 200 required numbers as of December 1, 1978 are shown by horizontal lines on the progress chart.

5. Steps 2, 3, and 4 are repeated for other milestones. For each milestone, the required number as of monitoring date will be shown by dark horizontal lines on the progress chart. These lines are connected together, forming a step-shaped Line of Balance for the monitoring date of December 1, 1978.

Use of the LOB charts

The progress chart shown in figure 8.4c represents the status of the project at a given monitoring date. It shows which milestones are ahead, on schedule, or lag behind the plan as represented by the LOB. The progress chart and other diagrams are used to analyze the causes of project delay. For example, it can be seen that delay in the delivery of panels and structural elements (item 5) has caused delays in items 6, 8, and 10 to 16. The overall actual progress of the project in terms of housing units delivered is shown by the dotted line on the objective chart.

Application of LOB in one-time projects

The LOB concept can be used in scheduling, monitoring, and controlling the progress of projects consisting of only one or a small number of systems in which many one-time activities and operations are involved. Here, instead of monitoring the quantity of items produced, the percentage of progress of the major milestones of the projects is monitored. Some necessary modifications are needed for this purpose.

The project objective chart is modified to represent the percentage of completion of the project versus time. For the whole project, this usually takes the form of an S-shaped curve. A typical project objective chart for a single-unit housing project is shown in figure 8.5a. The construction plan for this housing unit is shown in figure 8.4e. The project objective chart also indicates the plan for completion of each of the activities in a percentage form. The horizontal axes of figures 8.5a and 8.5b indicate the working days elapsed from the start of the project. The vertical axis of the objective chart is from zero to 100 percent. Milestones representing the start and finish of various activ-

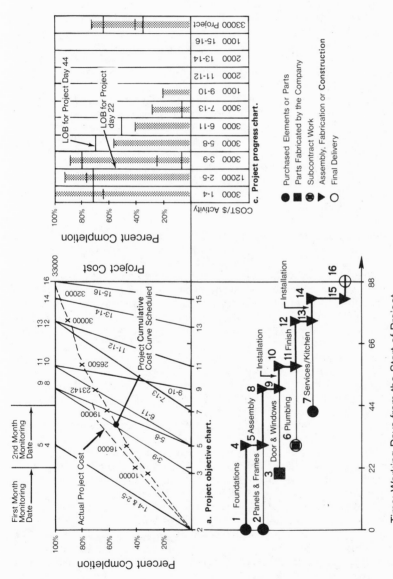

Fig. 8.5 a,b,c. Line of balance diagram for a one-time project.

148

ities are laid out according to their time of occurrence on the lower or upper (zero or 100 percent lines) horizontal axes of the objective chart respectively, where each activity is shown by a straight slanting line connecting its starting event to its ending event.

The progress chart is shown in figure 8.5c, where each position on the horizontal axis represents an activity indicated by the number of its start and end events. The vertical axis is similar to that of the objective chart and shows the percentage of completion of the project and individual activities from zero to 100 percent. An additional column at the extreme right side of the chart represents the progress of the whole project.

On a given monitoring date, the Line of Balance can be obtained from the objective chart in a similar manner, as discussed before. The actual percentage progress of each activity is estimated by those people responsible for carrying out that activity, and is shown by a shaded bar at the position of that activity. In the progress chart (figure 8.5c), the scheduled status of the project and its various activities on the 44th project day (44 working days elapsed since the start of the project) are shown by the LOB. The actual status of the activities is shown by the shaded bars. The project completion curve on the objective chart (S=curve) represents the planned expenditures or percentage of the estimated cost of the whole project as a function of time from the starting date. The shaded bar representing the actual progress of the project on the progress chart reflects the actual expenditures or the percentage of accrued costs as of the date of project monitoring.

Advantages and disadvantages of LOB

LOB has been used for monitoring progress, and generating management reports and financial status reports.(3) It is an easy management technique for learning, teaching, installing, maintaining, and updating, and is best suited for application in industrial production and manufacturing. Some organizations that have used network techniques in their projects have switched to LOB in some cases for control of the related manufacturing processes. It uses a single type of display and reporting method for project control from beginning to end, where all planning, scheduling, control, and reporting information are presented in one sheet.

LOB also has several shortcomings. It does not provide simulation capability when it is desirable to obtain the effects of alternative courses of action in eliminating certain bottlenecks. LOB is also a deterministic approach and cannot consider uncertainty. Additional extensions of LOB, such as day control LOB, are discussed by Heyel.(4) Merged with network techniques, however, the LOB method has become a powerful production and project management control technique.

NETWORK TECHNIQUES FOR PROJECT MANAGEMENT

This chapter will briefly consider three network techniques: the Critical Path Method (CPM), the Program Evaluation and Review Technique (PERT), and the Precedence Network.

Application of network techniques in various types of projects throughout the world has increased immensely during the past two decades.(5) Due to their success in reducing the cost and duration of various projects, CPM and PERT were recommended by the United States Government in 1962 for use by its contractors. Network techniques have been modified and extended further since their development. Many new features have been added to their basic structure to increase their applicability and the scope of their service in project management.

Network techniques can be used manually without the need of a computer for small size projects; their immense power for handling large and complex projects, however, can be explored only by using high-speed digital computers. Today many computer programs and software services in project management using network techniques, especially CPM and PERT and their extensions, are available in most countries.

Critical Path Method (CPM)

The CPM, which has been called Critical Path Scheduling (CPS) or Critical Path Analysis (CPA), was developed by a private industry; therefore, the method was not made available to the public for fear of competitors.(6) Thus, various management firms, universities, and consultants have developed their own CPM-based routines and provide these routines for other users for a fee. During past decades many new, elaborate, and sophisticated additions have been developed and added to the basic technique, making CPM a very powerful and comprehensive technique for management of complex and large projects.

CPM networks are produced by carrying out the following four steps:
1. Identification and listing of project activities
2. Preparation of the project graphic model or arrow diagram
3. Estimating activity durations and introduction of time in the network
4. Calculating the scheduling times of the activities and events and determining floats and critical paths

The steps are discussed briefly in the following sections, and applications of CPM are discussed later in this chapter.

Identification and listing of project activities

Project activities can be identified in various ways, such as by analyzing and systematically dissecting a project into its component parts, as in preparing PBS and Gantt charts. In CPM the breakdown of projects into component activities is usually carried out in greater or lesser detail depending upon project requirements, management needs and interpretations, and the intended use of the final network for the particular level of the project management concerned.

Early recognition of natural subgroups or cluster of activities within the main body of the project, such as repeating cycles or certain activities, important activity chains, subprojects, and project segments, simplifies the project breakdown and saves considerable time and effort in preparation, analysis, and use of CPM networks.

An activity is a work item, a job, or a task necessary for completion of a project that uses time and other resources, and has a definable beginning and ending. The amount of work involved in an activity should be of such magnitude to allow reliable estimates of activity resources and duration and the application of control measurements.

Preparing the project graphic model or arrow diagram

A graphic model is used for representation of the project activities and the sequence of their execution. This graphic model, which uses the so-called activity-on-arrow network system, is the backbone of the Critical Path Method. The main element of this graphical model is the arrow.

Each activity in the project is represented by an arrow; therefore, the graphic model is called the arrow diagram. The arrow diagram shows the plan and the logical interrelationships among the component activities of the project. Each arrow is a separate entity representing one activity; therefore, it has only one tail and one head and cannot be interrupted. The tail represents the start and the head represents the completion of that activity. Arrows are not scaled vectors and can thus be freely drawn as needed to clarify the diagram. The arrows in the network are arranged in such a way as to represent the logical sequence of carrying out the project activities.

The starting and ending points of activities or the intersection of two or more activity arrows are called nodes or events, which represent a point in time. All activities ending into an event must be completed before any activity starting from that event can begin. Key events representing accomplishment of important intermediate project objectives within the network are called milestones (see figure 8.6).

The logic of the network may be described as follows:
1. The position of each arrow within the network implies the logical precedence of the activity represented by that arrow in relation to other activities.
2. In some cases, the precedence of one activity over another can be represented by a broken-line arrow, which is called a dependency or dummy arrow and represents a dummy activity that uses zero resource or time. In figure 8.5, three typical dummy activities are shown.
3. An activity cannot begin unless all its preceding activities are completed.

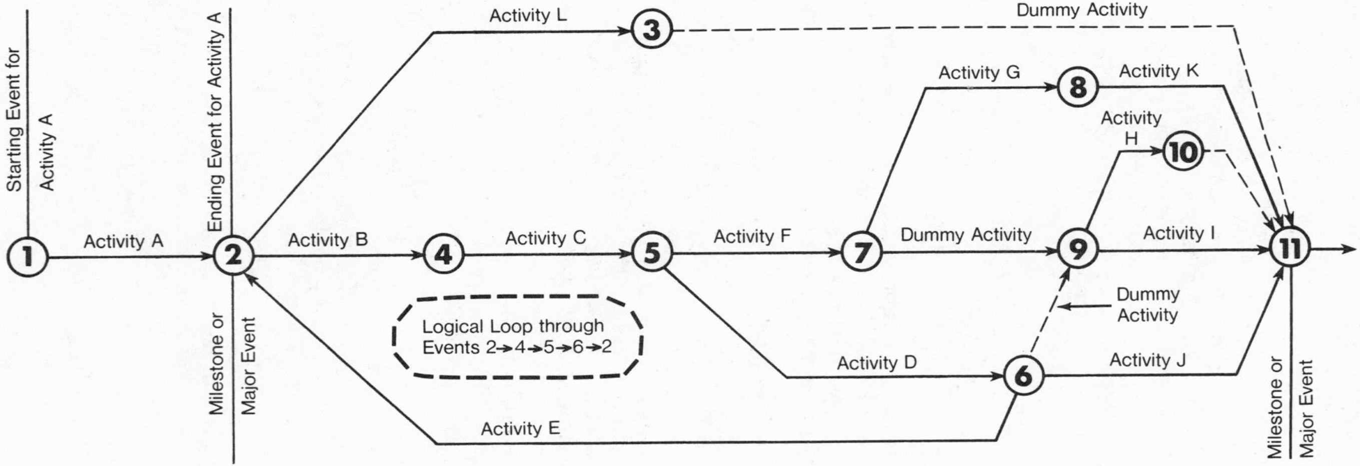

Fig. 8.6. Milestone activities.

152

4. An activity that succeeds a sequence of activities cannot precede any activity within that sequence; otherwise, a loop in the network logic, called the <u>logical loop</u>, occurs, showing that the planning is illogical and absurd. In figure 8.6, the chain of activities B-C-D-E forms a logical loop.

The following rules and recommendations should be considered in drawing arrow diagrams:

1. Each activity is bounded by a starting and ending event. Each event should be represented by a unique number. For example, in figure 8.6, activity I is represented as activity 9-11.

2. Only one arrow (activity) should span directly between any two events. When two or more activities span directly between the same events, it must be ensured that each arrow representing those activities has a unique i-j event number. This is only possible by introducing broken-line dummy arrows in proper places.

3. Each network should have only one starting and one finishing event. No activity should be left dangling. All the dangling activities should be connected directly or by means of dummy arrows to the last event of the project.

4. For each activity, the number representing the ending (or j) event should be greater than the number representing the starting (or i) event. This is called the j   i rule. This rule is not very strict, especially when using computers whose programs allow random numbering of events. Observing the j   i rule of event numbering simplifies locating the events on the network and identifying logical loops, because in a loop at least one activity can be found, where i   j. For example, in the logical loop formed by activities B-C-D-E shown in Figure 8.6, activity E is numbered as activity 6-2 where i   j.

5. For assigning a number to events, the Fulkerson procedure, which observes the j   i rule, can be used.(7)

6. It is a good practice to write the activity description on the upper part of the horizontal portion of the arrows. Instead of using codes to identify each activity, the summary description of each activity should be written down on the corresponding arrows.

7. The main chain of activities, which are also often the critical activities, should preferably be located at the center of the drawing to form the so-called <u>backbone</u> of the network.

8. The CPM network is a diagram for recording and communicating planning and scheduling information to various people in all levels of management and field operation. Therefore its appearance, format, and physical layout should be well organized, neat, and concise to facilitate communication and reduce the chances of error. The physical layout of the arrow diagram must be logical and well organized; a disorganized network often reflects confused and disorderly planning.

9. For large networks consisting of hundreds of activities, suitable organization of the network is very important; otherwise, confusion will result. The activities must be organized into logical and natural

groupings and the groupings located in suitable areas of the drawing. The natural approach is to organize the network by the physical and/or organization subdivision of the project. For example, in a construction project, the groupings may be: foundation works, building floors, site works, irrigation canals, spillway, and so on.

For preparation of the network, the project manager has to think through the project from start to completion. In doing so, the manager can find many problem areas needing advanced planning, specialized solutions, and early preparations. When the arrow diagram is drawn, the project manager has mentally built and completed the project.

Introduction of time estimates in networks

The third step in the preparation of a critical path network diagram is the introduction of time estimates. The arrow diagram obtained at the second step lacks the dimension of time. It describes how the project has to be carried out and in what sequence various activities have to be accomplished; it does not, however, say how long it will take to carry out various activities or the whole project, or when various planning targets and milestones are to be met.

In this step, the durations of various activities are estimated and added to the network. The result is a working network ready for carrying out scheduling computations. Because the timing of activities may necessitate some changes in the plans and assumed sequence of activities, some refinement of network is often needed at this step.

Activity duration is the amount of time most likely needed for completion of an activity, assuming it is carried out in a "normal" way by a "normal" work crew under "normal" conditions, using a "normal" level of resources. The word "normal" here implies conditions that lead to the most economical way of proceeding. Due to the impossibility of predicting various future uncertainties, such as weather conditions, strikes, and so on, the only sound policy is to obtain the best estimate of activity duration available at the time and to update that estimate later when more accurate information becomes available. Depending upon the type of project and organization involved, activity duration estimates can be obtained from different sources, such as work measurement studies, activity analysis, published standards, the recorded data of past projects, past management and personnel experiences, and so on. The accuracy of the scheduling information obtained from the network is proportional to the accuracy of the activity duration data used.

Scheduling the activities

After determining activity durations, the scheduling calculations can begin. In CPM scheduling, the important basic scheduling dates and information are the earliest and latest times of occurrence of events, the earliest and latest times of starting and finishing various activities, and various types of activity floats. Activity floats or slacks are the measures of scheduling flexibility and can be used later or in scheduling that activity. For determining these times and information, it is necessary to make a forward and then a backward "computing pass" through the network. Before describing these passes, let us define these terms and show their relationships by means of graphs and formulas, as follows:

Nomenclature and Formulas for Computing Scheduling Times

i and j = Number of starting and finishing events of $Activity_{i-j}$, respectively

D_{i-j} = Duration of $Activity_{i-j}$ in days, weeks, months, etcetera

TE_i = Earliest time of $Event_i$; this is the earliest time at which $Event_i$ can logically happen (that is, all its preceding activities can finish). It is obtained by a forward computing pass through the network.

TL_j = Latest time of $Event_j$; this is the latest time at which $Event_j$ can logically happen without increasing the duration of the project. It is obtained by a backward computing pass through the network.

ES_{i-j} = Earliest start time of $Activity_{i-j}$; this is the earliest time at which $Activity_{i-j}$ can be logically started. It is equal to the earliest time of $Event_i$ (TE_i): $ES_{i-j} = TE_i$ (1)

EF_{i-j} = Earliest finish time of $Activity_{i-j}$; this is the earliest time at which $Activity_{i-j}$ can be logically completed. It is equal to the earliest start of $Activity_{i-j}$ plus the duration of that activity: $EF_{i-j} = ES_{i-j} + D_{i-j} = TE_i + D_{i-j}$. (2)

LF_{i-j} = Latest finish time of $Activity_{i-j}$; this is the latest time at which $Activity_{i-j}$ can be completed without extending the duration of the project. It is equal to the latest time of $Event_j$ (TL_j): $LF_{i-j} = TL_j$ (3)

LS_{i-j} = Latest start time of $Activity_{i-j}$; this is the latest time at which $Activity_{i-j}$ can logically be started without lengthening the duration of the project. It is equal to the latest finish time of $Activity_{i-j}$ minus the duration of that activity:
$LS_{i-j} = LF_{i-j} - D_{i-j} = TL_j - D_{i-j}$ (4)

TF_{i-j} = Total float of $Activity_{i-j}$; this is the total amount of flexibility in scheduling $Activity_{i-j}$ as shown in figure 8.7. It has to be shared with other activities along each chain. Once it is used in any activity along the chain it is lost and other activities along the chain have no further float.
$TF_{i-j} = (TL_j - TE_i) - D_{i-j} = (LF_{i-j} - ES_{i-j}) - D_{i-j}$ (5)

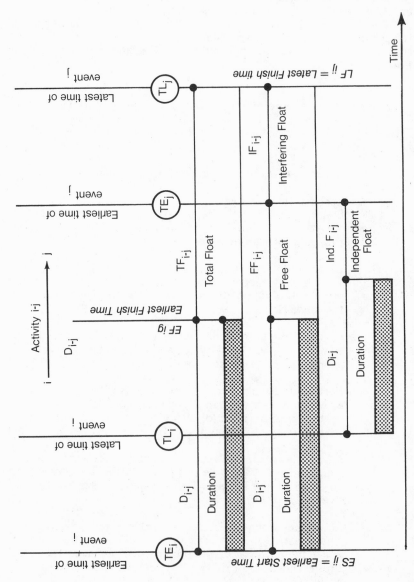

Fig. 8.7. Various types of floats or slacks in scheduling a typical activity$_{i\text{-}j}$.

FF_{i-j} = Free float of Activity $_{i-j}$; this is the amount of flexibility in scheduling Activity $_{i-j}$ as shown by figure 8.7, which if used, will neither delay nor interfere with scheduling the succeeding activities:

$$FF_{i-j} = (TE_j - TE_i) - D_{i-j} \tag{6}$$

IF_{i-j} = Interfering float of Activity $_{i-j}$; this is the amount of flexibility in scheduling Activity $_{i-j}$ as shown in figure 8.7, which must be shared with the succeeding activities:

$$IF_{i-j} = TF_{i-j} - FF_{i-j} = TL_j - TE_j \tag{7}$$

Ind. F_{i-j} = Independent float of Activity $_{i-j}$; this is the amount of flexibility in scheduling Activity $_{i-j}$ as shown in figure 8.7, which can be used exclusively for that activity and its use will have no effect on scheduling the preceding or succeeding activities:

$$Ind.\ F_{i-j} = (TE_j - TL_i) - D_{i-j} \tag{8}$$

DETERMINATION OF BASIC SCHEDULING TIMES

The times used in these computations are the elapsed times from the start of the project, expressed in suitable time units such as working day, working week, etc. For example, when the time is described as project-day 12 (or simply day 12), it means the end of the twelfth working day elapsed since the start of the project. The forward and backward computing passes are as follows:

Forward Computing Pass: Determination of TE, ES and EF

From the forward computing pass the earliest time of occurrence of each event (TE) and the earliest start and finish times of each activity (ES and EF) are obtained. It is assumed that projects start at time zero (the beginning of the first project day; the end of the first project day is time 1 or project day 1). In the forward computing pass, it is assumed that each activity starts as soon as its preceding event occurs. It was mentioned before that an event occurs when all the preceding activities merging into that event are completed. Thus, the earliest time that an event can occur is equal to the largest (or the maximum) of the earliest finish times of the activities merging into that event, as shown by the following equations:

$$TE_j = Max\ (EF_{k-j} \ldots, EF_{l-j} \ldots, EF_{h-j}) \tag{9}$$

where activities $k-j$, $l-j$ . . ., $h-j$ are those merging into the event j. As an example, in the simple network shown in figure 8.8, the project starts with event 1. The earliest time for this event is zero, that is, $TE_1 = 0$. The earliest event times are recorded on the network in the left-hand side square below each event. The earliest start times of activities 1-2, 1-3, and 1-4 are equal to the earliest time of occurrence of event 1,

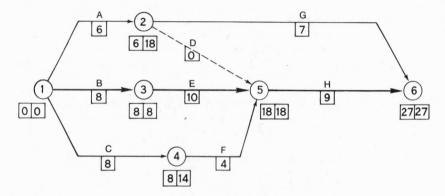

Fig. 8.8. Forward and backward computing passes
through a CPM network.

Table 8.1. Activity times, Floats, and Duration for
CPM Network shown in Fig. 8.8

i	j	Title or description of activity	Duration Days	Activity Times				Activity Floats			
				ES	EF	LS	LF	TF	FF	IF	Ind. F
1	2	A	10	0	10	2	12	2	0	2	0
1	3	B	8	0	8	0	8	0	0	0	0
1	4	C	12	0	12	2	14	2	0	2	0
2	5	D	0	10	10	18	18	8	8	0	6
3	5	E	10	8	18	8	18	0	0	0	0
4	5	F	4	12	16	14	18	2	2	0	0
2	6	G	15	10	25	12	27	2	2	0	0
5	6	H	9	18	27	18	27	0	0	0	0

Table 8.2. Resources, Duration, Times, and Floats for
CPM Network in Fig. 8.8

i	j	Title or Description of Activity	Total Cost $	Cost/ Doz. $	Man/ Day	Duration Days	Activity Times				Activity Floats			
							ES	EF	LS	LF	TF	FF	IF	Ind. F
1	2	A	6000	1000	5	6	0	6	12	18	12	0	12	0
1	3	B	12000	1500	8	8	0	8	0	8	0	0	0	0
1	4	C	6400	800	6	8	0	8	6	14	6	0	6	0
2	5	D	0	0	0	0	6	6	18	18	12	12	0	0
3	5	E	20000	2000	10	10	8	18	8	18	0	0	0	0
4	5	F	10000	2500	12	4	8	12	14	18	6	6	0	0
2	6	G	14000	2000	10	7	6	11	20	27	14	14	0	2
5	6	H	27000	8000	15	9	18	27	18	27	0	0	0	0

$$ES_{1-2} = ES_{1-3} = ES_{1-4} = 0.$$

The earliest finish time of each of these activities is at the end of project days 6, 8, and 8 is equal to the duration plus the earliest start time of each activity respectively. Only one activity precedes each of the events 2, 3, and 4; therefore, the earliest time of occurrence of these events is equal to the earliest finish times of activities 1-2, 1-3, and 1-4 respectively, that is,

$$TE_2 = EF_{1-2} = 6, TE_3 = EF_{1-3} = 8, TE_4 = EF_{1-4} = 8.$$

The earliest start times of activities 2-5, 3-5, and 4-5 are equal to the earliest time of their branching events 2, 3, and 4, respectively.

$$ES_{2-5} = TE_2 = 6, ES_{3-5} = TE_3 = 8, ES_{4-5} = TE_4 = 8,$$

the earliest finish times of these activities according to equation 2 is equivalent to their duration plus their earliest start time, that is, 6, 18, and 12 respectively.

No event can occur until all the preceding activities merging into that event are completed. Therefore, event 5 cannot occur until activities 2-5, 3-5, and 4-5 are finished. This happens at the end of the eighteenth day of the project when activity 3-5 which has the largest earliest finish time is completed. Therefore, according to equation 9, the earliest time of event 5 is

$$TE_5 = Max (EF_{2-5}, ER_{3-5}, EF_{4-5}) = Max (6, 18, 12).$$

Following the same procedure, the earliest event times and the earliest starts and finish times for other events and activities are calculated and recorded on the network. The earliest time of event 6 is

$$TE_6 = Max (EF_{2-6}, EF_{5-6}) = Max (13, 27) = 27.$$

Thus, the earliest time for completion of this small project is the end of the twenty-seventh day elapsed from the start of project.

Backward Computing Path: Determination of TL, LF, and LS

From the <u>backward computing pass</u>, the latest time of occurrences of each event (TL), the latest start and finish time of each activity (LS and LF) are obtained. To start the backward pass, it is necessary to specify the expected latest completion time of the project. This time will be equivalent to the latest time of occurrence of the last or terminal event of the network. This time must be greater than or equal to the earliest time of occurrence of the last event. To simplify the identification of critical activities, it is customary to assume that the latest time of occurrence of the last event of the project, event n, is equivalent to the earliest time of its occurrence, that is,

$$TE_n = TL_n.$$ (10)

In the backward computing path, it is assumed that each activity finishes at its latest finish time, which is equivalent to the latest time of occurrence of its ending or succeeding event. The latest time that an activity can start is equivalent to its latest finish time minus its duration, which was shown by equations 4 and 6. It was mentioned earlier that all activities branching from an event cannot start unless that event occurs. Therefore, the latest time that an event can occur without delaying the completion of the project is equal to the smallest (or minimum) or the latest starting time of the activities branching from that event. According to the following equation:

$$TL_i = Min\ (LS_{i,h}, LS. . ., LS_{i,h}) \tag{11}$$

where activities i-h, i-1. . .and i-j are those that succeed and branch from the event i. As an example, for the sample network shown in Figure 8.7, event 6 is the last event of the project. The latest time of this event, TL_6, is assumed to be equivalent to its earliest time, $TE_6 = 27$. The latest event times are recorded on the network in the right-hand side square below each event. The latest finish times of activities 2-6 and 5-6 are equal to the latest finish time of the succeeding event 6, that is,

$$LF_{2-6} = LF_{5-6} = TL_6 = 27.$$

The latest start time of these activities LS_{2-6} and LS_{5-6} are 20 and 18, respectively, which is equivalent to their latest finish time minus their duration. Only activity 5-6 succeeds event 5; therefore, the latest time of occurrence of this event TL_5 is equal to $LS_{5-6} = 18$. Continuing the same procedure, the latest finish and latest start times of activities 2-5, 3-5, and 4-5, the latest time of events 2, 3, and 4, the latest finish and latest start times of activities 1-2, 1-3, and 1-4 are obtained. All the latest time of events are recorded on the network. The latest time of occurrence of event 1 is equal to the smallest of the latest start times of the succeeding activities branching from that event, that is,

$$TL_1 = Min\ (LS_{1-2}, LS_{1-3}, LS_{1-4}) = Min\ (12, 0, 6) = 0.$$

When the latest time of the ending event of a project is taken equal to its earliest time, then the latest time of the starting event of the project becomes equal to its earliest time. This also serves as a check to control the accuracy of calculations.

Determination of activity floats.

After determining the earliest and latest event times TE and TL for all events, and the activity times ES, LS, EF, LF for all activities, various types of floats as described by equations 5 to 8 can be calculated. The significance of these floats, which represent flexibility in scheduling each activity, was discussed earlier and is shown in figure 8.7. For the network shown in figure 8.8, the values of the activity times, duration, and floats are computed and are shown in the table below that figure.

Determination of the critical path

Figure 8.8 demonstrates that the earliest time of occurrence (TE) of some events, such as 1, 3, 5, and 6, is the same as their latest time of occurrence (TL). These events are critical because no flexibility exists in their time of occurrence. They must happen at a particular moment of time, not sooner and not later. If they happen later, the whole project will be delayed. Therefore, all those events, for which TE = TL, are called <u>critical events</u>.

From figure 8.8, we can see that the earliest start time ES of some activities, such as activities B, E, and H, is the same as their latest start time LS. Also, the latest finish time LF of these activities is equivalent to their earliest finish time EF. These activities are also critical because no flexibility exists in their scheduling. They must start at a particular moment and finish at another particular moment. No sooner time is possible and no later time is allowed because the entire project will be delayed. Therefore, all these activities, for which ES = LS and EF = LF, are called <u>critical activities</u>. Figure 8.8 also shows that the total float TF for these critical activities is zero.

Critical activities are located between critical events; this condition, however, is not sufficient to make an activity critical. The condition for an activity to be critical is that it has zero float, or TF = 0. Where TF is zero, other types of floats are also zero.

If we start from the first event, we can trace a continuous chain of critical activities through the network which passes through the critical events. This chain of critical activities is called the <u>critical path</u>. It has been proved that through each network there is always at least one continuous critical path, which passes through the first and last events. Sometimes there may be more than one critical path in all or some parts of the network; these must, however, form a connected chain. The critical path is shown by thick dark or colored lines on CPM networks as shown in figure 8.8.

Summary

This section has discussed methods for preparing the CPM network, calculating scheduling time, floats, and critical path. The final results of these efforts is a CPM network or arrow diagram similar to the one shown in figure 8.8. This network indicates a model for programming the execution of various activities of the project. On this diagram, the earliest and the latest time of occurrence of each event is recorded in two adjacent squares under each event. Also on this diagram, the critical path representing the chain of all critical activities is shown by bold lines. In addition to the CPM network, the results of the time calculations are obtained in tabular form similar to the one shown in figure 8.8. This table lists all the network activities as well as the earliest start time (ES) for each activity, earliest finish time (EF), latest start time (LS), latest finish time (LF), total float (TF), free float

(FF), interfering float (IF), and independent float (ind. F). This information is sufficient for scheduling project activities and the control of project progress, a subject discussed later in this chapter.

THE PROGRAM EVALUATION AND REVIEW TECHNIQUE (PERT)

In 1958 a network system similar to the CPM was developed by the United States Navy for monitoring and control of the Polaris missiles program. This network method was later called Program (or Project) Evaluation and Review Technique (PERT).(8)

PERT was initially designed to handle research and development projects using a computer.(9) The first important step in this technique is identification and scheduling of key events or milestones, which, if they are not met on schedule, will cause the project to fall behind schedule. Minor milestones within the major ones also are identified, scheduled, and their occurrences monitored regularly.

Because the PERT system was originally developed for monitoring and controlling the progress of projects, the major emphasis in the PERT network is on accomplishment of events or milestones, in contrast to the CPM network, in which the major emphasis is on the status of activities. Consequently, in the past decade there has been a trend in the PERT network toward recognition of the importance of activities.

Another important difference between CPM and PERT is in the way each considers uncertainty in estimating the activity duration and the project completion date. CPM assumes only one time estimate for each activity duration, while PERT uses three time estimates for each activity duration. In addition, by using statistical calculations, the probability of the earliest and latest occurrence of important project milestones is obtained.

Preparation of the PERT network is carried out in four steps:
1. Identification of activities and milestones

In PERT, the project events and activities can be identified by using PBS or other approaches in the same way as described for CPM; then their sequence must be determined. In CPM, events are not very important and are used only as indices for drawing the network and for ease of calculation; therefore, they are identified by simple numbers. In PERT, however, events are very important; therefore, each must be represented by both a number and a suitable description. To identify each activity, two events are needed to represent the activity's start and finish. This practice introduces redundancies in the network for description of each activity. Describing the events that are either a merging or a branching point for two or more activities is usually a difficult job.

2. Preparation of the project graphical model

In this step, various project events will be linked together to construct a graphical model of the project very similar to the arrow diagram in the CPM. As an example, figure 8.9 shows a typical PERT network for a simple project whose CPM network was shown in figure 8.8.

3. Introducing the time element

Originally PERT was developed for the R and D projects in space and weapon systems in which there was a large level of uncertainty in assigning duration times to the many various activities involved. Therefore it was decided to use three time estimates for each activity as follows:

a: optimistic time or the shortest expected time, if everything happens in a favorable way,

m: most likely time or the normal time that an activity will take. It is similar to the activity duration D_{ij} used in the CPM.

b: pessimistic time or the maximum time an activity may take if everything happens in an unfavorable way.

The following formulas are used to obtain the average expected time (t_e), and the standard deviation (σ) for each activity.

$$t_e = \frac{a + 4m + b}{6} \tag{12}$$

$$\sigma = \frac{b-a}{6} \tag{13}$$

4. Calculating event times, critical path, and slacks

Earliest and latest events TE and TL. For calculation of event times TE and TL, the expected time t_3 calculated from equation 12 is used in the same fashion as activity duration D_{ij} in the CPM network calculations. The event times are obtained in exactly the same manner as described for CPM and then are recorded on the PERT network as shown in figure 8.8.

The critical path

In figure 8.9, TE and TL are equal for some events, called critical events. As in the CPM, the critical path passes through the critical events. It should be noted that not all the activities spanning two critical events are critical. An activity spanning two adjacent events i and j is critical if the following conditions exist:

$$TE_i = TL_i, \ TE_j = TL_j, \ TL_j - TE_i = t_{eij}.$$

The critical path(s) are shown by thick dark lines on the PERT diagram, as shown in figure 8.9.

Slacks

In PERT, the word slack is used to represent the same concept as the word float in the CPM. There are two types of slacks in the PERT, the event slack and the activity slack. The event slack SE is the difference between TL and TE for event i, that is,

$$SE_i = TL_i - TE_i.$$

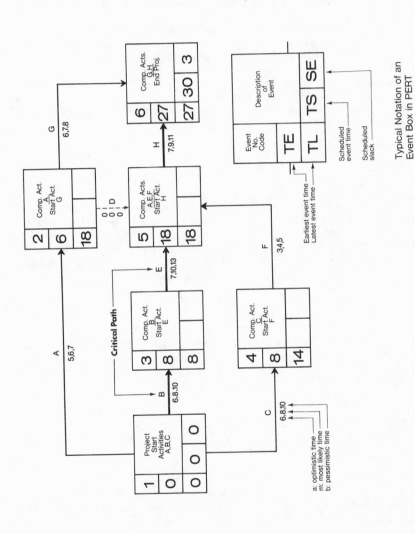

Fig. 8.9. A typical PERT diagram for a simple project (for its CPM diagram, see fig. 8.7).

The activity slack TF_{ij} is similar to the total float in the CPM, and is for each activity:

$$TF_{ij} = TL_j - TE_i - te_{ij}.$$

The slack of a critical activity or event is zero.

PERT was originally developed to monitor an existing schedule. Therefore, TS was introduced for each event value to represent the scheduled completion dates of that event. For any event TS is assigned by the project managers, it does not have any specific relationship with TE or TL; usually, however, it is someplace between TE and TL. In some cases, TS may be smaller than TE.

If the scheduled event times TS are known, then, for an event, the scheduled slack of that event and the adjacent activities are obtained by substituting TS for TL in the above equations, respectively. When for some events the scheduled event time TS is smaller than TE, then the above calculations lead to negative slacks. Also, in some cases the scheduled slacks of the critical events or activities may be different from zero (positive or negative).

Calculation of probabilities

The standard deviation σ calculated by equation 12 for each activity represents the magnitude of uncertainty in the estimates. If σ is small in comparison with te, then there is more certainty to complete the work in the expected time t_e. The standard deviation for any event in the PERT network is the sum of the square roots of the variance (σ^2) of all the activities along the longest path from the start of the project to that event, according to the following formula.

$$\sigma_{TE} = \sqrt{\sum_{i=1}^{m} \sigma_{tei})^2} \tag{14}$$

The probability of meeting any given scheduled date for the occurrence of an event TS is determined by calculating the Z factor for that event, as follows:

$$Z = \frac{TS - TE}{\sigma_{TE}} \tag{15}$$

The value of Z is used to obtain the probability from the existing statistical tables.

As an example for event six in Figure 8.9, the longest path is B-E-H passing through events 0-3-5-6, TE = 27. The standard deviation of activities B,E,H are

$$\sigma_B = (10-6)/6 = 4/6, \sigma_E = (13-7)/6 = 1, \sigma_H = (11-7)/6 = 4/6$$

The standard deviation of event six according to equation 14 is

$$\sigma_{TE_6} = \left[(4/6)^2 + 1^2 + (4/6)^2\right]^{1/2} = 1.36$$

The probability of meeting event six at the twenty-seventh or the thirtieth project day is obtained by calculating Z from equation 15 as follows:

$$Z_{27} = (27-27)/1.36 = 0.0, Z_{30} = (30-27)/1.36 = 2,205$$

From the statistical table showing the area under the normal curves for the above values of Z, the probabilities are 0.50 and 0.986, respectively.(10) Thus, there is a 50 percent chance to complete the project on the twenty-seventh day. There is about a ninety-nine percent chance, however, to complete it by the thirtieth day.

Precedence Networks

Precedence networks were first introduced in 1962 as the Method of Potentials (MPM),(11) or Precedence Network.(12) In this method, each activity is introduced to the computer in terms of its immediately preceding activities, not by its starting and ending events as in the CPM.

In the precedence method, the identification of activities and estimation of their duration are carried out exactly as for the CPM. There are, however, some differences in the preparation of the network diagram. The precedence network or diagram uses the so-called "Activity-on-Node" network notation system, where the activities are graphically shown by nodes instead of arrows. In this method, the descriptions of an activity are shown in a box diagram instead of on the arrows. The sequence of activities and their logical connection are shown by arrows connecting the boxes together. Arrowheads show the direction of the flow of activities and their precedence to one another.

In the precedence diagram, there is no need to use events except to show the start and end of the whole part. In preparing the network, the activity boxes can be connected together in many ways, as shown in figure 8.10 where their equivalent CPM representation is also shown. In these cases, the precedence diagram clearly does not need the use of dummy arrows. In practice, overlapping activities occur when it is possible to start a job after a certain percentage of the preceding activity has been completed. In the precedence diagram, this situation can be handled easily, as shown in figure 8.10, where their equivalent CPM representation, requiring lead and lag arrows, is also shown. Figures 8.10 and 8.11 demonstrate that there is no need for dummy arrows in the precedence network.

Calculation of activity times

Because the precedence diagram shows no events, we can directly calculate the earliest and latest start times and finish times (ES, LS, LF, and LF, respectively) of each activity in a similar fashion, as was done for the CPM. First, the activities are numbered according to the Fulkerson Method.(13) Then, assuming the ES of the first activity is

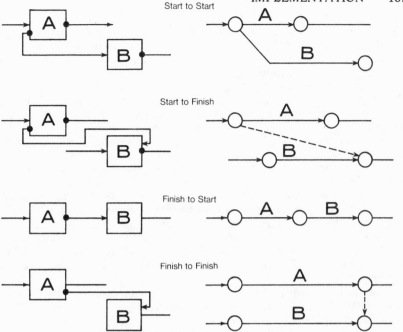

Fig. 8.10. Comparison of CPM and precedence notations.

Precedence Notation   CPM Notation

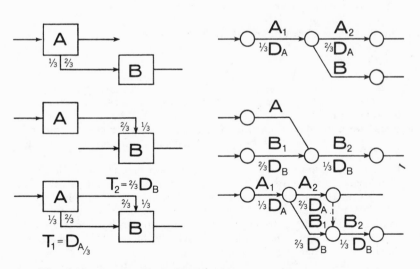

Fig. 8.11. Comparison of CPM and precedence notations for
activities with overlap.

zero, a forward pass is carried out through the network and the ES and EF are obtained for all activities, as in CPM. In calculating ES, it should be noted that whenever more than one activity precedes a given activity, all the preceding activities must be completed before that given activity can begin.

At the end of the forward pass, the EF for the last project activity is obtained. This is the earliest time that the project can be completed. As in the CPM, here it is also assumed that the earliest completion time of the project is also the latest anticipated date for its completion, that is, for the last activity of the project EF = LF. Then a backward computing pass is carried out through the network and the LF and LS for all the activities are obtained as in CPM. In calculations of LF, it should be noted that whenever more than one activity succeeds a given activity, then the latest finish time of that activity should not be later than the latest start times of its succeeding activities.

The results of these forward and backward computing passes through the network are the ES, EF, LS, and LF for each activity. Their values are written down on the four corners of the box representing that activity, as shown in figure 8.12.

The floats used in the precedence diagram are similar to those defined for the CPM. Some of them are usually shown on the activity boxes, as in figure 8.12.

The critical activities are those for which ES = LS and EF = LF or have zero float TF = 0, as in CPM. These activities are easily identified in the network. Connecting these critical activities together forms the critical path which is indicated by marking their connecting arros with thick dark or colored lines, as in the CPM.

Figure 8.12 represents the precedence diagram for the project whose CPM diagrams were shown in figure 8.8.

Advantages and disadvantages of the precedence network

The relative merits of the precedence network, as compared to CPM, may be listed as follows:
1. It is a simpler technique for presentation of networks to project managers, people in the field, and shop-floor personnel who do not appreciate more complicated diagrams.
2. It can be viewed as a natural link between the bar chart representation of a project and its network representation, as shown in figure 8.3(f).
3. It does not use many of the symbols and jargon used in CPM or PERT, such as events and dummy, delay or time-lag arrows, etc. Therefore, the amount of necessary calculation is reduced.
4. It is often used manually for planning, scheduling, and control of small projects. Here the precedence diagram can be directly used as a bar chart. For this reason, Mulvaney has called this method Analysis Bar Charting (ABC).(14)
5. It can model repetitive and dovetailed activities more efficiently; therefore, in this type of project, the use of the precedence network is preferred.

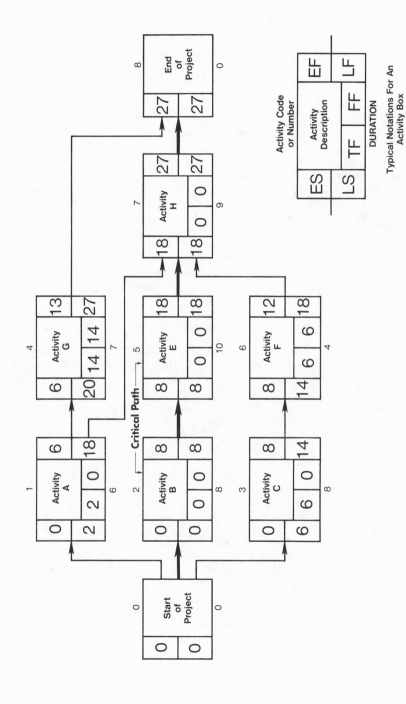

Fig. 8.12. A typical precedence diagram for a simple project (for CPM diagram, see fig. 8.7).

169

6. At present, it is seldom used for large projects, because it is not standard and because most computing centers do not have precedence programming support available.
7. For projects with overlapping or repetitive activities, the precedence network looks much simpler than CPM or PERT networks. Interpretation of the network, however, is more difficult.

APPLICATION OF NETWORK TECHNIQUES IN PROJECT IMPLEMENTATION

Network techniques are used for planning and programming the implementation phase of the projects and for their scheduling and control. Project planning and programming is carried out during preparation of the network diagrams. Addition of the activity durations to the network diagrams and determination of activity and event times, floats, and critical path completes the project planning and programming. Thus, a network diagram as determined in the previous section represents the project implementation plan and program. In the following sections, the application of networks for project scheduling, monitoring, and control is briefly discussed.

Project Scheduling by Networks

Project scheduling determines the definite dates (usually calendar dates) each project activity should start or finish and each event should happen. The first step in scheduling a project is to determine the project completion date. This date is sometimes established by external requirements or constraints. Often, the earliest time of the last project event, TE_n, is assumed to be the project completion due date. When the earliest computed project completion date, TE_n, is longer than the desired or required project completion date, TS_n, the project duration must then be shortened as much as $TE_n - TS_n$ by the following methods.

1. <u>Shortening the project completion date by revising network logic.</u> This is possible by carrying out some of the critical activities in parallel or in overlap form instead of in a series.

2. <u>Shortening the duration of critical or semicritical activities.</u> This is possible by allocating more resources to such activities from noncritical activities or other sources. A good approach to shorten the duration of critical or semicritical activities is to choose the activities that occur early in the project and have the longest duration. In most cases, reduction of the project duration increases its cost. Some activities are cheaper to reduce than others. A suitable policy for reducing the duration of any project is to choose to shorten the activities that lead to the cheapest overall cost. This policy can be obtained from the project time-cost tradeoff curve.

Time-cost tradeoff curves

A typical time-cost tradeoff curve for a project and an activity is shown in figure 8.13. Methods for determining this curve are discussed by O'Brien(15) and others.(16) Certain terms in figure 8.13 need definition. Crash time for an activity is the shortest time possible to carry out that activity by using as many resources as available technology permits. The cost of carrying out an activity in a crash form, which is generally more than its normal cost, is called the crash cost. A project is said to be in full crash when all activities are carried out in the crash form. A project is said to be in crash when some critical and semicritical activities are carried out in a crash form in such a way that no further reduction in project duration is possible by further expenditure of resources or money. These terms are shown in figure 8.13. Time-cost tradeoff curves indicate the crash situations for the project and prevent the project manager from using the unnecessary and costly full crash approach.

Finalizing the project schedule

After obtaining a satisfactory project completion date, the final schedules of critical activities or events are obtained directly from network calculations. For small projects, network-based time-scale Gantt charts can be used to obtain the final schedule of activities.

Network-Based Time-Scaled Gantt Charts

A typical time-scaled Gantt chart for the CPM network of figure 8.8 is shown of figure 8.14. Activities B, E, and H are critical. They form a continuous connected bar from the start to the end of the project. Activity A has twelve days float; therefore, it can be scheduled somewhere between zero and the eighteenth day of the project, which are its earliest start and latest finish times, respectively. Noncritical activities, such as A, G, C, and F, can be scheduled in many ways. The two extreme cases are earliest start schedule and latest start schedule, shown in figures 8.14a and b respectively. In the earliest start schedule, each activity starts at its earliest start time and finishes at its earliest finish time. There are many possible schedules between the two extreme cases.

The time-scaled bar chart is used for scheduling the noncritical activities. The two extreme cases discussed above act as limits. The time-scaled bar chart is similar to a Chinese abacus where the noncritical activities can slide back and forth like beads between the two limiting cases.

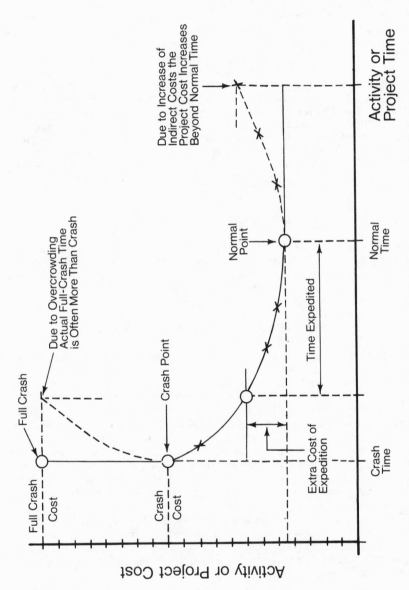

Fig. 8.13. Typical time-cost trade-off curve for a project or an activity.

172

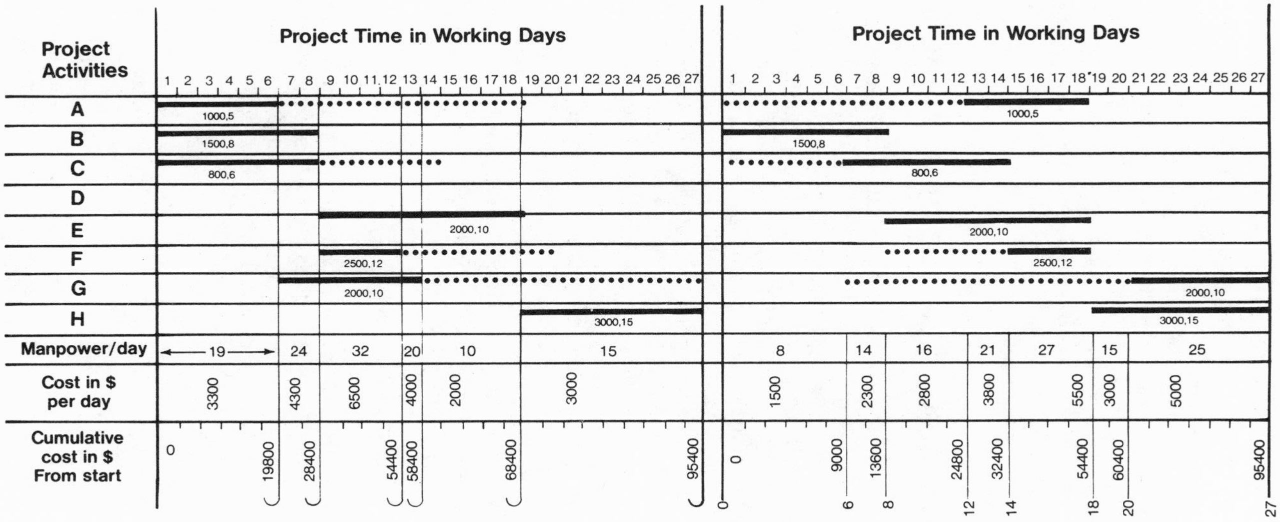

a – The earliest Start Schedule
(all activities Start at their Earliest)

b – The latest Start Schedule
(all activities Start at their latest)

Fig. 8.14. Network-based Gantt chart for a CPM project of figure 8.8.

Factors to be Considered in Scheduling

In reviewing the final schedules for intermediate activities and events, many factors such as bad weather, delay in delivery, strikes, shortages, and other contingencies should be considered.

When there are resource or other types of scheduling limitations, special dummy arrows called schedule sequence, lag, or lead arrows are used to sequence the activities in such a way that these limitations are satisfied. This subject is treated in more detail in the upcoming section on resource allocation. The final schedules are usually converted into calendar dates manually or by computer, and the results are published and distributed to all concerned.

RESOURCE SCHEDULING, ALLOCATION AND SMOOTHING

Resources such as workers, money, material, and machinery are seldom available in an unlimited amount for use in any project. When resources are limited, the project manager has to schedule the activities in such a way that the available amounts are not exceeded. In some cases, the project manager wants to prevent the day-to-day fluctuation in the level of required resources and obtain an even resource requirement during the project duration. This problem is called <u>resource leveling smoothing</u>. Resource scheduling and smoothing are achieved by:
1. Scheduling the critical and semicritical (low float) activities first.
2. Juggling around those resource-consuming activities with high float and using them as fill-in jobs.
3. When step two does not lead to a satisfactory solution, there may be no choice except to elongate the duration of certain activities, which may lead to elongation of project duration.

Various manual and computerized network-based techniques are available for resource scheduling, allocation, and smoothing; these are briefly discussed in the following sections.

Manual methods for resource scheduling

Manual methods are used for simple, small-size projects. The network-based time-scaled Gantt chart in figure 8.14 shows the two limiting activity schedules. It is assumed that the resource in question is humanpower (other types of resources can be treated the same way). For each activity, the number of workers per day is indicated on the bars. At the bottom of the chart the total number of workers required on each project day for all activities is added up and recorded. The workforce requirement for the two limiting schedules of figure 8.14 is shown in figure 8.15 by histograms A and B, respectively. Histogram C shows the workforce requirement for critical activities B-E-G.

In figure 8.15, the earliest start schedule results in an early peak in worker requirements while the latest start schedule results in a late peak.

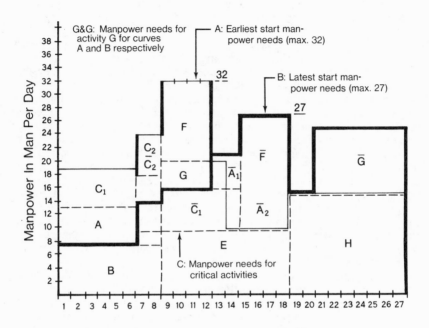

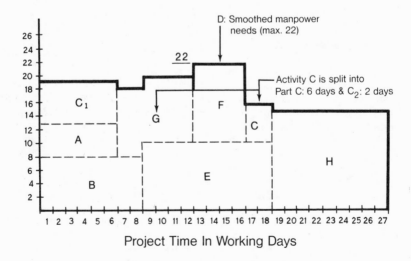

Fig. 8.15. Manpower scheduling and smoothing.

The areas under histograms A and B are subdivided into segments representing the worker requirement of one of the activities. The objective of resource scheduling and leveling is to shift around the uncommon segments in such a way as to achieve an allocation not exceeding the available resources as smoothly as possible (if required), so that the logical sequence of activities is not violated.

Manual handling of this task, which is similar to solving a jigsaw puzzle, is time-consuming because of the many possibilities and constraints. For figure 8.15, a typical final smooth schedule of workers has been obtained and is shown by histogram D.

Limited resources add a new constraint in project scheduling which requires extension of project duration. Many activities become critical or must be sequenced and scheduled in a different way than required by the network logic due to resource limitation. In fact, resource limitation forces its own logic on activity scheduling. In general, two types of project schedules exist. Those that have strict limitations on the level of resources with no time limits are called the resource-limited schedules. In contrast, those projects that have strict limitations on project duration with no limitation on resources are called the time-limited schedules. In some cases, it may be necessary to extend both the project duration and the level of resources required. In general, it is not possible or realistic to limit both the project duration and the maximum level of the available resource.

In many projects, certain activities require more than one type of scarce resources. These are called multiple resource-limited projects. The scheduling of these activities is much more difficult than those with one type of resource. Detailed descriptions of methods of single or multiple resource scheduling and smoothing have been discussed elsewhere.(17)

Computer Methods for Resource Scheduling

It has been found that only computerized scheduling analysis is feasible and economical for large, complex, or multiresource projects. There are many computer programs and software supports available for resource scheduling and smoothing, such as RAMPS (Resource and Manpower Scheduling Systems), RPMS (Resource Planning and Scheduling Methods), RPC (Resource Planning and Control). These methods are discussed in detail elsewhere.(18)

Monitoring and Control of Project Progress

Monitoring of a project involves determining the project status, maintaining network logic, updating the project schedules, and reporting. Determination of project status is carried out by collecting activity progress reports and displaying them against the schedule so that discrepancies can be easily observed. The activity progress can be marked directly on the network in regular intervals. For example, in the CPM diagram the completed activities are shown in red. The activities in progress are marked to a length proportional to the percentage of the progress. The line representing the monitoring date passes through the network and crosses each activity in progress at its scheduled percentage of completion on that date. In this fashion the actual project status at each monitoring date can be checked against the schedule in a glance. The frequency of monitoring depends on the management requirements, project duration, and the time-distance from completion date or important milestones.

In some organizations, full project monitoring is required days prior to regular official dates of project-control meetings. For short duration projects, weekly monitoring may be necessary. For long duration projects biweekly, monthly, or even quarterly monitoring may be sufficient. On the average, a monitoring interval is about twenty to thirty time units, or five percent of project duration.(19) There is no need to update the network each time the project is monitored.

Network updating

As the project progresses, sometimes, due to some "real world" problems, the sequence of a few activities may have to be changed. In some cases, new activities may have to be added to or eliminated from the network. In addition, as the project moves forward, more accurate information about the activity durations and project resources and environment is obtained. At the same time, the differences between the schedule and the actual status of project become clear. Therefore, it is necessary to review the network regularly, to check and revise the network logic, and to introduce the new and more accurate information regarding the project status, activity duration, delivery dates, and other necessary revisions in the network. This regular revision is called network updating. As a result of network updating, new project completion dates, new activity and event times, new activity schedules, and in some cases, new critical paths, are obtained.

Networks have to be updated at regular intervals; the frequency of updating depends upon the intensity and frequency of changes that have occurred. For many projects, monthly updating may be sufficient.

Project control

Network techniques are used for control of project resources – in particular, for cost control and budgeting. Controlling the cost of the projects relates the expenditures to the work being accomplished. Network cost control is obtained by determining the cost of each project activity in totality and as a function of activity duration, and by drawing the two limiting cumulative cost curves for the network, as shown typically in figure 8.16. One of the limiting cumulative cost curves is obtained by assuming that all project activities start at their earliest start times. This curve is called the early cost curve; the other,

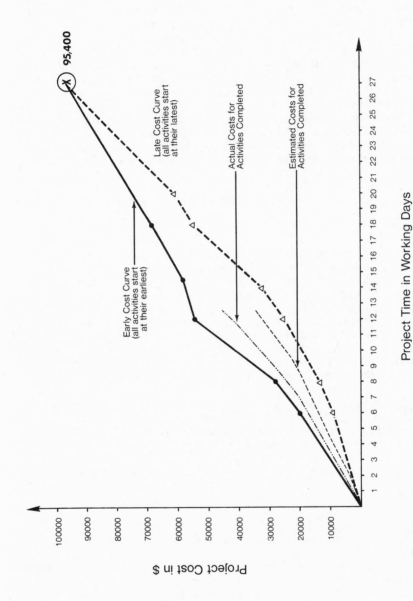

Fig. 8.16. Cumulative cost curves for CPM network of fig. 8.7.

called the <u>late cost curve</u>, is for the case when all project activities start at their latest start times. Depending upon the final schedule adopted, the project cumulative cost curve is at some point between these two limits. These curves are used for project cash management and financial planning. Moder(20) and O'Brien(21) have discussed this subject in detail.

During project implementation, due to many change orders, cost increases, inflation, etc., the actual cost of many activities and of the whole project often increases, leading to cost overrun. Using network techniques, the amount of cost overrun or underrun can be monitored regularly, and its impact on the whole project can be predicted. This problem called cost forecasting, is discussed in detail elsewhere.(22) Sophisticated techniques such as PERT/cost,(23) CPM-based cost systems,(24) and precedence-based cost systems are presently in use.

The problem of cost expediting – where, by using the project time-cost tradeoff curve, the optimum project time is obtained – was discussed earlier; this subject is discussed in more detail elsewhere.

Similar approaches can be used for controlling other resources. The problems of resource scheduling, allocation, and smoothing, all resource control tasks, were discussed earlier.

Extensions

Network techniques have been extended to handle planning scheduling, monitoring and control of complex projects, sometimes each consisting of many interrelated projects. Many of these systems,(25) such as the PMS (Project Management Systems), PCS (Project Control Systems), PMIS (Project Management Information System), etc., are discussed by O'Brien, Burnam, and Archibald.(26)

COMPARISON OF TRADITIONAL AND NETWORK PROJECT MANAGEMENT TECHNIQUES

Table 8.3, reproduced from Heyel, compares the important traditional and network techniques on the basis of factors such as ease of installation, operation, applicability to planning and scheduling, output, suitability for control, and usage.(27) The information given for CPM, it should be noted, is also applicable to precedence networks.

Other advantages of network techniques, compared to traditional methods, are as follows:
1. The network concept brings a logical and scientific discipline to the planning, scheduling, and control of projects.
2. It separates planning from scheduling and control, leading to more effectiveness and flexibility.
3. It presents the interdependencies among various activities and the effects of their changes on one another.

Table 8.3. Factor Comparison of Current Project Management Techniques

Factors for Consideration		Gantt Charts	LOB	PERT	CPW
Installation	Training of personnel to operate and maintain	No problem: only one or two persons usually required	Involves some training of two to four specially qualified personnel	Requires extensive training of four or more qualified personnel	Requires extensive training of three or more qualified personnel
	Orientation of personnel concerned	No problem	No problem	Considerable amount required: procedural manual usually necessary	Brief orientation required
	Records system required	No problem: majority of records maintained at working level	No problem	Extensive: tends to be complicated	Extensive
	Special requirements	None	Minimum of outside help required	Outside consulting services are required	Outside consulting services are required
Operation	Up-dating	No problem: maintained on daily or weekly basis: up-dated by working level supervisors	No problem: maintained on bi-weekly basis	Voluminous input data required: but easily processed by computer	Considerable input data required: normally processed by computer
	Monitoring	Good	Good	Very good	Good
	Need for computer	Not required	Not required	Ordinarily required, especially with more than 100 events	Required
	Output	Graphs: readily analyzed by inspection	Easily understood graphic form	Computer tab runs: require group presentation	Computer tab runs: requires group presentation
Applicability for Planning and Scheduling	For planning	Excellent for manufacturing control; on R&D projects, effectiveness decreases as activity interrelationships increase	Good	Very good: networking presents all essential information	Very good: networking presents all essential information
	Cost-schedule alternates	Poor	Fair: but no provision for minimizing cost	Good	Very good
	Provision for uncertainty in estimates	None	None	Very good	None
	Flexibility	Good: self-adjusting for delays and inaccurate estimates	Fair	Very good	Very good
	Usefulness for allocation of resources	Fair	Good	Good	Very good
Output Information	Management summary information	Good; however, amount of details given calls for close examination	Good: basic and not complicated: group presentation may be required	Very good: available in variety of forms: adequate but complicated	Very good: available in variety of forms, excellent for cost-minded management
	Program status and progress reports	Good	Very good	Good but fails to show incremental activity progress	Good but fails to show incremental activity progress
	Cost information	Good	Very good	Good	Very good
	Timeliness and quality of danger signals	Excellent for manufacturing control; not effective for detailed control of complex R&D projects	Good	Very good	Very good
	Availability of historical information	Poor	Poor	Poor	Poor
Suitability for Control of:	Research projects	Fair	Fair	Very good	Good
	Development projects	Fair	Fair	Very good	Good
	Production	Very good	Very good	Poor	Poor
	Subcontracting	Fair	Very good	Good	Fair
Usage to Date		Short period planning and continous manufacturing planning Widely accepted by many companies as a fundamental control technique	Design and production, e.g. DEW line, control of subcontracting for Polaris Navigation Sub-system followup production of preceding PERT and CPM efforts	Research Weapon Systems and other large complex government projects e.g. Polaris Project Skybolt Program	Commercial industries, fields of construction, development projects and new product introduction

Source: Reprinted by permission of Van Nostrand Reinhold Company, from The Encyclopedia of Management, 2nd edition, Carl Heyel, editor (New York, 1973). Copyright 1973 by Litton Educational Publishing.

4. It presents the project plan and schedule graphically. Plans are no longer hidden in the thoughts of the project manager; networks allow other people, whose activities are interlocking, to review the network and express their views.
5. It usually reduces the total duration of the project.
6. It estimates project duration more accurately.
7. In the process of preparing the network diagram for a project, the attention of the project manager is focused on one activity or a related group of activities at a time. Therefore, the manager has to think about the project from the start to completion. The manager cannot draw the network unless he or she makes decisions about the sequence of various project activities one at a time. Thus, preparing the network diagram facilitates project decision making.
8. A network simply represents the logical sequence of the execution of activities. If activities take a longer or shorter time than estimated, the network diagram does not generally change.
9. It considers the constraints on project time or resources.
10. It can be used as a simulation model to examine alternative methods for carrying out one or a number of activities with different time and resource requirements.
11. Change in plans and modification of policy can be easily incorporated into the network. The impact of these changes on the project as a whole can be assessed easily and quickly.
12. It identifies the critical sequence of activities or events from project beginning to completion.
13. Network analysis identifies the most critical activities in the plan and focuses the attention of project management on these critical activities, thus leading to management by exception.
14. Promptness and delay in the performance of all groups involved in carrying out various activities are easily discovered.
15. Deviation and slippage from the network schedule is easily and quickly discovered, thereby allowing better monitoring and control of the project.
16. Costs can be incorporated into the scheduling of activities. The whole project can be finished on schedule at minimum cost. The extra cost of expediting a project can be estimated by time and cost tradeoff curves. Networks can be used for cost control and forecasting.
17. Networks encourage a more detailed and long-term planning of projects.
18. The resources needed for the project can be scheduled by shifting noncritical activities, or the peak demand for use of scarce resources can be reduced to available limits by extending the project completion date.
19. Networks provide a standard method for communicating and documenting project plans, schedules, and time and cost information.

The Network Is the Language of Planning and Project Management

Network and traditional control techniques are, finally, simply the tools available to the project manager in her or his overall supervisory and control role during the implementation of a project. The use and maintenance of these techniques are only part of the manager's supervisory responsibilities, which are outlined more generally in Chapter 9. Unquestionably, however, these techniques lay the groundwork for the successful and systematic execution of these responsibilities, ensuring the smooth flow of project operation.

NOTES

(1) H.N. Ahuja, Construction Performance Control by Networks (New York: John Wiley & Sons, 1976).

(2) Russell D. Archibald, Managing High-Technology Programs and Projects (New York: John Wiley & Sons, 1976).

(3) Carl Heyel, ed., The Encyclopedia of Management, 2nd ed. (New York: Van Nostrand Reinhold, 1973).

(4) Ibid.

(5) Mats Ogander, ed., The Practical Application of Project Planning by Network Techniques, vols. 1-3 (New York: John Wiley & Sons, 1972).

(6) James J. O'Brien, CPM in Construction Management – Project Management with CPM, 2nd ed. (New York: McGraw-Hill, 1971).

(7) H.R. Hoare, Project Management Using Network Analysis (New York: McGraw-Hill, 1973).

(8) O'Brien, CPM in Construction Management.

(9) Heyel, Encyclopedia of Management.

(10) J.J. Moder and C.R. Phillips, Project Management with CPM and PERT (New York: Van Nostrand Reinhold, 1964).

(11) Hoare, Project Management.

(12) P.J. Burman, Precedence Networks for Project Planning and Control (New York: John Wiley & Sons, 1976).

(13) Hoare, Project Management.

(14) John Mulvaney, Analysis Bar Charting – A Simplified Critical Path Analysis Technique (Washington, D.C.: Management Planning and Control Systems, 1969).

(15) O'Brien, CPM in Construction Management.

(16) See Burman, Precedence Networks, and Moder and Phillips, Project Management.

(17) See Burman, Precedence Networks; Hoare, Project Management; Mulvaney, Analysis Bar Charting; and O'Brien, CPM in Construction Management.

(18) See Archibald, Managing High-Technology Programs and Projects; Burman, Precedence Networks; and O'Brien, CPM in Construction Management.

(19) Hoare, Project Management.

(20) Hoare, Project Management.

(21) O'Brien, CPM in Construction Management.

(22) Hoare, Project Management.

(23) Andrew Toal et al., PERT/CPM: Program Evaluation and Review Technique/Critical Path Method (Melbourne: Australian Executive Development Foundation, 1967).

(24) See O'Brien, CPM in Construction Management.

(25) Ibid.; Burman, Precedence Networks; Archibald, Managing High-Technology Programs and Projects.

(26) Heyel, Encyclopedia of Management, pp. 380-81.

SELECTED BIBLIOGRAPHY

Ackoff, R.E. Management Systems. New York: John Wiley & Sons, 1971.

Ahuja, H.N. Construction Performance Control by Networks. New York: John Wiley and Sons, 1976.

Archibald, Russell D. Managing High-Technology Programs and Projects. New York: John Wiley and Sons, 1976.

Burman, P.J. Precedence Networks for Project Planning and Control. New York: McGraw-Hill, 1972.

Cleland, David I. and William R. King. Systems Analysis and Project Management. New York: McGraw-Hill, 1975.

Hartman, W., H. Matthes, and A. Proeme. Management Information Systems Handbook, New York: McGraw-Hill, 1968.

Heyel, Carl, ed. The Encyclopedia of Management 2nd ed. (New York: Van Nostrand Reinhold, 1973.

Mulvaney, John. Analysis Bar Charting — A Simplified Critical Path Analysis Technique, Management Planning and Control Systems, 5828 Rockmere Drive, Washington, D.C. 20016, 1969.

O'Brien, James J. CPM in Construction Management — Project Management with CPM 2nd ed. New York: McGraw-Hill, 1971.

Toal, Andrew et al. PERT/CPM: Program Evaluation and Review Technique/Critical Path Method. Melbourne: Australian Executive Development Foundation, 1967.

9 Supervision and Control

The difference between maintaining a project's activities, once they have been set in motion, and all the tasks that have gone before, has been ably pinpointed by one commentator: "Planning, organizing, staffing, and directing are steps taken in preparing to execute decisions, whereas control is the step taken in making certain that the decision is properly executed."(1) After a project has begun functioning in its assigned areas, regulatory and supervisory measures assume prominence in the project cycle.

Control has been classically defined as "verifying whether everything occurs in conformity with the plans adopted, the instructions issued, and the principles established."(2) It therefore follows that, first of all, the plans, instructions, and principles must be clearly defined and understood by everyone, forming the standards or criteria by which performance can unequivocally be measured; lack of initial benchmarks makes control virtually impossible. The purpose of control, then, is to find deviations, correct them as early as possible, and prevent them in the future. The nature of project supervision and control thus requires a constant flow of information so that deviations from plans may be spotted and decisions and corrective actions may be taken on time.

It is important to remember, however, that a deviation between performance and plans is not always the fault of project implementors; a lack of conformity to plans can result from inappropriate plans rather than inadequate performance. Whether the villain is the plan or the nonconforming subordinate is sometimes difficult to determine. Planning decisions frequently have to be revised due to errors in judgment and forecasts. Subordinates are sometimes penalized for the superior's planning failures rather than their own performance failures.

The logic used to formulate planning and performance information should be the same. For example, the premises used in preparing budgets should be the same as those used to compile accounting and other performance data. The technical drawings used for inspection purposes should contain the same specifications as those used to plan operations.

Managers should also recognize that a comparison of plans with performance information may not adequately measure efficiency. The words or data used in the comparison between plans and actual performance must be capable of exact comparison. A great deal of knowledge about environmental, technological, and sociopsychological factors cannot, however, be defined or measured in precise terms.

And because the mechanisms for supervision and control are complex, any extended discussion of these mechanisms must be specific to the actors in this process, the content covered by the process, and the manner in which the process is carried out. This chapter therefore discusses supervision and control in three sections that deal with the who, the what, and the how of project supervision and control. To understand the range of pressures brought to bear on this seemingly limited task, we must retrace our steps somewhat and once again view the project cycle as a whole.

PRINCIPALS IN THE SUPERVISION AND CONTROL PROCESS

Ultimately, every project must have been put forth and commissioned by some individual or group as the final authority. This authority may be a national or regional unit of government, a private corporation, a social organization, or an individual investor. For the purpose of our discussion, this first principal will be referred to as the "owner" of the project.

The owner, of course, soon realizes that he must secure financing if the project is to succeed, and must engage the services of a second principal to conceptualize the project and prepare preliminary studies that will lead to a more definite and detailed design. This second principal, whom we will call the "designer," can again be an individual or a group, and can be architects and engineers if the project concerns infrastructure, or social scientists if it is a human-development project. If the results of initial studies are favorable, the designer goes on to prepare full-scale feasibility studies and design.

Assuming selection and approval by the owner, a third principal is usually called in, referred to here as the "contractor." Again, depending on the nature of the project, the contractor could be a building organization contracted because it submits the lowest sealed bid to the owner, or an agency that implements a social development or social-service project.

In addition to these three principals, there must be another actor, known to all three, whose main function is to coordinate their mutual efforts. This actor is usually an individual or organization who is a trusted representative of the owner; for larger projects, she will be supported by a separate specially qualified staff. This principal could be a professional engineer, an architect, or a government bureau chief, and she may be known by a number of titles such as project engineer, clerk of works, works engineer, or resident engineer for infrastructure projects, or auditor for other projects. She may be an associate or an employee of the designer. More often, she is employed directly by the owner to see that the contractor or whoever implements the plans follows them specifically and correctly, not by way of policing the contractor, but in such a way that she is a help to the implementing agency. For our purposes, we will refer to this individual as the "project manager." An organization usually cannot supervise each and every person in a firm, especially when a thousand or more persons are involved. The larger the project, the greater the possibility that human error will occur. Thus, it becomes a primary supervision responsibility of the project manager to check the contractor's work and spot such errors in a spirit of cooperation and help.

The interrelationships of these principals constitute a complex situation, the details of which will be covered later. In a broad sense, however, all the principals of the total operation must work together as a team to accomplish the best finished product in the most expeditious and economical manner. The individuals involved in the control of a project for the owner may vary all the way from an individual owner, who is both authorizing agent and project overseer, especially for small jobs, to officers of a corporation or organization, who will constitute a committee or board assisted by a staff of competent technical individuals. Such a group will normally be made up of one or more of the principal corporate officers of the company, including perhaps the general manager or the chief engineer. Other members may include legal and financial personnel and the necessary specialists of the project. If the contemplated project is large, this committee in turn may be broken down into subcommittees, each responsible for certain phases of the total operation.

Usually for infrastructure works, a project that has been defined and approved is turned over to the designer for development. The person who functions as the designer prepares the plans and writes the specifications to fit the needs, desires, and capability of the owner. The designer's relationship with the owner is one of trust similar to that of a surgeon-patient relationship. In technical matters, the designer is an agent of the owner and acts in the name of the owner. One member of a designer's organization is usually in overall charge of the specific project from start to finish. If the design contract so provides, as in some cases, the designer furnishes a resident in full charge of project supervision at the site who is, as mentioned previously, the works engineer, or the clerk of work – that is, the project manager. If the project is a large one, the project manager will be assisted by a substantial staff. The cost of this kind of service for the owner is in addition to the usual supervisory fee of the designer.

Some degree of control supervision is necessary for effective managerial action. There is a level, however, beyond which, from an economic standpoint, additional information is too costly. The revenues or savings that result from a correction of planning and performance errors must at least be equal to the cost of obtaining the required information.

For infrastructure work, the contractor executes the plans prepared by the designer. The contractor has a direct contract with the owner covering financial matters, but the contract is under supervision of the designer for technical matters. The liaison among these three organizations – the owner, designer, and contractor, who are usually independent of each other – is a critical link for various management functions. The importance of this liaison may be indicated by a study of the implications of the following sketch representing the overall structure. This is a triadic situation, each element of which must be kept coordinated and under control from within, while the entire operation, an important function in its own right, must be maintained as a closed system at all times for efficient functioning (see fig. 9.1).

CONTENT AREAS OF SUPERVISION AND CONTROL

To be effective, comprehensive project supervision must encompass all aspects and areas of the project. Control must, by its own definition, concern itself with plans, instructions, and principles. More specifically, the progress of a project must be monitored to see that the correspond-

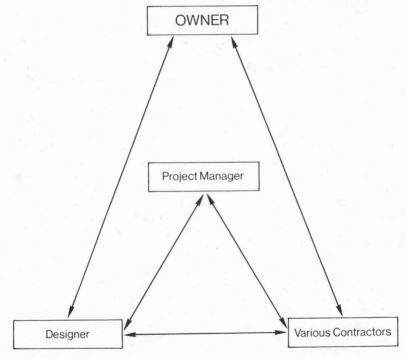

Fig. 9.1. Interrelationships of principals.

ing amount of work is done within the prescribed period of time and within the resources allocated for it. As Cleland points out, "Standards used in project management are based on the basic parameters of cost, schedule, and performance."(3) General control mechanisms, often based on personal values, are also used to monitor other standards, such as ethics, organization morale, and personnel development. More sophisticated control procedures may be used for asset management, worker-hour utilization and efficiency, and so on. Because they are quantitative, however, the basic three parameters of cost, schedule, and performance are the most concrete for framing factual premises and redirecting work activities and are, therefore, the most universally useful. Superiors must be taught to use these, along with value premises, in their decision making, and then be given enough time to gain acceptance of their newly-framed decision.

At any rate, for purposes of this discussion, the three categories of operation for supervision and control discussed individually here are those identified by Goetz: accomplishments, expenditures, and investments.(4) It is true that several techniques currently in practice, such as the ACP (Accomplishment/Cost Procedure), have succeeded in measuring and controlling accomplishments and expenditures simultaneously,(5) but for purposes of conceptual analysis, these three divisions of operation will be discussed separately.

Accomplishments

Management establishes a standard of accomplishment which is used as a measure. For example, the amount of work accomplished by a housing firm's sales department can be measured against a predetermined sales volume. Work accomplished in a construction job is measured against the plans and specifications provided by the designer. A family planning or rice productivity project is measured against pre-identified targets it has set out for itself. Moreover, the project manager is expected to see that certain parts of the project are accomplished within a given period of time. The actual accomplishments, as verified by an independent group, are compared to the original plan prepared for the project. The auditors or inspectors who report to management check the minute details of the implementation of the project. Such checks verify, among other things, whether the size of beams are according to plans, that the excavation meets the type of soil expected of the site, that the correct number of beneficiaries of a social project are indeed receiving the service, and so forth. The inspectors, who collate the information, report these measurements to the project manager. The project manager then passes the data on to the owners, contractors, and to the designer, who may evaluate the progress of the work and make necessary comments and recommendations.

Because of the finite life of the project, it is imperative that accomplishment and progress be measured within a specific time dimension. For this purpose, the management and control information tool of PERT/CPM discussed in Chapter 8 is particularly useful.

Many of these standards are merely restatements of managerial selections of rival policies, designs, or resources. Policies originate from studies which may take the form of comparative cost-benefit analysis, comparative safety, and sometimes comparative times of completion. Records of actual performances are gathered and compared with those of originally-determined standards in order to arrive at a parameter that can be used and refined. These data may be the basis for future estimates of costs. Deviations from a certain set of records lead to managerial investigation and possible remedial action. Most standards of achievement are applied item-by-item. These are usually not incorporated in the system of records and reports, although records of successes and failures are customarily accumulated and reported.

Expenditures

Accomplishments are attained through the allocation and expenditure of resources – financial, human (worker-hours), material – though these are normally discussed at the common denominator or monetary amounts. Each task assignment is accompanied by an expense limitation. Very often these values are the best estimates, based on past experience adjusted to meet present conditions. These limitations, or standards of expenditures, enter the system of standards, records, and reports and are therefore matched against the records of performance. Excessive deviations indicate need for managerial investigation, reviews, and action. Investigation can take the form of checking the values used as standards for the project against actual expenditure. Standards and measures of expenditures may be in quantity or price, and are established in both. Material expenditures may be stated in tons or in monetary values, labor in worker-hours, days, months, or also in monetary values. Many expense items are sometimes based on physical terms such as kilos of steel or kilowatt hours.

The physical and monetary standards of expenditure are the baseline values that may be used to measure the standard of achievement. Progress of infrastructure work tends strongly to be measured solely against physical norms; in other projects, the use of social indicators is a recent phenomenon. More generally, standards and measures of expenditures are stated as relatives, or ratios or percentages of achievements, that is, the number of hours a mason needs to finish plastering 100 square meters of wall area, or dollar cost per ton-kilometer carried by a truck, or dollar cost per square meter of building area. Employees are expected to attain standards of achievement without exceeding estimated expenditures or employing more than standard investments. In any project, the ideal situation occurs when the expenditures are equal to or less than the collections or allocated funds.

Larger projects tend to have monitoring subsystems for each major category of expenditure. Thus, for example, worker costs, both in absolute terms and in terms of ratio to overall costs, are controlled separately. More particularly, worker-power reports by cadre categories, reporting worker-hour utilizations for specific aspects of the project, are tabulated and kept, to be compared with original projections.

In the monitoring of financial resources and comparing performance with plan in this category, there is no more pervasive or effective instrument than the budget, at once a planning tool in its formulation and a supervisory and control tool in its demand for adherence. The performance of managerial and operating personnel can be measured by a comparison of budget estimates with accounting and other data. The planning and foundation of an operating budget is concerned with forecasting relationships between revenues and costs. The budgeting process generally begins with the preparation of the revenue forecasts, based on estimates from sources such as interest from investment and royalties, revenues from sales, appropriations from governmental sources, and other information.

From this forecast, the budget for the activities of the project and other subsidiary budgets are prepared. The materials budget lists the kinds and quantities of raw materials, parts, and supplies specified in the activities of the project. The purchase budget specifies the quantities of materials that must be purchased, together with estimates of purchase costs. The labor budget specifies the amount of direct labor necessary to meet activity schedules. Information from the sources can be used to estimate funds needed to meet payrolls during the budget period. The administrative expense budget is essentially concerned with the expenses that result from the performance of general management functions, including top executive salaries and traveling expenses, director's fees, professional services fees, and general office expenses. Two highly significant subfinancial budgets are the cash budget and the capital additions budget. The primary purpose of the cash budget is to prevent a lack of sufficient liquidity to finance operations. The cash budget is an estimate of cash receipts and cash disbursements during the budget period. Capital additions budgets detail planned expenditures for additional plant, machinery, and equipment, improvements in existing facilities, and replacement due to depreciation and obsolescence.

Budgeting is concerned with the expected consequences of planning and operations, and accounting with the actual consequences measured in monetary and other quantitative terms. Quantitative variations between expected and actual results can be used to gauge planning and operating efficiency. An analysis of such variations is frequently useful in determining the kind of problem that may be involved. But a quantitative approach is inadequate without an understanding of the nature of accounting and budgeting systems and the manner in which they relate to environmental and organizational conditions.

Many managements require their accounting departments to prepare daily or weekly reports covering the data. Close watch is kept over cash balances, receipts, and disbursements. Fixed assets are controlled through plant ledgers, appropriation procedures, and loading records. The plant ledgers contain an account for each price of equipment owned by the enterprise, each account carries such data as date of acquisition, price, source, description, depreciation rate, repair and maintenance records, and final disposition date and price. The appropriation procedure requires that each project be detailed with savings and costs estimates. After authorization, a record is maintained and compared to the estimation on the request for the appropriation. Loading records show the backlog of work ahead for each piece of equipment, thereby revealing inadequacies and chronically idle items. The record indicates what additional equipment is needed and which items can be liquidated without curtailing operations.

Investments

Managerial control of investments follows the same general pattern as managerial control of achievement and cost. Standards are set and performance measured and compared with the standards. Short-run solvency depends largely on the managerial control of the current assets. A large portion of the cash available is paid out for worker-hours; this is an expenditure that cannot be postponed or delayed. The receivables and collections from clients or from a national budget as sources of funds and the inventories must be carefully monitored. This is where accounting helps management a great deal, providing answers to such questions as: What is the cash balance? How much money will be collected from accomplishments? How much money will be needed to meet the current expenditures or maturing accounts payable for materials purchased on credit? How much cash must be reserved for payroll and current operating expenses? Are there long-term obligations maturing, and how may we treat them? Do we pay the loan or should this be structured for later payments?

Subsidiary to investment supervision and an integral aspect of asset management is materials control. Just as supervision and control demand that effective use be made of available financial investments, so they also demand that effective use be made of materials and equipment, not having an unnecessarily large supply or inventory on one hand to tie up the assets, but not having a supply or inventory so low as to impede operations. The tools of materials and equipment management explained in Chapter 8 provide the basic avenues for supervision and control of this area.

THE PROCESS OF SUPERVISION AND CONTROL

Having examined both the principal actors in the control process and the three general areas they concern themselves with, let us now turn in greater detail to the project control process itself.

Control and Coordination, Supervision and Superintendence

Before embarking on a detailed description of this process and the common pitfalls encountered in its course, let us clarify the ambiguity of terminology that is often present in this area.

To start with, control as used here does not mean active supervisory control of the operation itself, which is actually the function of the various contractors' organizations. The task considered here includes the project manager's responsibility for the coordination, preparation, and approval of schedules, records, and reports of committees as well as material and equipment deliveries, progress estimates and reports, and project requests. Many of the specific operations involved in this overall task will be carried out by the contractor's forces, the exact division of the work being defined by the contract documents. The project manager, however, will normally be charged with the project-site approval of such documents involved. The manager's organization should provide legal support for such approvals on the basis of accomplishments. Administration is always present as an internal function to provide for suppliers, personnel, and equipment incidental to the project manager's operations, personnel office space, laboratory facilities, and interorganizational communication and coordination. On large projects in remote locations, this element of the organization may also be charged with the provision, maintenance, and operation of a camp or even a community or with all the facilities of a town. Alternatively, this latter function may be a direct contractual obligation of the contractor, in which case the project manager will normally be charged with general supervisory responsibilities only.

On the other hand, coordination and interaction of the various organizations working for the project are the basic reasons for the existence of the project manager's operation. For the personnel involved in the position to discharge their duties faithfully, reasonable consideration should be given to the character of the investigation procedures. While the inspector is responsible for inspection of the work, provision must be made for the variety of craftstage operations involved in the project, for the several materials and items of equipment to be incorporated in the work, for the normal sequence of the various elements of the total project, and for the degree of coverage contemplated in the contract documents. The inspector's technical services will require substantial amounts of survey and ample use of laboratory equipment. But the project manager's fundamental responsibility to the owner cannot be avoided. The manager must be sure that the control and supervisory services are adequately provided for at every stage of the work.

A second major source of ambiguity is the sometimes interchangeable use of the terms supervision and superintendence. Supervision, the broader term, is used here in the sense that Albers specifies, as the lead instrument of control.(6) Every executive below the apex of the hierarchy, whether a vice-president or a foreperson, is subject to supervision from a higher level. Observing a subordinate's behavior under various conditions is sometimes the best way to evaluate one's own performance or potential. Much of the process is informal and indirect and becomes an aspect of the sociopsychological dynamics of the superior-subordinate relationship. Superiors, however, cannot constantly keep watch over their flocks if they are not to be overwhelmed with work. There are also good motivational reasons for not carrying supervision to an extreme. Accounting and other indirect control devices make possible a greater degree of decentralization and tend to give more personal freedom to subordinates. Therefore, the control process generally involves some combination of supervision and indirect techniques.

Superintendence, however, takes on much more specific meaning in the context of project management. While supervision is an act or oversight to inspect with authority, superintendence is an act or oversight for the purpose of direction.

To further illustrate this distinction, we can say that supervision is the responsibility of the designer; superintendence, that of the general contractor. As a supervisor, it is highly desirable for the owner to provide funds separate from the design fee for the employment of a person responsible for the superintendence and overall control of the project; this is the role of the project manager. The project manager thus provides countersuperintendence as a valuable and usually welcome check to the activities of the contractor and subcontractors. The coordination and superintendence of the progress of the entire project is principally the responsibility of the project manager and demands detailed personal attention on the manager's part. The progress of the work is under the command of the various contractors' superintendents over their respective scopes of work, and the resulting installation is inspected by the project manager. Thus, the carrying out of the work is under the continuing analysis of two competent, responsible individuals, each representing one of the principal parties to the contract; the project manager representing the owner and designer, and the superintendent or project engineer of the contractor representing the latter. Should they disagree, they must promptly suggest the proper changes to clarify the matter and go through the established lines of communication and authority to the designer and owner for a final decision.

The implementation and control in the execution of plans for infrastructure works rests with a general contractor. No general contractor, however, performs all parts of the project with his or her own forces because some parts of the work are subcontracted; other highly technical work is given to specialized contractors. Very often, for example, the general contractor in an infrastructure project takes care of the excavation, concreting, and erection of steelwork, but the specialized work, such as finishes, tinsmith, electrical installations, and plumbing, are subcontracted to specialists. The general contractor, however, controls all parts through established lines of communication and authority. With the general contractor's own workers, the control is direct through the contractor's own organization channels. With the subcontractor's workers, the control requires a definite means of clearance with the subcontractor so that there is no interference with the orders given by the subcontractor's own organization to comply with the elements of the work or any of the details affecting the subcontractor's related activities. It is imperative for a general contractor at the start of the project to work out with each subcontractor definite channels of authority and specific procedures for using them. If the project is allowed to get underway with policies made on a day-to-day basis, meeting new situations as they come up without any reference to an overall plan of operation, confusion will prevail.

The broad responsibilities of general superintendence are discharged by proper performance of a great many detailed operations, namely:

o   Hiring, assignment and discharge of personnel
o   Purchase and delivery of materials and equipments
o   Contract changes in the form of change orders due to corrections or changes in the original plan
o   Keeping of cost records, including labor, materials, and miscellaneous expenses
o   Project office control, including job meetings, office operation, financial transactions, and maintenance of safety standards(7)

The Sequence of the Project Manager's Control Process

The project manager's area of control begins with ensuring that the implementation contracts and agreements are in order.

1. Based on these agreements, the first step is the preparation of a complete and realistic implementation schedule, not only in terms of timetables but also in terms of financial, human, and other resource allocations. This is required as a basis for the evaluation of the contractor's progress.

The contractor will, in the preparation of an estimate, prepare a schedule. If the invitation document states a required completion, this will be accounted for; and equipment, workers, and material delivery schedules will be planned accordingly. If no completion date is specified, the contractor will plan work for the maximum operating efficiency for the equipment and personnel available, with due regard to seasonal, climatic, and environmental conditions of the project.

Normally, the designer will also have a schedule, taking into account the requirements of the owner and making all possible allowances for the known social, political, and environmental conditions of the locality. This schedule will usually be available to the project manager's personnel charged with control operations, and will be referred to as the basis on which the manager estimates rates of progress, percent completion, and whether or not the construction is on schedule.

The development of a workable schedule is an area requiring considerable experience and a high order of informed judgment. Since this first step establishes the benchmarks for the ongoing supervision of the project, it cannot be overemphasized.

2. Next, the project manager must have an organized and systematic method for gathering information comprehensively, thoroughly, and promptly, and this is best accomplished through consistent and uniform record keeping. This procedure is essential, not only for the project manager, but also for the owner and the designer. The project manager functions on behalf of the designer for job control, and on behalf of the owner for financial control. The manager must therefore keep accurate records for the numerous transactions involved as part of his or her responsibilities. These records consist essentially of the following documents: a) drawings and revisions; b) specifications and revisions; c) correspondence; d) actions of committees; e) minutes of conferences; f) control surveys; g) inspection reports; h) implementation progress information; and i) progress payments. Other reports peculiar to each type of project, whether social, infrastructure, health, or agriculture, are also of course required.

3. The project manager must establish channels of communication – and authority to use them – through which information on progress is conveyed.

As indicated earlier, the supervision of the field operations by the project manager involves interrelationships among the owner, the designer, and the contractor. Ultimately, the project manager may be employed directly by the owner or by the designer. Whichever the case, the exact relationship should be clearly and specifically defined in the contract documents and clearly understood by all concerned. The project manager's scope of responsibility, it should be noted, is subject to revisions mutually agreeable to all the parties concerned. But one thing is certain: the manager should always be at the project site or be readily available at all times to fully exercise responsibility and authority in the inspection and control functions described here.

Many large projects may have two separate divisions: the project site inspection and control operation, under the office of the project manager, and the owner's overall inspection and control agency, which will maintain a continuing overview on all projects within the organization. Representatives of this latter agency will report directly to the owner or representative, while the project manager will report to the designer in matters of technical problems or design. When visiting the project site, the owner's control agency people will usually report to, and operate through, the agencies of the project manager. Their exact functions and authority will depend on the specific details of the organization involved. This is the manner in which the project manager and the other principals normally clarify authority and communication lines for control purposes.

Besides a central office and a field site, large projects will have attached to them a number of professionals, whom the project manager will need to supervise, guide, and advise. The authority of the project manager needs to rest in an individual with experience who can provide the leadership to young professionals keen to advance in their careers. The project manager must bring the project staff together as a team to work together toward a common goal. Supervision or direct observation of a subordinate is important and should not be neglected.

The professional character of these positions introduces further responsibilities. These are suggested by the wording of many standard contract forms which provide that the project manager should have final decision on a wide range of project site questions. This provision places the project manager in a quasijudicial position between the parties of a contract and implies an objectivity in the manager's point of view which in no way should be influenced by the ultimate sources of her or his compensation. Thus, it will sometimes happen that the project manager will defend the contractor's performance above and beyond the requirement of the applicable plans, specifications, and contract documents. This is not an agreeable situation, particularly when it is clear that the performance desired by the owner is in fact more than what is usually accepted as good practice. When the contract documents are specific, however, they must govern. Even when they are ambiguous, in fact, the contract documents must rule. The latter case is even more troublesome, because in resolving ambiguities compromise solutions become necessary. Usually such solutions please no one. The general exception to the principle of adherence to the contract document arises when it is obvious that the documents are in gross error and would lead to the production of works that are hazardous to the users or to the general public. In such a case, the project manager is professionally responsible and due notice of such error is given to all concerned. Adequate corrective measures should be taken to include work stoppage if it becomes necessary.

Generally, however, and especially for major changes, the final arbiter in technical matters of a project is the designer. Where the project manager may make certain decisions in the field, final decisions have to be made by the designer, who is ultimately responsible for the project. In some countries, the designer is, by civil code, responsible for the safety of the design for a considerable number of years. Hence, the project manager becomes the eyes and ears of the designer who assumes these responsibilities. The designer is not on the site but must rely on the project manager's inspection report. For this reason, and also to preserve professional objectivity which gives the managerial position its quasijudicial character in everyday decisions, the project manager must be supported by a system of comprehensive records and information channels.

Thus, the organizational structure of the project manager's staff follows, in a general way, the organizations of the general contractor and the designer, since there will be a corresponding project site function related to each element of these organizations. These inter-related functions must further be more organized in an orderly fashion for smooth and efficient operation.

4. Once communication channels are established, the information on project progress should flow through them regularly and fill the project manager's records and reports. Supervision and control in this sense is thus not so much direction of the operation (which is much more the contractor's task) as maintenance of continuing up-to-date information on the current status of the project, primarily in the form of reports to the designer and the owner.

The compilation of data for the progress report will normally begin either with the contractor's field forces or with the project manager's inspectors in the field. When the contractor initiates the information, it will usually be set up a day or two in advance of the cutoff date, based on projected progress of the work, and turned over to the field inspection personnel concerned in time to allow a check on the status of the designated time period.

The information thus flows into the project manager's office for synthesis. It is important, of course, that the project manager provide input, even taking the extra precaution of maintaining a separate, careful chronological record or daily logbook of every development, including weather conditions and special situations. The synthesized progress reports are finalized by the project manager's organization and are distributed through channels prescribed by the owner, the designer, or the contractor, depending on the level of detail of the project information involved. When there is a high level of popular interest in the project, as in the case of a service facility being contracted by a public agency, the progress report may also be released publicly by the project manager.

Since these data reflect a complete cognizance of the status of all elements of the work, including the preparation of payment estimates, they are also usually gathered under the supervision of the same group responsible for the final form and check of such estimates. Similarly, since this group has in effect been carrying out a systematic check of the progress of each element of the work, it is usually charged with the compilation of the formal completion report prepared under the project manager's direction. In a broad sense, these operations represent the owner's continuing control of the construction, for which the manager is paying.

Obviously, the communication flow cannot be only one way, toward the preparation of the reports. The possibility of planning errors also requires a constant inflow of information about such environmental forces as product markets, resources markets, and innovation. A two-story control and feedback system indicates both planning inadequacies on one hand and implementation delays and variations on the other hand. It provides for adjustments in organizational behavior and proper adaptation to environmental changes.

If this feedback is regular and frequent, variations can be spotted and corrected promptly before they become serious problems, much like a thermostat operates.(8) The analogy is useful: the desired temperature is communicated to the system by setting an indicator. The chillers respond by turning on or off as the actual temperature varies by some amount from the desired level. A good thermostat will keep a room at fairly even temperature, but a badly designed thermostat will send the temperature into violent oscillations. A similar situation can arise from feedback failures in business and other organizations.

A lag in the flow of information about an environmental change and a failure to take prompt action can cause a sequence of adjustments in wrong directions. An organization such as an agricultural co-operative project, faced with severe fluctuations in the demand for its products, may find itself increasing production when it ought to cut production, and conversely. Production schedules may never be in accord with the actual market situations because information about an increase or reduction in demand is received or acted upon after demand has again moved in an opposite direction. Although the transformation period, lead-time requirements, and planning considerations limit adaptability, an organization can often increase its survival power if information about an environmental change is received in sufficient time. Similar problems can arise internally in an organization. For example, a relatively minor morale problem can become a serious labor problem because a lack of information precluded prompt corrective action; top management may not become aware of the problem until a horde of union officials storm the executive suite. Such a development might have been avoided with timely information about the problem. Costly consequences can also result from inadequate information about such matters as the quality of production, customer complaints, industrial accidents, a shortage of personnel, and research and development difficulties.

5. The comparison between the information gathered on project progress and the specifications in the master implementation schedule is the next logical step.

The objective of the analysis of the variations and discrepancies between plans and implementation is to institute prompt and effective corrective action. If, for instance, a set of plans shows details that are not workable in the field, the field person notifies the designer of these conditions and suggests possible practical solutions that may require plan modification. Thus, plans as well as policies may have to be revised to accommodate site conditions that were not foreseen during the design stage. Reports flow back to the organization to indicate discharge of responsibilities, degree of success achieved, and changes made to fit site conditions. Such reports are necessary in laying further plans, revising policies, and issuing further orders so that the implementation of the project may continue. In view of these activities, the project manager must be able to supervise and control the implementation of the plans to realize the established goals in a rational manner.

6. On occasion, the regular analysis of variance calls for more than routine adjustments handled at the level of the project manager and the contractor. Sometimes substantial contract changes in the detailed provision of the plans, specifications, and requirements are likely to become necessary. Changes may emanate from the owner, who in the course of the implementation receives inputs that changes requirements, or from the planners themselves, who have to conform to actual conditions as they become evident in lieu of the assumed or projected conditions used in the preparation of the plans. Since any modification of terms of a contract must be a matter of legal necessity, it must be put on formal record and be the subject of a supplementary agreement. This is important for each and every set of changes. These changes must be properly accounted for, as normally any change in the plans

will affect not only the cost but also the time of completion. The full formalization of the contract must be accomplished by the original contract between the owner and the contractor, and usually the designer is the party that undertakes the negotiations.

Insofar as such modifications reflect project site developments, the information must come from the project site itself. The owner's source of such information, as well as the designer's, is usually the project manager's organization. On a small project, this may not require much effort, but on a large project it will usually be found advantageous to establish specific responsibilities for change-order records in a group so designated within the field office. The construction control group of the project manager's organization will sometimes be responsible for preparing revisions to the basic implementation schedule in connection with change orders, because of their more direct contact with the current situation from an overall point of view. Such changes will usually be complete enough and may require changes in the critical path network.

Change orders arising on the project site will usually be of two types: one type arises from the development of unexpected conditions. Normal subsurfacing exploration may fail to reveal some important foundation condition or the presence of some important variations of subgrade material through which the contractor's operations must proceed. Seasonal climatic conditions may be exceptionally severe, necessitating special protective or remedial work, or seriously disrupting schedules in such a way as to interfere with normal sequences and develop the desirability of some sort of change in the contractor's schedule. A particular material or equipment supplier or a resource person who has to submit certain data may, for reasons not connected with the project, be unable to meet precise commitments, requiring the substitution of some other material or items of equipment or the modification of some related element. These unexpected situations are by definition impossible to predict. The second type of change order arises from field operations that necessitate a revision of contract estimate quantities or a revision of schedules to conform to the exact conditions occurring in the field, or exact quantities actually used.

It is usually a relatively simple matter to devise appropriate and entirely adequate alternative procedures and go on with the work. Often such changes will involve no change in the monetary value of the work, or else will balance the cost of the changes against the costs of the original contract. In such cases, all that is required is a proper record of the changes, all the information about their developments, and finally the negotiation and recording of the supplementary agreement covering them. Any change, whether initiated by the contractor or by the owner, must be under the control and approval of the designers. In other cases, changes arising from unexpected project site developments involve substantial changes in the contract costs. Unexpected added costs may be possible or substantial technical changes may be required for proper accomplishment of the owner's purposes. In such situations, the detailed record of the changes, while of no great legal significance, acquires in addition the usually recognized importance of added financial obligations to be met.

Since a proposal for change order may be initiated at any level in any of the organizations involved, the change-order record should include specific information, as available, concerning the individual who initiated the action and the reason for proposing the change. The authority for the approval of a change is critical, and should be clearly defined in the relationships set up among the owner, the contractor, the designer, and the project manager. Often the organizational level at which a change order will be approved is established in relation to the amount of change in the contract cost involved. Thus it will be noted that the exact change in the cost resulting from the summation of the items noted earlier may be the determining factor in who finally authorizes or disallows the proposed change.

7. As the project draws to its conclusion, the last control function will be the preparation of a final report embodying highlights of the progress reports, deviations from original implementation schedules, reasons for these deviations, and corrective actions taken. This report will supplement the "as-built drawings" on the implemented works, including notations and any changes made in deviation of the original plans, and will include notation of special circumstances or situations arising during the progress of the work. The completion report or final report will be generally based on the inspection of the field personnel, whose assignment gives them first acquaintance with the project. Thus, project diaries become advisable for many reasons. They are the logical basis, the first draft, of the final report. A full narrative of such diaries may not normally be incorporated in the completion report; rather, only unusual and particularly significant items. The logical outlines of the key steps of the work, however, and the tabular and graphical summaries included in the progress report can be made part of the final report.

The final inspection, from its name, is the last thorough checking of the features of the contract. This should be scheduled only when the work is substantially completed. Any deficiencies noted during this inspection by the inspection personnel should be recorded on the final inspection checklist, sometimes referred to as the punch list. Items in this list must then be completed and rectified or redone as directed before the contractor is released from liability and before final payment is made. Because of the contractor's interest in a prompt settlement of a contract, which requires satisfying the items on the checklist, and because of the distinct possibility of a difference of opinion concerning the existence of deficiencies, the final inspection should be made personally by the project manager or by a completely responsible, properly designated representative who has the authority to come to final agreement with the contractor.

The Project Manager's Attitude During the Process

There is one other consideration worth noting at this point. The project manager's operation is but one element of the total project, which exists for the purpose of providing a facility, or delivering a service, or achieving a target desired by the owner. Both contractor and project manager should keep this fundamental purpose in mind and cooperate in carrying it out. It has been noted earlier that the interest of the owner and that of the contractor diverge on the question of cost. The owner's financial interest is preserved by securing the most valuable facility under contract provision at the least possible cost. The contractor's financial interest is preserved by accomplishing the construction facilities in the most economical manner possible under the contract provision in order to increase profit. As the owner's representative, it is normal for the project manager to demand the highest type of output with the best resources, or the highest type of installation with the best materials and equipment within the scope of the contract. A reputable contractor is as interested as the project manager in completing a sound and honest project and will be genuinely grateful for a conscientious assistance in checking for errors or mistakes or defective materials and equipment.

The project manager's personnel are supposed to maintain vigilant checks for any defects in the completed work, and the contractors, among others, expect them to do this. They should not be allowed to obscure the basic fact that the fundamental responsibility of the project manager is in complete accord with the fundamental responsibility of the contractor's personnel for the completion of a soundly built facility or a satisfactorily delivered service, in full accordance with the intent of the contract documents. Projects organized and carried out with this underlying concept in mind will normally proceed with less friction and are bound to produce better results.

CONCLUSION

This chapter has attempted to provide a systematic overview of the supervision and control phase of project management, describing the principal actors in the process, the three general areas of supervision, and a sequential description of the process itself. The treatment should provide general guidelines, although the nature of the particular project will dictate specific differences and approaches. Nevertheless, attention to the broad guidelines underlying supervision and control pays off in rich dividends in the long run, and will be particularly useful when the project enters the completion and handover stage, to be discussed in Chapter 11.

NOTES

(1) D.I. Cleland and W.A. King, Systems Analysis and Project Management (New York: McGraw-Hill, 1968), p. 246.

(2) Henri Fayol, General and Industrial Management (London: Sir Isaac Pitman and Sons, 1949), p. 107.

(3) Cleland and King, Systems Analysis, p. 249.

(4) Billy Goetz, Management Planning and Controls (New York: McGraw-Hill, 1949).

(5) "Accomplishment/Cost Procedure (ACP) correlates cost with schedule accomplishment, comparing the difference between actual cost and budgeted cost with the difference between actual accomplishment and planned accomplishment. The posture of both elements of information is depicted at the same time." Ellery Block, "Accomplishment/Cost: Better Project Control," Harvard Business Review, May-June 1971, p. 111. Cf. also Arnold Saitow, "CSPC: Reporting Project Progress to the Top," Harvard Business Review, January-February 1971, pp. 88ff.

(6) Henri H. Albers, Principles of Management: A Modern Approach, 3rd ed. (New York: John Wiley and Sons, 1969).

(7) Elmer Munger and Clarence Douglas, Construction Management (Englewood Cliffs, N.J.: Prentice-Hall, 1970).

(8) Albers, Principles of Management.

SELECTED BIBLIOGRAPHY

Ahuja, H.N. Construction Performance Control by Networks. New York: John Wiley & Sons, 1976.
Block, Ellery B. "Accomplishment/Cost: Better Project Control." Harvard Business Review, May-June 1971.
Cleland, David I., and King, William A. Systems Analysis and Project Management. New York: McGraw-Hill, 1968.
O'Brien, J.J. CPM in Construction Management, 2nd ed. New York: McGraw-Hill, 1971.

10 Completion and Assimilation

Project activities are brought under a unified form of management to achieve a given objective within a specified time period. Once objectives are achieved, the project must be dismantled and its remaining resources, both human and physical, transferred to other organizations. Completion prepares the project for phasing out and handover to the new administration; handover transfers project activity and resources to the new administration. These are critical tasks of planning which are sometimes neglected in traditional project management. Resources are rarely completely expended at the close of a project, and failure to utilize and transfer them efficiently is a common weakness in project management.

Phasing in and phasing out of resources, in fact, is a process that occurs throughout the project cycle. After the project has been approved, the project organization will require resources to implement project objectives. Sometimes each phase requires a different set of resources; often skilled specialists or specific equipment will be needed only for short periods. At the close of the project, all remaining resources must be smoothly transferred to the new organization or another project. But because few project-operation plans include detailed planning for completion and assimilation, the utility of the resources is often treated as nil after the project is completed, thus substantially adding to total project costs.

COMMON PROBLEMS OF PROJECT COMPLETION

International assistance organizations found the following to be common causes of difficulty upon project completion.

1. Failure to expeditiously terminate "unsuccessful" projects due to inadequate monitoring and control by central govern-

ment authorities and international assistance agencies, political defensiveness and unwillingness to admit failure, or resistance on the part of constituency groups.

2. Restriction of benefits and outputs to a smaller group of recipients than intended by project design; demonstration and spread effects of the project are limited except where special efforts are made to amplify them.

3. Failure to prepare and submit project completion reports, complicating project evaluation and delaying formal closeout of loans and grants.

4. Inadequate or inappropriate utilization of outputs of completed projects by beneficiaries; failure of the government and international assistance agencies to plan for user training.

5. Difficulties of the donor agencies in terminating their contribution to a successful project prior to completion without jeopardizing continuation of the project.(1)

To avoid these pitfalls, project managers must plan for this stage of the integrated project cycle in a systematic way, with the goal of smooth and efficient handover of authority, assimilation, and transfer of resources. Before discussing specific procedures, however, let us examine what the actual process of project completion involves.

The completion of a project can take place in several ways: Some projects will be completed and ready for operation immediately, while others will phase out on a stage-by-stage basis over a period of time as various segments of the project are completed. The completion of a project requires an array of different organizational activities to be prepared so that the project can be integrated into an ongoing organization for future administration and operation. With some projects, however, a new organization may need to be established. In the case of a hydropower project, for example, where the main construction involves a dam and a power station, the construction phase may have been completed before the transmission and distribution systems have been installed. This may create a need for an intermediate organization to maintain the dam until it becomes operational.

Where projects are completed, but not fully operational, clear responsibilities and organizational settings under which the project will exist until it is completely operational must be established. This requires a great deal of detailed planning prior to the stage of completion being reached, because of the numerous responsibilities and liabilities involved in a project. Where a contractor completes an operation, questions such as insurance, responsibility for public liability, security measures, and protection of assets must be clearly recognized and the responsibilities clearly defined.

THE PROCESS OF PROJECT COMPLETION

The completion procedure for all projects should include a completion report and a phase-in strategy for the permanent or temporary organization that will be responsible for the continuing operational activities. Where a project is completed in parts, as each part is completed its handover may take place. The lead time between the handover of the first completed component and the final one could be several years, so a number of activities must be considered:

The completion procedure must be planned and thoroughly analyzed by the project manager. Several steps are involved in this plan.

1. A project completion schedule should be prepared. The schedule will involve the estimated completion dates of the whole project and of the various stages of the project. It sets down the terms of completion for the contractor and for the final user, as well as for the funding agency concerned. To accomplish this, several factors need to be established:

   a. The financial aspects of the project, including the amount that may be retained by the funding organization following completion of a particular stage;

   b. The responsibility for the risk of the completed project once agreement to hand it over has been reached;

   c. The resources including workers, commodities, and physical and technical aspects required by the organization given the responsibilities for the project operating it;

   d. Notification of change of the control status must be made to outsiders concerned with the project in both a direct and indirect manner.

2. A special reporting and management information system should be established as the project or the stages of a project come nearer to completion, so that full information relating to the project is available for the contractor, funding authority, and the organization who will be taking over the completed project. A number of reports must be completed for the funding organization and the policymakers, together with details the future administrators of the project will need.

3. All the contracts must be finalized, loan facilities terminated, and institutions such as local banks, insurance organizations, and other authorities notified of the proposed changes in administration. Unexpired contracts will also have to be negotiated and a number of other activities, such as maintenance and insurance, may need to be carried over. At this stage, technical reports to enable future projects of a similar nature to learn from the project's experience could be prepared.

The completion of a major project may create a major disruption within a community. Every effort needs to be made to ensure that where resources are withdrawn from a community, as little upset to the social life as possible is experienced. This is particularly the case where local tradespeople, workers, and others have developed businesses and employment opportunities around the project's activities.   Wherever possible, the warnings and implications of completion and handover should be made known to the community so that steps can be taken well in advance to avoid what could be serious social disruptions.   Most projects are implemented with the purpose of increasing the welfare and bringing benefits to a community. Where a large section of the community becomes deprived of employment or of income through a project's closing down and large numbers of personnel are forced to leave the district, this prospect should be made known well in advance, so that people and businesses are not encouraged to go into business or become dependent on an activity that has a limited life.

HANDOVER

Many projects do not show a clear line between areas of responsibility at the handover stage. Thus project planning must take into account the important task of operation as an ongoing production unit for projects. The objective of project development is to enable an output to be used for the benefit of the country or organization initiating the project. This can only happen if sufficient skills and resources are available to ensure that the project can be utilized as a working arrangement. A checklist for handover includes such factors as:
1. The appointment of a management team to take over the project as an ongoing operation.
2. The preparation of an outline scheme with budgetary estimates to ensure that the project will operate within the financial resources available.
3. The securing of approval for the project to become operational from government, local government, or other authorities.
4. Contracting with suppliers or service organizations to ensure that necessary resources flow into the project.
5. Forging an understanding with authorities regarding such matters as taxation, union requirements, etc.
6. Obtaining necessary licenses to enable the operation of the project to get underway, ordering of special equipment or training of special staff so that the project is ready to begin on schedule.

Handover can, therefore, be a complex procedure. Since both the project managers and the receivers of the completed project are unlikely to have had much experience at handover, great care needs to be taken that all eventualities are covered.

DIVESTMENT PLANNING

According to Berger, all resources in project organization can be divided into two main categories: durable physical resources and human resources. The proper utilization of durable physical resources after a project is completed requires the arrangement of an appropriate maintenance and scheduling system; failure to provide for maintenance may result in rapid depreciation of these assets. This system, it should be remembered, differs from the system required to organize construction, for example, during the project's actual lifetime. Many instances can be cited of projects developed without integrated and systematic planning whose equipment, with several years of life remaining, was abandoned at the end of the project along with special equipment that had been used for specific purposes during the course of the project. Such neglect of the tasks of project completion and assimilation occur frequently in the case of projects that are heavily influenced by political considerations.

The physical resources will vary from equipment, plant, and machinery to small tools. Unfortunately, some projects do not properly utilize or maintain equipment, such as tractors, after the project is completed, causing considerable wastage. Buildings constructed specifically for the project are sometimes left abandoned. If the future use of buildings has been considered in the early stages of the project, demountable buildings could perhaps have been used, which could have been relocated fairly cheaply. Or a rice project, for example, may require earth-moving equipment in the construction of irrigation ditches. The project life may be five years, but the greatest use of the equipment will come in the first three years. Thus the life of the project is three years in terms of this particular resource utilization. It would be possible to discover that the average life of the earth-moving equipment in the project country is estimated at five years. The resource concerned has, therefore, a two-year period in which it can be utilized in some alternative activity. It is necessary to consider alternative uses and the available activities. Earth moving equipment can also be used for other projects such as building roads, construction of buildings, drainage of swamps, etc., and there would be a likelihood that some of these activities would occur within the two-year period of resource availability. The project manager would have to find out details about the alternative activities so that joint or collaborative planning for divestment and acquisition can occur. There are, however, built-in constraints to resource transfers. One problem might be the question of the type of equipment. Large earth-moving equipment, for example, may not be able to be moved into the area where it is needed. With some resources it is necessary that special skills are available to maintain equipment; otherwise serious breakdowns can occur.

Human resources must be one of the most important concerns in project completion and assimilation. Human beings have hopes or fears about their future. It is essential that long before a project ends, the project manager provides some means for accommodating the employee's personal goals. Planning is needed to reallocate such personnel to other projects or organizations. Human resources can be transferred to a permanent as well as a temporary organization. Persons working on a project are conscious that the life of a project is limited. They are also conscious that their skills, while useful on that project, may not be readily saleable in areas close to the project location. The key to successful divestment of human resources is that the particular skills and competencies of the persons be well known and that there be a matching of the person with opportunities the project manager should seek out. The problem of constraints because of accommodation and family commitments can also create problems. The cost of relocating people is often expensive. Cultural and ethnic considerations may also have to be taken into account. A significant difference between physical resources and human resources is that people will have set ideas as to what they want to do at the end of a project, and these should be known as early as possible by the project manager so that appropriate steps can be taken.

Attention must also be paid to the recruitment and training of personnel to manage the newly-established facilities. Not only resources allocation, but the transfer of administration and the organizational system from project status to "normal operation" is also an important concern at this stage. Wherever possible, suitable project personnel who want to remain under the new organization should be given the opportunity to do so.

A third category can be added to physical and human resources, namely, intangible resources. Intangible resources are those developed through goodwill generated within a community, such as the agreement to gain access to a project through private land. If they are positive, these resources may be turned into an advantage by ensuring that cooperation on future projects is obtained from the community concerned. The resources may enable development that would not normally occur to be implemented, and this should be recognized as an important aspect of a project's outcome.

The orderly transfer of all these resources must be contained in a project divestment plan. The process of divestment planning must commence well before the project is due for completion. Divestment planning should, in fact, take place before the project begins, along with the other aspects of project planning, so that management and employees alike on the project all have a fair understanding of what the final outcome will be.

Two prerequisites are necessary for intelligent planning of project completion and assimilation: 1) information about alternative activities where resources can be utilized, and 2) the capability of acting on this information.(2) In this case, sectoral or regional planning agencies have to collaborate with project managers to transfer resources with leftover utility from one to another project. Berger also points out that the project manager must possess four kinds of information to make good decisions about this stage:(3)

1. The expected duration of the project and the use of the resources in the project.
2. The expected life of the resources.
3. Alternative uses of the resources and available activities.
4. Inherent constraints on the transfer of the resources.

In some cases, it should be noted, future projects may be planned and based around equipment and resources presently being used in another locality. The multiple use of resources both physical and human can, in fact, play a major part in the planning of development within the planning system of the country. A great deal of the responsibility for divestment planning here will fall upon the project manager, who must be conscious of the future use of personnel and the physical resources, so that inquiries can be made as soon as completion deadlines become a reality.

For divestment planning to be successful, reliable information is necessary. For proper planning to take place, decision makers must be aware of the extent to which resources are being used in the project and the life and availability of each. Strategies on alternative uses of resources should be developed and the problems of transferring resources recognized at an early stage of the project.

Care must be taken, finally, to see that maintenance of physical resources does not slacken during the divestment process. Similarly, personnel should be encouraged to work during divestment at as high a capacity as they have throughout the rest of the project. Sustaining employee performance at the project's end can best be accomplished by ensuring that they have a job to go to once the project is completed.

The success of a project is usually measured in terms of achieving stated goals. The tasks of completion and handover, however, provide the opportunity to measure the project by a rather different yardstick: the manner in which available resources were divested. The importance of intelligent divestment becomes even clearer in the process of evaluation, the next task in the project cycle.

NOTES

(1) Michael Berger, R.A. Johnson, James Lowenthal, and Raymond Radosevich, "Divesting Project Resources" (Vanderbilt: Graduate School of Management, 1974), p. 1.

(2) Ibid.

(3) Ibid.

SELECTED BIBLIOGRAPHY

Berger, Michael, Johnson, R.A., Lowenthal, James, and Raymond Radosevich. "Divesting Project Resources." Graduate School of Management, Vanderbilt, 1974.

Phase 4 – Evaluation and Refinement

11 Post-Project Evaluation

Evaluation should be an ongoing activity throughout the phases of a project's lifetime and it should not end with the project itself. A post-project evaluation should be conducted to measure whether the project did meet its desired objectives, and if not, where and why it failed; such an analysis is a minimum requirement. The post-evaluation phase of the project cycle is an all-important one, as it links the project with the planning phase of the wheel; it links the specific with the general, the project itself with the policy that formulated it.

In the project cycle, project evaluation appears chronologically as the last of several phases in project management. Unfortunately, this is sometimes also indicative of the low priority and importance it gets from project managers. Project implementation has traditionally received the lion's share of the effort; recently, project planning has received greater and greater attention. Project evaluation has yet to come into its own. There are many reasons for this neglect.

In some cases, failure to provide adequate evaluation has been due to the sociopolitical nature of projects – thus, accountability for funds that have been spent or blame for project failures are not actively sought. In other cases, given the scanty resources of a country's economy, funds are thought to be better spent toward new and necessary projects, not to the review of old ones. In still other cases, reasons have been loss of interest in past projects; absence of an agency directly responsible for evaluation and follow-up; absence of a team or agency responsible for the entire project; lack of appreciation for evaluation; or lack of adequate planning for the whole project – meaning that standards or objectives were never comprehensively determined and the project, like Topsy, "just grew."

Some of these reasons do not necessarily exist only in developing countries. They happen everywhere, a circumstance that accounts for the only recent emergence of literature on techniques and procedures in project evaluation. Even less literature is available on aspects related to the scaling down, termination, and reallocation of project resources.

213

Yet the importance of post-project evaluation cannot be under-emphasized. The limited resources of developing countries certainly demand that their administrators should ensure that projects are well planned and efficiently initiated. But even more, administrators must see that these projects are well maintained, effectively and efficiently achieve the objectives of the individual project, and contribute to the development of the country as a whole. While this may seem obvious in theory, all too often the dictates and pressures of short-run perfor-mance indicators shift the allocation of priorities away from evaluation toward new, more activity-oriented areas.

EVALUATION IN VARIOUS STAGES OF THE PROJECT CYCLE

It is important to note that post-project evaluation is distinct from, but assumes as necessary for project success, both ex ante and ongoing project evaluation. Indeed, because post-project evaluation is linked with different types of project evaluation in earlier phases of the project cycle, the following section briefly examines the activities involving evaluation at each point in the history of the project.

Evaluation During Planning and Appraisal

In the early days of a project, evaluation is conducted when project proposals, prefeasibility studies, and feasibility studies are considered. In effect, these evaluation processes involve different sets of docu-ments and different evaluating bodies at each point, and can be summarized as follows:

Project Stage	Documents Evaluated	Evaluating Body
Project Identification	Interagency memo-randa or preliminary project proposals	Internal to agency
Initial Feasibility Analysis & Appraisal	Prefeasibility study	Internal to agency
Project Selection & Approval	Feasibility study	Top manage-ment of agency Financial Institu-tion National planning agency Other national agencies -Pollution

Project Stage	Documents Evaluated	Evaluating Body
		Commission -Energy Com- mission -Regional Council -Regulatory Industry Commission

The criteria used by each evaluating body may be different. For the agency involved, the yardstick may be return on investment, whereas for the national planning agency, it may be national security or net social benefits.

Evaluation During Operation and Control

Ongoing evaluation can and should be conducted while a project is being implemented. This will allow corrective measures to be installed while the project is active.

During implementation, the project manager concentrates on effective utilization of resources – getting the project accomplished at the right time, with the lowest cost, and at the acceptable level of quality. The project manager needs to stay informed on the progress of project as measured against performance, cost, and schedule standards. This level of evaluation for efficiency is often referred to as the control function. Usually, however, it is higher management that conducts a running evaluation of the impact of the project – that is, changes in the environment that affect the project's objectives.

Evaluation documents at this stage include:

- progress and status reports
- contractor's reports
- works engineer's reports
- budget reports
- year-end reports of all projects in process
- funding agency's project status reports

These are generally reviewed by top management of the agency and, at times, by the funding institution.

Evaluation During Completion and Handover

Once a project is completed, a project completion report may be required of the project manager. Again, this is an evaluation tool which can be used to measure whether expected project output levels are actually attainable, and whether problems were incurred in resource input conversions.

The project completion reports are submitted to top management of the agency; they may also be submitted to the national planning agency and the funding agency for further evaluation.

Post-Project Evaluation

This evaluation, coming at the end of the project, reviews all previous evaluations made. The culmination of post-project evaluation is a formal report analyzing the project itself, as well as recommendations for future projects. Main components of the post-project evaluation report are: a study of project objectives; a study of resources available and utilized for the project; alternatives, opportunities and constraints at each decision point; an analysis of the overall project with regard to its outputs and impact; and implications for project planning.

The post-project evaluation is intended to produce recommendations that will benefit the agency not only in projects of similar kinds, but in project management in general.

Documents available for the post-project evaluation effort would consist of the previously itemized project documents:

Internally Generated Reports	Externally Generated Reports
Prefeasibility studies	National planning agency reports
Feasibility study design studies	Studies prepared by consultants
Various progress and status reports	Studies made by funding agencies Project feasibility studies Status report End-of-project reports
Year-end reports	
Project completion reports	

OBJECTIVES AND SCOPE OF POST-PROJECT EVALUATION

Examining post-project evaluation here rather than ongoing project evaluation, then, it may be well to start with this definition provided by the Organization for Economic Cooperation and Development (OECD): "the attempt to assess the results of an activity and, as a function of the results, of the means employed to achieve them."(1) The description clearly indicates that the activity must have already been completed and that there are measurable results. It also indicates that the scope includes considerations both of effectiveness (dealing with results) and efficiency (dealing with means).

The concepts of effectiveness and efficiency take on specific meanings in the context of government and development projects. The following definitions are probably the most functional:

> Effectiveness concerns the extent to which government programs achieve their objectives. This presumes that decisions about what and how much governments do are based on considered judgments of the relative importance and cost of meeting public needs. . . . Efficiency concerns the organization of resources to carry out government programs and functions at minimal cost. Efficiency may be expressed in several ways, including output per manhour, capital-output ratios, and more broadly, least-cost combinations of resources.(2)

Various funding and project-oriented agencies further modify and define these concepts for their evaluation purposes. The United States Agency for International Development (AID), for instance, defines these and then adds the concept of significance ("contribute to economic development or higher goals beyond the project purpose") to constitute their three basic areas for post-project evaluation.(3)

In any event, those responsible for post-project evaluation must, by definition, assume a comprehensive point of view. Whereas components of the project may be worked on individually during implementation, the evaluator looks at the project as a package. Success or failure is determined by the achievements of the whole project measured against its objective. Thus, the project evaluator must be a generalist; he or she cannot bring to bear one specialization or one discipline as he or she might be able to do in some other technical tasks of project planning or implementation.

Evaluation, it is important to emphasize, should not be an end in itself but should look forward to the future. Evaluation is not designed to produce a compilation of reports about past projects for the shelves of libraries or for archival files. It is meant to provide lessons or information for use in assisting decision makers – now and in the future. Much has been written on actual and potential wastages caused by poor project management. To make a mistake once or twice is human and sometimes inevitable, but to make the same mistake over and over (as recurring project failure patterns seem to indicate) is to neglect the tool of project evaluation and its use for future project policy guidelines.

This future-oriented role of evaluation becomes especially relevant when viewed against the magnitudes of project funding by both international agencies and national governments. The Asian Development Bank, now averaging forty project loans a year, has a total loan commitment of US$3.3 billion for some 266 projects in twenty-three developing countries.(4) To take another example, the public investment outlays, principally for power and irrigation in a country such as the Philippines, are expected to reach US$10 billion over the next ten years.(5) Clearly, evaluation must provide guidelines for the future;

otherwise, if it is "not oriented to better decision making and there is little commitment to applying results, the project is probably a poor candidate for evaluation."(6)

POST-PROJECT EVALUATION IN DEVELOPING COUNTRIES

As stated earlier, post-project evaluation has not been systematized in developing countries. At the Asian Development Bank and the World Bank, major funding agencies for developing countries that have promoted the efficient utilization of project management techniques, this form of evaluation was pioneered and implemented several years ago, but is still being further refined.

A review of five case histories written on development projects in Asian and Pacific countries reveals that post-evaluation on the whole is not institutionalized in government planning or implementing agencies.(7) In an Indonesian transmigration project, the World Bank conducted the intensive research and evaluation. In a Pacific island livestock development project, no formal post-project evaluation was conducted either by the local agency or by the funding government agency. In a Korean national family planning program, ". . . no system of evaluative research was built into the administration of the Korean operation. . . .Any systematic follow-up after evaluation was not institutionalized." In a Philippines rural social development project, the funding agency commissioned evaluation studies to be done by an independent academic and research institute; the implementing agency itself did not conduct post-evaluation studies.

In the Bangkok water improvement program, however, attention was given to evaluation studies. The departments concerned reported on the projects in the annual reports, and made final reports on each project following its completion.

Officials at the major international funding agencies admit that they have not yet "debugged" their post-project evaluation procedures and techniques. There is still much room for improvement and institutionalization in this area. For the developing countries and their local agencies, as we have seen, post-project evaluation is an even newer concept. In the Philippines, the national planning agency implemented a post-project evaluation scheme only in 1978. The National Economic Development Authority (NEDA), whose activity consists in the planning of projects, will prepare evaluation reports on projects with the aid of the implementing agencies. Basis for the evaluation is the implementing agency's project completion report. In each approach, the objective of the post-evaluation effort is essentially to analyze what happened, using objectives as the basic criteria.

EVALUATION APPROACHES AND GUIDELINES

Two handbooks published by international agencies provide interesting overviews of current approaches and guidelines in use by the larger project-monitoring bodies. These are Evaluation Handbook, by the United States Agency for International Development, and Guidelines for Project Evaluation, by the United Nations.(8)

The Evaluation Handbook first distinguishes between the different levels of activity – multicountry-level studies, program-level studies, sector-level studies, and project-level studies. Obviously, there will be a significant difference in evaluation scope and emphasis, depending on the level of activity and degree of complexity being reviewed.

For a project with a definite beginning and completion date, a post-evaluation is possible. Furthermore, the objectives of the project are relatively more specific on the project level.

The starting point for the evaluation is the project's objectives as defined and stated in project documents. An evaluator's first task then is to determine whether the project as conceived would really accomplish the set objectives. Next would come an analysis of the inputs, process or project implementation, and the outputs of the project.

To a great extent, the project documents, such as the feasibility and design studies, provide the blueprints as plans to be implemented. The progress/status reports and other ongoing evaluation documents at the implementation stage provide the "actual" data – or "what happened." The project completion reports present an initial analysis of the inputs, process, and outputs.

The more difficult aspect of the evaluation task consists of measuring the impact of the project. (Impact, outcomes, or purpose here will be used interchangeably to mean the final benefits or effects the project intends to achieve.) Since the evaluator has determined that the project as conceived will result in outputs that will lead to a certain level of net benefit, concern at this stage is with measuring net benefits.

A simple example would be an irrigation project to benefit the small farmers in a particular area. The output of the project is water, but the expected net benefit is water to help irrigate the crops of the small farmers in the area.

A study of output will simply determine if the project design to turn out water for irrigation was done efficiently. The study on impact will go further and study if the small farmers in the area are in fact benefitting from the irrigation project. This can be related again to the earlier-mentioned tests of effectiveness, efficiency, and often significance.

Thus, as Koppel suggests, a number of approaches must be considered when comparing original project targets with actual results:

1. Evaluating objectives: that is, clarifying explicit and implicit objectives. Also, reference should be made to inputs, transformations, outputs, and effects.

2. Evaluating subjectives: emphasis here is on process. The question mainly tackled is the "who" – who decided, who benefited, and who paid.

3. Evaluating levels: making a distinction between the level of activity – program, projects and activities – and identifying the objectives according to each level.(9)

A guideline in project management that will greatly influence evaluation is consistency. Consistency here refers both to format and requirements in project documentation, as well as consistency in procedure. To the extent that projects are documented at each different level or stage, and that some degree of uniformity in approach is utilized, then the evaluator's task is facilitated. Consistency in procedure points to routing of documents in such a way that the evaluating office has access to all the various documents pertaining to projects. A data bank with up-to-date records for projects and all other related materials would be extremely helpful to evaluators.

Essentially, the procedure should approximate the "wheel" of the project cycle, with project evaluation close to project planning and policy formulation. For established international agencies, this procedure and format have recently been somewhat formalized. For developing countries themselves, project management procedures are yet to be institutionalized.

EVALUATION TECHNIQUES

The usual approach in measuring impact is by social cost-benefit analysis. This is because a project is usually considered part of a means to attain a national objective, and is computed either at the project feasibility or selection stage.

What is involved, then, is measuring the social benefits and costs accruing to a project. The term cost must be distinguished from its commercial meaning. Cost in the context of social costs and benefits refers to the opportunity losses of a government by its undertaking a particular project. Prices, for example, is a term that is also not used in the usual sense. In this context, prices are adjusted to reflect the values we want to attach to a particular commodity or service.

Social cost-benefit analysis attempts to determine what success the country will have toward achieving national objectives by pursuing a particular strategy against opportunities lost because it did commit its resources to this particular project.

The biggest factors affecting an evaluator's assessment are the country's objectives and priorities. If a country, for example, aims to set up a petrochemical complex to produce raw materials for local industry, it does so for several reasons. One may be to hasten the industrialization of the country, another may be to increase employment. If the country previously imported the resins and chemicals and collected tariff duties on these goods, this "cost" will mean losses to the government from tariffs on the imports. If the assumption is that net outputs of the plant would be equivalent to previous imports, then gross benefits of the project will be equivalent to the foreign exchange that would have been used for importing. Other cost and benefit items would then likewise be adjusted to reflect the relevant social or national values.

The procedure, once these cost/revenue items are so adjusted, will be to proceed with calculating the discounted rate of return using present values. The resulting rate of return is a social rate of return, again distinguished from a commercial rate of return.

The basic formula used for present value computations is:

$$V(i) = \sum_{t=0}^{n} \frac{Pt}{(1+i)t}$$

where $P_0, P_1, P_2 \ldots P_n$ is the stream of profits, the present value of the project at interest rate i, is $V(i)$, and t is time.

The country can determine a social rate of discount to be used as a cutoff point. Projects offering a higher rate of return would be "acceptable," projects with lower rates of return would be "unacceptable."

In post-project evaluation, the evaluator's task is to measure if the computations made for social benefits and social costs done in the planning stage did, in fact, reflect what actually occurred. This could mean a recomputation or remodification of social costs and benefits in the light of changing government priorities. The resulting figures would give implementors a more realistic perspective of the project in relation to national objectives.

Other approaches or techniques in evaluation would be the use of control groups for comparative analysis, baseline measures, sampling, and various data-gathering methods such as field surveys, questionnaires, and interviews.

These techniques, again, largely occur at the beginning of a project if a study or research design is planned. If this type of study is done, an experimental test group and a control group may be determined. Furthermore, baseline measures such as size and number of irrigated farms for an irrgation project can be set. Tests or interviews conducted can reveal certain critical aspects or situations prior to the start of the project.

At the time of evaluation, the comparisons made would be the experimental group before and after the project, the control group before and after the project, and an evaluation of results based on the critical aspects studied. Other techniques used would be financial techniques, such as variance analysis, where a study of the budgeted versus actual financial performance is made. If the project did not utilize a budget, however, such analysis would be very difficult, if not impossible.

In any case, the present state of project evaluation techniques is such that we must maintain the dynamic tension between regarding it as a science and regarding it as an art. On one hand, there is an increasing body of scientific and systematic techniques and tools, largely quantitative, that facilitates the evaluation process. On the other hand, the sought-for social and nonquantifiable benefits from projects often defy rigorous scientific analysis and demand much more case-to-case methodology for project evaluation.

THE CHOICE OF EVALUATORS

As the previous sections of this chapter imply, post-evaluation can be more effectively conducted if attention is given to establishing standards, criteria, and indicators from the time a project is planned.

The ideal arrangement, then, is for the central or national planning agency to be responsible for post-evaluation. On a company level, such as in the private sector, this would mean that project evaluation should also be the responsibility of the corporate planning department.

Another implication is that the staff for project evaluation must work closely with the implementing agency in evaluation work. It is universally recognized that the nature of the evaluation processes requires the input of more than one individual, so that a multidisciplinary team with enough resources and enough time, and autonomy from the project-implementing group, should be put together.

Opinions differ, however, on the composition of the project team. Some funding agencies rely heavily on "in-house" teams, that is, project evaluators from within the agency who use standard agency frames of reference. Others rely on teams of external experts and consultants who bring different frameworks, and thus less structure, to the evaluation exercise, hopefully guaranteeing greater objectivity. Still others prefer a mixed project team composed of both "in-house" evaluators and external consultants. The factors that determine the optimum mix of a project team have been identified as administrative confidence, objectivity, understanding of the program, potential for utilization, and autonomy.(10)

The debate on the relative merits and demerits of a preponderantly external team over an institutionalized evaluation staff within an agency is far from over. External teams have objectivity at the cost of possible lack of understanding, perspective, or access to background hard and soft information; internal teams enjoy familiarity and access at the expense of possible subjectivity.

In any case, once a project is chosen or slated for evaluation, a project team is selected. The selection is sometimes made by a committee headed by the project evaluation department head. Names are suggested and negotiations ensue – in cases of outside teams – to ensure that the nominees are available and willing to do the evaluation work. Next, timetables are set and team members agree to a deadline for the complete project report.

The team is usually composed, at minimum, of a technical expert and a project management expert. The group may consist of three to five individuals from various disciplines with recognized expertise in the line of the project. They are sometimes from universities or research agencies, as well as from various government offices. Their expertise and experience are of primary consideration in their selection, however, as the quality of the evaluation work will only be as good as the evaluators themselves.

It has become standard practice for funding agencies to send project teams on missions to evaluate the effectiveness of projects for which loans, often in millions of dollars, have been given. Ironically, the international agency often seems more interested in the impact of the project than the recipient country itself.

Another area requiring much more serious attention than it has previously received is the development of local expertise for project evaluation. It is notable that international funding agencies rely mostly on Western experts for the evaluation of projects. This practice is both costly – considering that a major cost for evaluation work would include salaries, transportation, and other fees for the management team – and in some cases, impractical. It is far more advisable that local experts be recognized and/or trained in the techniques and processes of project evaluation.

PROJECT EVALUATION PROCESS

Given all of the foregoing considerations, how then is the actual process of post-project evaluation conducted?

As discussed earlier, project evaluation begins right at the planning stage, and post-project evaluation mentality must be evident in the planning process itself. In particular, the post-project evaluator should also be involved in this early planning stage, or, more realistically, a member of the project-evaluation team must be drawn from people involved from the beginning.

During feasibility, selection, and approval, the major planning documents should be supplied to the central project evaluation office or division. Most important, a section of the feasibility and planning documents should include a separate section on the evaluation plan. This section should explicitly identify:

1. Criteria to be used in post-evaluation. If the main body of the feasibility document is done properly, these criteria will naturally emerge out of the time schedule, cost and budget limits, and productivity output targets. Key result areas, specified in measurable terms where possible, will be the criteria for post-evaluation. This is equally true of concrete technical projects as of social projects, though the latter are admittedly harder to quantify.

2. Evaluation techniques. This section would identify, where appropriate, the use of control groups, surveys, baseline measures, and questionnaires, as well as the points in time when these techniques are

to be used to provide before/after pictures, and so on. It would also lay out the cost-benefit premises against which future evaluations could be set.

3. Time schedules for conducting the evaluation. Besides scheduling implementation, proposals should schedule evaluation, so that it is not indefinitely postponed, or indicate an acceptable lapse time in instances where a project's desired results – especially social – are not evident immediately after project completion.

4. Budget for post-evaluation. This section should include, besides the total amount and the program breakdowns, the promised or possible sources of funding and the schedule of budget releases.

5. Organization and staff requirements for evaluation. This section should outline the size of the evaluation team, its qualifications, the reporting relationships, and access to project information and staff.

Thus stated at the outset of a project's history, these considerations on project evaluation can then be presented and taken into account in the selection and approval process.

During project implementation and control, copies of the various status reports and progress reports should likewise be furnished to the central evaluation office or division, as should various studies on the project made by or made for external agencies and groups.

Even as implementation continues, the central evaluation office should begin the process of selecting the evaluation team specifically constituted for that project. Recruiting, identifying, and – importantly – providing adequate orientation at least at the head office level, should all hopefully be completed by the time the implementation stage draws to a close, so that the team is ready as soon as it is needed.

As this selection and orientation takes final shape at the head office, the project manager and the field staff should be simultaneously drawing up a comprehensive project completion report. Though this is not itself the post-evaluation report, it becomes the objective basis and starting-point document for the evaluation team.

It is true that, except for specific infrastructure projects, most projects that deal with ongoing concerns and problems tend to require an ongoing mechanism or structure even after the specific project is over. This means that projects, like old soldiers, never die; in fact, they do not even fade away. What does happen is a transformation from a project status to an ongoing agency status. This often means also a handover from an initiating and temporary set-up team to a less high-powered operations group that becomes part of a larger bureaucracy. In some instances, the project team itself becomes absorbed and assumes regular operations, but the transition from project status to regular operating status must be made clear to the project team.

Thus, the evaluation team will be conducting its work in the context of an ongoing concern. Besides the performance of the original project stage, it will also have to evaluate the capability and the success of the second stage, the continued existence under nonproject terms of the activity, and the adequacy of provisions for the transfer of technology, insights, and recommendations from the project manager, who is a major source of recommendations for future activities.(11)

As the evaluation team conducts its work, it will eventually crystallize its findings, judgments, and recommendations in a detailed post-project evaluation report. This report will include judgments on effectiveness, efficiency, and significance. It will present the findings of the various statistical and quantitative techniques of evaluation used. In particular, it will comment on the following:

- the extent to which articulated objectives are valid, and the extent to which they were achieved
- the extent to which the assumptions upon which the feasibility study depended were proven true or untrue as the project was implemented
- the deviation in cost-benefit analysis terms between anticipated results and actual results, and the internal and external causes of this deviation
- the deviation in the three areas of time and schedules, budgets and costs, and quantity and quality of productive output; the causes, justified or unjustified, for the deviation
- the impact of the project on development in general, on the intended beneficiaries in particular; the unintended other impacts and side effects of the project
- prescriptions and recommendations for continuity, replication, scaling up, or phasing out of post-project activity
- identification of opportunities for further project or investment opportunities, as well as backward, forward, and lateral linkages based on elements of generalizability (that is, those elements with applicability to several projects(12)); recommendations and proposed guidelines for future similar projects, and indeed for policy at the supraproject level in general

The post-evaluation report should hopefully be completed within the time originally specified within the evaluation plan section of the feasibility study, and submitted within its deadline.

The central project evaluation office or division receives this report, but it should not just stay there. The agency should articulate a clearly defined policy for appropriate circulation that protects confidentiality and prevents indiscriminate perusal on one hand, and guarantees that those who will find the report useful do get a chance to see it on the other hand. This latter group· would include the project manager and staff (except in rare instances), the central planning agency, the funding agency, and the necessary executive and legislative enabling authorities. For some in this group, brief executive summaries of the comprehensive report would be most useful.

Hopefully, the document will be specific in its treatment of the project and yet generalizable, so that findings can apply beyond the specific project context. This document, which represents the output of this phase of project management, should be useful for policy reformulation or, at best, for refinement of operating practices. A report of an ongoing evaluation serves as the occasion to identify deviations of project implementation from program planning, and to re-schedule or correct the current project.

The report of a post-evaluation is, by definition, submitted after the project is over and therefore of little use to the project itself. It is, however, valuable, using the principle of generalizability for similar future projects and often for indicating the manner in which the activity of the project can be turned over or regularized.

POLICY ISSUES AND PROBLEM AREAS IN PROJECT EVALUATION

To ensure that the evaluation phase of the project management cycle is effectively carried out using optimum procedures and methodologies, it is important, finally, to resolve a number of policy issues and potential problems relative to project evaluation. The resolution of these policy issues will differ according to the particular country's government structures, to the requirements of the funding agency, and to the scope and nature of the project itself. Nevertheless, these issues require explicit attention for successful project evaluation.

The General Development Planning Context

The planning infrastructure for evaluation in a given national government should be clearly delineated. To the extent that the government of a country has planned a project, has provided the necessary continuing administrative support and funding, and has rationalized the project in the country's overall scheme of operations, then precisely to that extent the evaluation work is facilitated.

The national planning authorities of countries such as Malaysia and the Philippines have, to a greater or lesser degree, specified their countries priorities and needs in development: a classification of the country according to regions for development purposes is made, providing an inventory of available human, financial, and natural resources; a listing and description of top priority projects per region follows. The national development plan is thus integrated, and the evaluating team for a project in a region can, at a glance, perceive the role of the project in the country's development scheme.

The Organizational Setting for Project Evaluation

Often a number of agencies are involved in development projects. This provides an additional problem in evaluation. Will it be the planning agency, implementing agency, funding agency, the Commission on Audit, or support agencies that should conduct the post-project evaluation?

In cases where an interdepartmental body is created to spearhead and coordinate the project,(13) this agency would be best equipped to conduct the post-evaluation. More generally, a separate central agency or organization should be mandated with the task of overseeing evaluation efforts at the supraproject level and of providing information inputs on the evaluation of projects and facilitating the flow of information on evaluation back to the persons affected, that is, the project implementors and planners. A number of national governments have taken steps toward consolidating a mechanism that analyzes and compiles data, feedback, and evaluation work on all major development projects in the country. In some countries, this may be a newly-created agency, while in other countries, it may not be an entirely new agency, but a function assumed by a special division of an existing central agency, such as the Evaluation Division, Programs and Projects Office of the Philippines' National Economic Development Authority.

An example may illustrate this mechanism. If an internationally-funded project on irrigation were to be evaluated in the Philippines, the evaluation mission would have to go to a variety of source documents, sectoral agencies, and other funding institutions to piece together a comprehensive picture on practices and priorities in Philippine irrigation. The team would have to look up a variety of different agency reports, unless a centralized project evaluation government agency would have this material assembled, not only for the evaluation mission but for future irrigation project planners as well.

In the Philippines, the preliminary proposal for institutionalization of post-evaluation of government projects was made by the National Economic Development Authority (NEDA), the national planning and coordinating body. NEDA recognizes the value of post-project evaluation as an instrument for improving both project planning and execution capabilities of implementing agencies of government, and also the related evaluation and appraisal functions of NEDA.

In other governments, project evaluators may be distinct from policy makers, central planners, and project formulators but would nevertheless be somewhat centralized.

Under any of these alternative forms, a centralized government office could participate actively in dissemination of current and relevant information to the government and planning offices. It would see to it that all projects – both successes and failures – would systematically undergo a prescribed evaluation, and not just those that some research agency opts to study. The task of coordinating with the different international lending agencies could also belong to this office. A centralized agency could thus minimize existing problems of project evaluation teams in generalizability, confidentiality (where either too many people or too few people, or not the right people, see the reports), and objectivity, especially where the specialized agency responsible for implementation also inputs heavily into the evaluation.

The Participation of Beneficiaries

The intended beneficiaries of a project must assume a vital role in the evaluation phase of the project cycle. Several large-scale projects, often commissioned by international funding agencies, undergo evaluation in the manner and even form dictated by these funding agencies. The beneficiary region or country, more interested in new projects rather than accountability, often complies with project-evaluation procedures not for their intrinsic value or for measuring the resulting benefit to the country, but rather simply to comply with the international funding agency's requirements – if only to position for another project loan. If this perspective were changed and the host regions, countries, or institutions were to undertake project evaluation as it should be done, then the effect of the project can more properly be assessed and policy directions implicit in this assessment can be made.

To accomplish this change of perspective, of course, it will be necessary to gear up organization and workers to conduct such project evaluation more thoroughly and tie it in more explicitly with public policy. This may be a large task, for it will involve a more adequate rationalization of government planning, executing, and evaluating agencies, an adequate worker training and development program and certain public policy modifications that may affect the legal, administrative, and economic dimensions of the country. It would, however, be worthwhile, for not only will it bring forth the value and usefulness of evaluation but it will be an opportunity to indigenize originally Western (and sometimes inappropriate) techniques, approaches, and guidelines, and adopt these to the sociocultural and administrative environment of one's own developing country.

The Inclusion of Evaluation Mechanisms from the Start

Although project evaluation is the next-to-last chronological task in the project cycle, we have emphasized that it be included in the project manager's conscious framework right from the start. Much of the failure of project evaluation attempts can be traced to the absence of such foresight in project planners and implementors, so that at evaluation time it becomes impossible adequately to design the criteria – expected outputs and benefits – against which the evaluation can be carried out. When the project planners and implementors are clear from the start about the methodology, criteria, and approach the evaluation will use, their task will not only become focused, it will also contribute immeasurably to the effectivity of the project evaluation task itself.

Post-evaluation must be preceded by an appropriate amount of ongoing evaluation. Although this presentation has focused on evaluation after the project is over, ongoing evaluations on a regular basis, especially if it is a multiyear project, should be built into the project design and carried out routinely, and documented as an essential part of the project manager's control and monitoring functions.

This is particularly true if the evaluator is new to the project, or does not come from a support office that assisted in the project.

While a fresh perspective indeed presents advantages, the new evaluator must carefully review the project from country documents as well as documents pertaining to the project itself, to ensure a balanced, comprehensive, and unbiased overview of the project. The evaluator, to a great extent, is limited in scope by the documents of the project. The evaluator's understanding of the project development and implementation will be based, first, on the availability and, second, on the accuracy of these documents.

The Timing of the Evaluation Itself

The timing of the post-project evaluation must be explicitly incorporated into the total project schedule. In many instances, this means that even before the project is completed, the processes of establishing project evaluation criteria, methodology, and the composition of the project team would have already been done. In fact, this should ideally take place at the planning stage.

In this way, post-project evaluation for technical projects can take place immediately after completion. Project completion reports will provide an evaluation of the outputs of a project.

Measuring the outcome or impact of a project, however, can usually only be done after a few years have elapsed. For projects with social impact, it may be wise to wait for a relatively longer period to measure such aspects as attitude change and social returns on the investment; for this purpose, although expensive, a longitudinal study may be best. The timing for making an impact study, therefore, is subjective depending on the nature of the project and its intended objectives. As a rule of thumb, five years is usually considered a "long enough time" by evaluating agencies. In any case, the proper timing of project evaluation requires that the on-site project evaluation already be preceded by the briefing at international headquarters (in the case of a funding agency's evaluation mission) on agency policies, country economic indices, and by pertinent discussions with government officials of the recipient country. While it is important to give adequate time to enable the evaluation mission to conduct an in-depth analysis, the evaluation report must not be so delayed as to prevent the findings from having direct influence on the policy formulation of subsequent similar projects.

Standardization and Cost Considerations

As a variety of projects are evaluated by a central governmental agency or international funding group, the issue of establishing relatively standardized criteria becomes crucial. All too often, projects with similar objectives and similar performance outputs are evaluated by teams from the same agency, but, because one team has different criteria or emphasizes different aspects, the prospects receive vastly different evaluation ratings.

Obviously, the need to establish workable and flexible, but somewhat standardized, criteria for evaluation must be addressed by agencies responsible for project evaluation on a continuing basis.

As far as costs of evaluation are concerned, these criteria should ideally be built into the project's budget. This, however, is not generally the case. The project's total budget usually includes only a budget for preoperating studies (and sometimes even this is not included, especially when funded from a different source) and for project implementation up to completion.

When post-project evaluation costs are included, they are generally in the context of a fund grant proposal, and even then the funding agency does not always include the amount in the approved grant, on the grounds that post-evaluation does not affect the completed project directly but is rather a supraproject policy responsibility.

A further complication arises when a project's impact can only be measured a few years after project completion and a complexity of research tools are required. Funding longitudinal studies then runs into difficulties of budget release several years after budget approvals are made.

But post-evaluations, like projects themselves, require not only time and effort, but also money, and managing the evaluation process must include the planned acquisition and efficient utilization of this needed resource.

CONCLUSION

Project evaluation is one of the last tasks in the project cycle. As in every cycle, the later steps are inexorably linked to the earlier ones. Thus, evaluation leads to policy which leads to planning which leads to further implementation. It has been said that ten years' experience is not the same as one year's experience repeated ten times. This is precisely the potential value of post-project evaluation. As the cycle operates, it remains the task of project evaluation to see that subsequent reiterations of the cycle continue to be maximally effective and beneficial and that the evaluation process results in the refinement of policy and implementation. In this light, the importance of project evaluation cannot be overstated.

NOTES

(1) OECD, Evaluating Development Assistance (Paris: OECD, 1975), p. 5.

(2) Research and Policy Committee, Committee for Economic Development (CED), Improving Productivity in State and Local Government (New York: CED, 1976), p. 14.

(3) USAID, Evaluation Handbook (Washington, D.C.: USAID 1976), p. 3.

(4) Minister Cesar Virata, "Perspectives in ADB Activities" (Speech delivered on the 10th Annual Meeting of the Board of Directors, Asian Development Bank, Manila, May 1977).

(5) IBRD report, "The Philippines: Priorities and Prospects for Development" (Washington, D.C., 1976), p. 315.

(6) Weiss, Carol H. Evaluation Research, Methods of Assessing Program Effectiveness (Englewood Cliffs, N.J.: Prentice-Hall, 1972), p. 13.

(7) East-West Center series of case studies in PPIPM Project (Honolulu: EWC, 1976-7), seven vols. Five are reprinted in Louis J. Goodman and Ralph N. Love, eds., Management of Development Projects (New York: Pergamon Press, 1979).

(8) USAID, Evaluation Handbook, and United Nations Industrial Development Organization, Guidelines for Project Evaluation (New York: United Nations, 1972).

(9) Bruce Koppel, The Evaluation Factor: A Handbook to Remind Evaluators of the Complexity of Their Task (Honolulu: East-West Center, 1976), pp. 8-13.

(10) Weiss, Evaluation Research, p. 20.

(11) J. Bainbridge and S. Sapirie, Health Project Management: A Manual of Procedures for Formulating and Implementing Health Projects (Geneva: World Health Organization, 1974).

(12) Koppel, The Evaluation Factor, p. 13.

(13) Ibid., p. 18.

SELECTED BIBLIOGRAPHY

Koppel, Bruce. The Evaluation Factor: A Handbook to Remind Evaluators of the Complexity of Their Task. Honolulu: East-West Center, 1976.
Organization for Economic Cooperation and Development (OECD). Evaluating Development Assistance. Paris: OECD, 1975.
United States Agency for International Development (USAID). Evaluation Handbook. Washington D.C.: USAID, 1976.

Weiss, Carol H. Evaluation Research: Methods of Assessing Program Effectiveness. Englewood Cliffs, N.J.: Prentice-Hall, 1972.

12 Refinement of Policy and Planning

As the IPPMC model clearly indicates, policy occupies a central position in the entire management cycle. It has become increasingly evident over the past two decades that the future of development projects is directly linked to the policy-making process. Without adequate communications or feedback channels, projects either become divorced from the arena of policy making or are doomed to be replicated uncritically without the benefit of policy refinement. Although refinement of policy and planning occurs in the IPPMC model as a discrete task in Phase 4 (Evaluation and Refinement), it is important to note that the model also indicates the ideal situation. The cycle proposes that continuous feedback occur between each major phase (as well as between the tasks contained within each phase) and that continuous linkages be formed during each phase with the central hub of the cycle, policy.

The primary focus of this chapter is policy refinement as a discrete process (for a complete discussion of policy per se, consult Chapter 13). In this sense, the IPPMC model proposes that both formative policy refinement as well as summative policy refinement be major components of every development project.

Policy refinement is an area of great complexity and one that has not been well researched. Although the literature on evaluation and policy making is voluminous, utilization of evaluation data by policy makers is inadequate and the structured mechanisms for policy refinement are conceptually weak. In fact, a data base is still being gathered on project management in general, each of the phases of the cycle, and especially on the processes of evaluation, refinement, and policy change. The experiences and data obtained during the course of the PPIPM project have, however, provided some observations and tentative conclusions regarding these phenomena. This chapter will briefly explore some of the issues, offer some suggestions for developing more appropriate policy refinement procedures and, finally, raise some questions that will hopefully encourage others to pursue this research topic more fully. Increasingly recognized as an indispensable process in the project management cycle, policy refinement should be a positive experience that the principal actors in project management and policy making look forward to.

THE ROLE OF POLICY REFINEMENT IN PROJECT DEVELOPMENT

The importance of policy refinement to project development and management is directly related to the process of evaluation. The interrelatedness of evaluation-refinement-policy change is clearly evident, but it is still necessary to understand how policy responsiveness or refinement actually operates.

How do we know when this phenomenon has occurred? One useful way to find out is to focus on the correspondence among evaluation data, recommendations, and agency (or policy maker) decisions and actions. In this chapter, policy makers and decision makers are essentially the same actors. Policy making and decision making may take place either as a general, national process or focus only on an individual project, and the points raised here could apply to either case. We are not talking about a mechanical cause-and-effect relationship, but rather an appropriate fit between evaluation and agency action. Many agencies recognize the importance of this process but fail to discuss it adequately. The World Bank, for example, utilizes a fairly autonomous organization called the Operations Evaluation Department (OED) to provide their policy makers with the kind of data deemed necessary for refinement of policy. In their project cycle, however, evaluation is listed as the final stage in the project management cycle. It is stated that evaluations are "proving (to be) a gold mine of information" but that, nevertheless, over ninety-one percent of all projects audited in terms of investments have proven to be worthwhile and not in need of even minor policy refinements.(1) This kind of statement raises questions about the importance of policy refinement as a major stage in the project-management cycle.

While the problem is recognized as important, there is little evidence, at least on the surface, that a strategy or structured mechanism exists for implementing a policy-refinement process. Likewise, a recent Ford Foundation report, extensively reviewing development policy and project management, stresses that a major problem for development agencies (the World Bank in particular) is the need to successfully "evaluate and explore generic issues of importance for policy and practice."(2) The importance of the role of policy refinement in project development, then, is well recognized. What are some of the more critical elements of the policy-making process?

Perhaps the pattern most deeply rooted in the minds of policy makers in both developed and developing countries is what can be termed the ideal-rational model of policy making.(3) In this model, several stages are identified as the essential elements of policy making.

The first stage consists of organized efforts to clarify policy goals and eventually enumerate these in a manner useful for implementation. Second, an analysis is made of past and recent trends in order to compare goals with social realities. The third stage involves the preparation of a resource inventory and a "menu" of alternative policies: in short, an analysis of conditions prevailing in the policy area under consideration. Fourth, a cost-benefit analysis is performed in order to calculate the net benefit for each policy alternative. Finally, the identification and selection of policy alternatives is formulated and it is possible to state that policy refinement has been carried out. Additionally, an entire array of methodological tools are utilized to complete each of these stages successfully (for example, expert opinion, technological forecasting, statistical comparisons, regression and correlation analysis, extrapolation models, cost-benefit analysis, and computer simulation, to name only a few). This model, while appearing eminently rational, is perhaps too "ideal." Developing nations rarely have the luxury of proceeding through each of these stages, nor do they possess the considerable resource pool of technologies and techniques necessary to adequately complete each policy-making task. One major problem of this model is that it often suffers from information overload, providing the policy maker with too much information and data to absorb and utilize in the refinement process.

An alternative policy-making role model moves to the other end of the spectrum of complexity and is seriously challenging the rational model just described. Originally proposed by Lindblom (1963), variants of this approach have been suggested as being more feasible, especially for developing nations.(4) This approach can generally be termed the incremental change model. This approach recognizes the excessive complexities and costs of the rational model and attempts to take into account some of the major problems associated with policy making in general. In brief, the incremental change model asserts that the appropriate role of policy refinement in project development is to "make small, exploratory alterations in existing policy," rather than macro-policy revisions as suggested by the previous approach. Ongoing, small-scale fine-tuning of existing policy is lower in cost, has fewer unforeseen consequences, and is politically less risky. The suggestion here is that policy refinement is a necessity but that greater success will be achieved in impacting policy if basic policy principles are not tampered with.

The point in discussing these two models of policy making is to indicate that regardless of the variant (or subvariant) to which one subscribes, both stress the important role that policy refinement plays in project development. They diverge, however, in the specific tasks of developing guidelines for policy refinement, identifying basic problems in the effective utilization of evaluation results, and finally prescribing solutions to these problems. In fact, the experience of most project planners, managers, and evaluators in attempting to influence policy makers reveals that they adhere to a view of the policy-making process that falls somewhere in between these two models. This chapter will propose another, perhaps more appropriate, model of policy making that is more consistent with the experiences of actual project managers.

THE USE OF EVALUATION FOR POLICY REFINEMENT

Because most key personnel involved in actual project management and development agree on the important role policy making plays in the future of development projects, some critical guidelines deemed essential for initiating the policy refinement process can be readily identified. Typically, these guidelines have focused on either the role played by the evaluation team or that of the project manager or policy maker. To understand more thoroughly the role of refinement in project development, these guidelines can be used as the basis for identifying problems associated with the refinement process and for eventually suggesting some solutions.

The previous chapter noted that both formative and summative evaluation are necessities to evaluate development projects effectively. The next logical step is for the evaluation team to perform two related tasks. First, the evaluation staff meets with selected project personnel to discuss the evaluation report and to identify mutually agreeable areas of policy refinement. In other words, they meet to answer the question: What policy implications are contained in the evaluation report?

Second, in most cases, a task force is formed consisting of key individuals from the project staff, middle-level policy makers, funding personnel, researchers who were prominent in the evaluation process (the number of these individuals is normally kept to a minimum), selected members of the evaluation team and a key person who will have the responsibility for transmitting policy recommendations to the upper-level policy makers. The selection of this final member of the task force is of crucial importance, because once a judicious decision of policy refinement has been made, it must be transmitted in a manner that is sufficiently flexible to ensure that mutual agreement can be reached between the task force and the policy makers. In many cases, if no agreement can be reached, then two sets of policy recommendations can be drawn up and the process can begin again. The key word in this phase of policy refinement is "consensus." Once consensus has been reached between the task force and the upper-level policy makers, then the entire set of recommendations can be prepared for the final authority approval, often in the form of written decision memoranda requiring signatures complete with budget proposals.(5)

While this process represents a logical attempt to influence policy makers, the success or failure of this effort often depends on the role and behavior of individuals in a managerial and/or policy-making position. Either the project manager or a member of the management team associated with the policy-making level is chosen to fill the position of the key individual on the task force (as discussed earlier). Some important characteristics of persons in this level of management position must be understood if the policy refinement process is to be carried out effectively. While generalizations are risky, as a result of research in the field of project development some significant manager behavior patterns have emerged that allow us to attempt a profile of the role of the manager in the policy-refinement process. Because of the extreme pressures often placed on managers (especially in developing countries), they are extremely work conscious, keep a fast pace, and seldom have time for extended meetings and discussions. The work activity they are associated with is sometimes fragmented and characterized by brevity. Managers on development projects and at the policy level must be action-oriented and appreciate concrete suggestions, especially for the policy refinement area. One important observation is that managers who have the responsibility for transmitting policy recommendations prefer verbal input, received through face-to-face encounters with members of the evaluation team. Written reports are of course compiled for the record and for eventual implementation, but in the initial stages of policy refinement, verbal relays of information and recommendations are highly preferred.(6)

There are some obvious (yet often ignored) lessons and guidelines in this profile of members of the evaluation task force. First, because of the action-oriented nature of managers engaged in policy refinement, it is advisable to avoid using evaluation data as the sole source information for policy recommendations. Many managers on development projects indicate that they prefer information in small amounts, directed toward specific problems, and received in stages. Second, managers are likely to take a greater interest in promoting policy refinement to the extent that the issues identified by the evaluation team are of direct interest to themselves and their superiors. One implication of this for evaluators is to make an effort to transform an evaluation issue imposed on them by outside forces into one that will be of direct use to the manager with whom they will be dealing. Finally, since the manager is in an extremely political position (as the link between the evaluation team and the policy makers, who are often the manager's superiors), it is important that the evaluation team understand the political nature of evaluation from the outset and devise a strategy to cope with this phenomenon.

Increasingly, these general guidelines for policy refinement are being practiced by evaluation teams and others interested in refining policy for project management and development. Yet problems continue to emerge. While some of the problems that block effective policy refinement have already been suggested in the material discussed earlier, it may be instructive to outline them briefly before concluding with some suggestions for future efforts in policy refinement.

PROBLEMS IN EFFECTIVE UTILIZATION OF
EVALUATION RESULTS

It has become a commonplace complaint of project evaluators everywhere that despite their best efforts to conduct rigorous, method-
ologically sound, and penetrating studies, the policy recommendations
that emerge from these labors are either totally ignored or distorted
for political purposes. Even when guidelines such as those just suggested
are followed to the letter, obstacles to influencing policy making still
seem to emerge. Depending upon one's point of view, the blame for this
disjunction between policy and evaluation is either with the policy-
making level itself or the evaluation team. A brief review of these two
points of view may highlight some of the problems inherent in the
policy-refinement process.

From the evaluation team's perspective, policy makers simply place
too many hurdles in the way of the effective transmission of evaluation
results to policy refinement. One major problem often voiced is that
policy makers do not take the time necessary to digest evaluation
information and reach appropriate conclusions suitable for policy refinement. They are in too much of a rush to get on with the next
project to worry about the problems of the previous project. Furthermore, they are ruled too much by political pressures, are too sensitive
on this issue, and are reluctant to take a policy-refinement position
that might damage their political standing with superiors. The bureaucratic nature of the policy-making level (whether it is located in a
complex private organization or a governmental agency) represents
another problem area for evaluators. There are often too many channels
to pursue to reach the level of policy making that will assure genuine
policy refinement. Finally, individuals at the policy-making level are
unfamiliar with the scientific method of project evaluation and therefore are unable to appreciate fully the soundness of the data provided
them for policy refinement.

Policy makers themselves, of course, see the problem differently.
In their view, the evaluation team (and particularly the individual or
individuals responsible for communicating evaluation data to the policy
level) is unable to communicate effectively with policy makers. Their
respective roles and styles are different, and from the policy perspective the evaluation team should take on the responsibility of effecting a
role change. On another level, it is precisely the methodological fetish
that irritates policy makers and encourages them to put aside evaluation data. Too much attention is paid to methodology and too little to
providing information in a useful manner. Related to this criticism is
one directed at the data itself. One common complaint of policy makers
is that evaluation data often answer the wrong questions.   The
fascination with methodology results in the generation of data that are
not high on the priority list for policy refinement. Perhaps the most
strongly voiced criticism of all is that evaluation results overemphasize
the negative aspects of a project rather than offering information on
the success achieved in each stage of the project cycle. Because of the

stress on negative criticism, the strengths of a project are not identified and may not be replicated in future projects.

This list of problems in effecting policy refinement is not exhaustive but tends to be rather typical. Clearly, neither the evaluators nor the policy makers are totally justified in placing the responsibility for lack of evaluation utilization on each other. The problems, however, are real, and any effort to devise a more efficient policy refinement strategy must require change and adaptation from both groups of individuals. It is this difficult and complex question that will now be explored. While the suggestions that follow are not empirically verified, they represent the accumulation of experience and data over several years and in the context of a variety of development projects. By viewing the project development cycle in an integrated manner through the IPPMC, some insight into this question has possibly been gained and is offered now for consideration and perhaps for experimentation.

SUGGESTIONS FOR A POLICY REFINEMENT STRATEGY

The previous sections of this chapter explored the process of policy refinement, including some more specific guidelines, and problems associated with the use of evaluation data by policy makers. Out of all this, one central observation can be made: There is a direct relationship between the policy-refinement process, the behavior of both evaluation teams and policy makers, and, as shall be suggested, the training of project managers and policy specialists. Earlier in this chapter it was suggested that neither the ideal-rational model nor the incremental change model of policy refinement was totally satisfactory as a realistic alternative for most developing nations. The former may be too rigid and complicated to be of much utility for a nation undergoing rapid change, and the latter may be too conservative.

While the incremental change model appears to be more useful as a policy-refinement method, an underlying assumption is that previous policies were sufficiently sound as to require only minimal fine tuning. For many developing nations, however, there may be a need for a more radical departure from existing policy, and the risks involved in this approach may be warranted, given certain critical problems. The energy crisis, for example, has forced developing and developed nations alike to seriously question existing energy policies and the projects associated with them. In the area of raw materials and food, many nations are also facing challenging tasks that cannot be sufficiently carried out under policies generated during the past two decades. In these and similar areas, the incremental change approach to policy refinement would be counterproductive.

An alternative approach might be called the policy refinement and prescriptive model (PRPM). This model deviates from the ideal-rational model in being more flexible and less complex, and it deviates from the incremental change model in allowing policy refiners and evaluators to suggest fairly radical policy changes. The key to this approach is a continual process of goal and objective clarification (represented in the IPPMC for every task of the project management cycle as a feedback loop). Feedback from every task of the cycle is essential to provide needed data for evaluators, but unless this information is translated into a clarification of policy goals and objectives that can then be translated into prescriptive policy recommendations, the refinement process will be stalled either during the cycle or in the final evaluation.

A second component of the policy refinement and prescriptive model is the continuous and judicious design of preferred alternative policies. These policy alternatives can depart as widely as possible from original policies, but precisely because they are alternatives (and not hard-and-fast recommendations), they can be rejected in whole or in part without presenting evaluators or policy makers with an either/or situation.

Finally, this model suggests a mix between theory and experience; between objective data and subjective perceptions. It has been the experience of many project managers that subjective data can also be a valuable source of information for the policy maker seeking to refine policy. Since conventional evaluation data are empirically based, this experimental dimension is ignored. An ongoing effort to summarize the experience of project personnel and managers in a manner that allows this information to be presented to policy makers will augment and enrich the more conventional evaluation report. Evaluators and policy makers alike should not be hesitant to consider extrarational suggestions for policy refinement. In fact, there is some evidence to suggest they may welcome this kind of input (similar to the process of "brainstorming" as a method of problem solving in the committee structure).

The PRPM model does not mean that other methods of policy refinement be excluded (cost-benefit analysis, for example), but rather that the process be characterized by its flexibility, its acceptance of a wide range of policy alternatives, and, most important, its willingness to prescribe policy changes.

How is such a model operationalized? How are the many obstacles to policy refinement outlined in the previous section of this chapter overcome? There are no magic solutions to these issues. However, the perspective of the PRPM policy refinement process does allow some tentative judgments to be made. A major weakness in the evaluator-policy maker link is that each group of actors utilizes different criteria in identifying overall policy goals and objectives. The evaluation team must take this factor into account from the beginning and attempt to understand the constellation of criteria and construct the evaluation study accordingly. Again, an ongoing effort to clarify policy goals and objectives will assist enormously in solving this problem. Many studies indicate that policy makers rely much more on unconventional data than on typical written reports (or statistically verified evaluation studies). Both the evaluation team and the policy makers can make great use of verbal, face-to-face encounters; brainstorming sessions; subjective suggestions for policy refinement; and so on. Again, from the outset, ample time for unscheduled meetings should be built into the feedback and refinement cycle. Perhaps the most important suggestion is that the evaluation team build into its structure, from the beginning, key persons from among the agencies likely to create barriers to policy refinement. The political character of policy making can be utilized effectively if the evaluation team draws political supporters into their team in the early stages of formative evaluation. If policy alternatives are clearly defined from the outset, and policy goals and objectives undergo continuous clarification, the policy refinement process will proceed in a more effective and positive manner.

Finally, there are problems associated with policy makers themselves, the perspective they have on projects and project management, and the educational and training experiences they have encountered. The use of simulation models has become increasingly popular as a means to provide policy makers with a training experience designed to sharpen their analytical and decision-making skills. Apart from training project managers, the PPIPM curriculum and the IPPMC model can also be utilized as training materials for policy makers. The case histories and the use of the cycle provide the policy maker with an immersion in actual project management experiences from which many important policy-related questions can be raised. Policy refinement can thus be enhanced through a consciousness-raising process on the part of the policy makers.

CONCLUSION

The observations and suggestions contained in this chapter should be regarded as preliminary, raising more questions than are answered. What is important, however, is that these questions are raised in the context of the actual experiences of development projects. The case histories associated with the PPIPM project provide a valuable data base for discussing the issue of policy refinement; the IPPMC model illustrates the complexity of the refinement process. It is highly likely that projects will continue to be the cornerstone upon which development policies are implemented. The projects themselves, however, are only as good as the policies that guide their identification, selection, approval, and implementation. The cyclical relationships within projects and between projects, then, are linked together by policy. In this sense, it is hoped that continued research into the policy-refinement process will indeed result in viewing refinement as both an end and a beginning.(7)

NOTES

(1) W.C. Baum, "The World Bank Project Cycle," Finance and Development (December 1978).

(2) The Ford Foundation, Report on the External Advisory Panel on Education (Washington, D.C.: The Ford Foundation, 1978).

(3) For a more complete and detailed discussion of these models, see R.E. Pugh, Evaluation of Policy Simulation Models (Washington, D.C.: Information Resources Press, 1977); and Y. Dror, Ventures in Policy Sciences (New York: American Elsevier, 1971).

(4) R.E. Pugh, Evaluation of Policy Simulation Models (Washington, D.C.: Information Resources Press, 1977); and J. Rothman, Planning and Organization for Social Change (New York: Columbia University Press, 1974).

(5) This process has been summarized in Larry Polivka and Eric Steg, "Program Evaluation and Policy Development," Evaluation Quarterly 2, no. 4 (November 1978).

(6) Gary B. Cox, "Managerial Style: Implications for the Utilization of Program Evaluation Information," Evaluation Quarterly 1, no. 3 (August 1977); J. David Hawkins, Roger A. Roffman, and Philip Osborne, "Decision-Makers Judgments," Evaluation Quarterly 2, no. 3 (August 1978).

(7) The problems enumerated in this discussion are a summary of those that have emerged in the case histories prepared during the course of the PPIPM project and represent critical areas for future research.

SELECTED BIBLIOGRAPHY

Dror, Y. Ventures in Policy Sciences. New York: American Elsevier, 1971.

Patton, M.Q. In Search of Impact: An Analysis of the Utilization of Federal Evaluation Research. Minneapolis: University of Minnesota Center for Social Research, 1975.

Pugh, R.E. Evaluation of Policy Simulation Models. Washington, D.C.: Information Resources Press, 1977.

Rothman, J. Planning and Organization for Social Change. New York: Columbia University Press, 1974.

Phase 5 – Overview: Projects and Policy

13 A Policy View of the Project Cycle

A major consequence of looking at development projects from the framework of the integrated and comprehensive project management cycle is the realization that responsibility for project success or failure spills over from the individual traditionally identified as the project manager and is shared by a number of people and entities, including planners, evaluators, the central budget authority, and so on. Perhaps more important, not only is the project manager a link in the chain, but the entire chain exists within a context, an administrative and political environment, defined and shaped by a number of policies. Some of these policies are made specifically for projects. Others are made primarily for other purposes but with frequently unintended impacts on projects. The most competent project managers are doomed to failure if they operate within a policy context that renders them ineffective.

Relatively little has been written on this overall policy context as it affects projects. This chapter will focus on significant factors of policy and their influence on decisions about projects.

We will define "policy" here as a goal made definite by the adopted prescription of a course of action to guide present and future decision making in the pursuit thereof. The emphasis is on adoption and pursuit – a conscious acceptance of a cause for action and an attempt to realize it. This view of policy is an ex ante one – and, as a result, an adopted course of action may not achieve the goal desired. It may not do so even if the prescribed course of action is efficiently pursued if this course is, in fact, inadequate for the purpose. It is certainly unlikely to do so if actual implementation is inefficient, untimely, or ineffective.

FACTORS IN AN OVERALL POLICY FOR
DEVELOPMENT PROJECTS

The complex processes according to which projects are identified, approved, implemented, and evaluated requires the development and use of social, economic, and governmental institutions. Within this framework, a considerable number of individuals – the links in the chain – can work in a coordinated way. This indicates the desirability of an "overall policy for ensuring effective projects," not so much to control and direct the entire range of institutions, but to recognize, develop, and utilize them to ensure effective projects.

Such an overall policy context would include the following factors:
1. The articulated acceptance of the goal of development projects.
2. The perceived role of a variety of social and economic institutions that are "given" in that environment.
3. The designation of a government agency to systematically review project development and implementation in its operating contexts.
4. The agency's function within a planning framework to generate a maximum number of project ideas, and then to establish mechanisms responsive to the best ideas.
5. The agency's function to monitor and effectively modify those policies that bear directly on project implementation.

There are several alternative approaches to each of these areas, and various national governments create differing policy contexts for projects, depending on which alternatives are taken. The next sections will take a closer look at these approaches.

THE ARTICULATION OF GOALS

Development projects and national plans are necessarily embodiments of a goal or a set of goals. Results achieved by independent instruments must be measured against some standard of acceptability.

In the first case, where do the goals come from? In the second case, where does the standard of acceptability arise? Possible sources include: 1) the approval of citizens via direct vote, issue by issue. This is possible only for a few important issues or within a small governmental unit. 2) The approval of a legislative body presumed to be representative of citizens, either because it is elected by them or is otherwise selected. Here, the "representativeness" of the unit on specific issues is always open to question. 3) The approval of a strong executive (an individual, or a strongly structured group of individuals). This may occur even with direct vote of a legislative body if the executive is sufficiently charismatic, adequately attuned to citizen interests, or possessing – and willing to use – informal and formal instruments of power. 4) The approval of the bureaucracy. In possession of the instruments of government power, they may operate through a legislative or an executive – indeed, they may utilize legislative/executive forms masking the bureaucratic reality. 5) Tacit acceptance of international

values imposed by prestigious individuals or agencies whose "suggestions" carry weight because they are backed by, on one extreme,
scientific knowledge and high moral purposes, or, on the other extreme,
by economic and military power.

This way of looking at goals – or at standards of acceptability –
focuses upon who sets them. In every case, they may be faulty (for
example, citizens can be ignorant of consequences, legislators may be
venal as well as ignorant, executives or dictators may pursue power for
their own ends, bureaucrats may protect their own fiefdoms, and
international agencies may protect existing national interests, etc.).
Or, in every case, they may work well (for example, citizens may
intelligently pursue their own interests with full knowledge of consequences, legislators may be public-spirited and selfless, executives or
dictators may intelligently assess and selflessly pursue the interests of
citizens generally, bureaucrats may be perceptive and expert, and
international agencies may exhibit high moral purpose). In any case,
they will need to count the costs of opposition to their actions.

Another way of looking at goals – or at standards of acceptability –
would focus on the goals or the standards themselves. In this view, the
emphasis is not on who makes the value decisions but on the goals or
standards themselves upon which the decisions are based.

In this view, the relevant questions relate not to "who" is in favor or
"who" is opposed, but what is intended and what will result, evaluated in
terms of a prior goal or standard. Resting upon this alternate view is
the widely used practice of striving for maximum net satisfaction of
citizens through a refined cost-benefit calculation. In this view, different combinations of government agencies and individuals exist from
country to country to provide this calculation and to develop and
administer the resulting plans, policies, programs, and projects.

In principle, this view – subject only to the availability of adequate
theory and data and time to apply them – would provide the "best"
results – a society in which the total of citizen satisfactions would be
maximized. Action taken not in consonance with its conclusions would
be either uninformed or selfish.

This view is most attractive to the disinterested professional
planners or administrators (that is, the "technocrats") and to those
international bodies seeking maximum development of the less developed countries per unit of investment. Indeed, these groups tend to view
actions taken by citizens, legislators, executives, and bureaucrats that
are not consistent with their goals as ignorant, "political," or venal.

It is clear, however, that (with present theory, data, and available
time), cost-benefit analyses leading to maximum net satisfactions
cannot always be accomplished to indicate the best action. Theory is
frequently inadequate, data are incomplete, and time is short. Yet
someone must choose – citizens, legislators, executives, or bureaucrats.
And they can choose, even if the information is much less definitive.
Based on as much information as can be brought to bear outlining the
consequences of alternative courses of action, they can choose the
course that, on balance, might seem most likely to benefit most
citizens.

Even when data indicate an action will give maximum satisfaction to the community, some groups, such as executives deprived of power by a decision, may want to forestall or modify the action. If the calculations of net satisfactions are complete, accurate, and clearly presented, those wishing to forestall an action will have difficulty in getting support for a move which could be disadvantageous to society as a whole. Projects, whether public or private, will serve to benefit society to the degree that decisions are made either precisely to maximize net satisfactions, or, if that is impossible, to the degree that more preferred actions can be identified, or, if neither of these is possible, to the extent that actions are taken by individuals and institutions citizens perceive as acting in their interests.

THE PERCEIVED ROLE OF OTHER SOCIOECONOMIC INSTITUTIONS

Individual countries pursue distinctly different policies regarding the uses of a wide range of nongovernmental institutions and instruments (for example, the family and tribe, religious institutions, schools, nonprofit associations of all kinds, business enterprises, international institutions) operating within both formal and informal frameworks.

In some countries, these instruments are seen as traditional defenders of a status quo defining an appropriate culture and way of life historically appropriate to the environment – even though incomes may be low and stagnant and levels of education and health well below those available elsewhere. Here, government itself is a traditional instrument as one with the others in an integrated, stable society. In this situation, governments do very little national planning in a systematic and formalized sense.

In other countries, the same instruments are seen as traditional defenders of a status quo that insist instead upon an inappropriate culture and way of life denying modernization and development – thereby keeping incomes low and stagnant and levels of education and health well below those available elsewhere. In this situation, government becomes a modernizing instrument designed to break the traditional power of the nongovernment institutions. Some governments accomplish this by simply replacing those nongovernmental instruments by governmental ones. Others work cooperatively with the nongovernmental agencies to change their modes of operation or change the environments in which they operate via government action. Because nongovernmental agencies are seen as inadequate unless they are explicitly guided, government consciously plans the development of nongovernmental and control mechanisms for them. In this situation, government plans for society as well as government in society.

In still other countries, the nongovernmental instruments are seen as dynamic agencies that have led – and are leading – society to the discovery and use of new technologies upon the basis of which incomes, along with levels of education and health, are rising. In this situation, government is seen as a cooperating agency maintaining the necessary

framework for the continued effective activities of the nongovernmental units. The government believes that the free responses of
individuals and nongovernmental units cooperating with existing government units within the existing framework (including the price-market
mechanism and a system of government-sponsored rules, regulations,
etc.) will yield generally acceptable results to be forecasted but not
planned, to be reacted to ex post, but not postulated ex ante. Planning
in these countries will be 1) to develop and maintain a set of
institutions, both governmental and private, that will yield satisfactory
results without detailed, conscious, quantitative planning, and 2) to
operate effectively and efficiently desired governmental units. Planning
is not for society, but for government as an institution in society. In
such a situation, most projects will be initiated, approved, and implemented by private agencies and existing governmental units within an
accepted framework without reference to an overall plan. Developed
countries with sophisticated price-market mechanisms tend to operate
in this way.

Finally, in still other countries, while the nongovernmental instruments continue to be seen as dynamic leaders toward positive change,
they are also seen as exhibiting specific defects (including, for example,
unemployment, an unsatisfactory distribution of income, spoilage of the
environment) which must be corrected by governmental actions. Again,
some governments will replace nongovernmental instruments with governmental ones while others will change the modes of operation or the
environments of nongovernmental units. In this situation – and many
developing countries fall into this type – government once again sees
the need of developing both the private sectors and the instruments by
which these sectors are controlled, if not taken over. It is, as in the
second situation described earlier, planning for society, as well as for
government in society.

No judgment is made here concerning which policy is "correct."
Each country will base its decision upon knowledge of its situation,
aspirations, and perceived and anticipated effectiveness of both nongovernmental and governmental instruments. Obviously, the nature,
number and diversity of sources of projects identified will be related to
the policy chosen.

THE DESIGNATION OF A CENTRAL REVIEW AGENCY

The embodiment of a nation's efforts to ensure maximum utilization of
its institutions and resources for effective projects must be the
designation of an agency of government which, within larger existing
socioeconomic-political frameworks, would systematically review the
process of project development and implementation, with a view toward
suggesting governmental actions designed to improve them.   These
governmental actions would, to the extent possible, lead to modifications in the socioeconomic framework for both public and private
projects or directly impact upon the organization and procedures of
government itself.

The agency selected for this task should be one that has broad interests covering society, the economy, and government, has regular and systematic access to the chief executive, is interested in development, and has a systematic position on this development. In many countries, the central planning agency best meets these requirements. In other countries, it may be the central budget agency, the controllers, or a central organization and methods unit. The agency will almost certainly be a staff, not a line, agency.

This is not to say that the identified agency should assume operating responsibility or even control of all development projects, though this in fact turns out to be the case in a few developing countries. But the intent is to encourage, stimulate, and coordinate projects – not to stifle them.

In fact, the agency should not be so burdened with active project development and implementation responsibilities of its own that it cannot look broadly at the much larger number of projects potentially developed and implemented by others. The extent of a government's stance toward decentralization affects this capability.

At one extreme, all – or a very large proportion – of decisions can be made and actions monitored "at the Center," at the level of the chief executive and the staff agencies. At the other extreme, decisions can be made and actions monitored on a functionally-decentralized basis (to separate ministries or agencies responsible for particular sorts of activities, such as agriculture, defense, and so forth), or on a geographically-decentralized basis (to identified provinces, cities, etc.), or simultaneously on both bases (for example, to a ministry of agriculture operating through provincial offices). This may be only decentralization of implementing activities according to centralized rules by a centrally controlled bureaucracy (for example, by a unitary government) or may include decentralization of law-making and action-taking authority in specific fields to local decision makers (for example, by a federal government).

Obviously, the degree and nature of decentralization has a dramatic impact upon the ways in which projects are initiated, evaluated, selected, and implemented. The more highly centralized the system, the greater the power of – and the pressures on – central executive institutions as operating institutions. The less centralized the system, the more disbursed become both power and initiative and the more important are the instruments – both governmental and nongovernmental – of overall coordination.

THE GENERATION OF PROJECTS WITHIN A PLANNING FRAMEWORK

The central planning agency or its equivalent responsible for the overall policy to ensure effective project management must see to it that a maximum number of project ideas from public and private sectors are identified and responded to in such a fashion that the most useful are considered, properly planned, implemented, and evaluated.

This means that the agency would wish to ensure that a sufficient number of agencies and individuals representing all functional and geographical areas of society were alert to project opportunities for which, at each stage of the project cycle, there was adequate technical, organizational, financial, and personnel support.

This also means that, having solicited an adequate number of project ideas, the agency would be able to provide mechanisms that would respond in such a way that the less useful project ideas are discarded in time and the more useful ones brought to successful implementation. This implies, in other words, a planning framework, whether for government as it responds to society, or for society.

It is unfortunate that on this point most of the literature – either explicitly or implicitly – views the sequence as planning → policies → programs → projects. In this view, goals are set and plans calculated to allow their achievement. In light of these plans, policies are formulated, programs are conceived, and projects are initiated. This is a top-down process. Rationality is to be achieved by moving from goals through ever more operationally specific activities until the actual "building blocks" – the projects – are implemented.

But when planning is introduced into the real world – as it must be – the sequencing will be entirely different. A great variety of public and private projects will exist at one stage or another, some isolated and others more or less explicitly encompassed into programs which, in turn, may or may not be responsive to articulated policies, and – since planning is only beginning – certainly not in response to a prior plan. In this situation, planning must begin with "what is" – the projects – and try to rationalize them by assembling related projects into programs implying acceptable policies which can – with modifications that are feasible in the situation – be termed a plan. This is a bottom-up process.

With the passage of time, the actual cluster of plans, policies, programs, and projects that come to exist is likely to reflect both processes – the ex ante intentions of the central planners with capacities to specify policies, programs, and projects limited by knowledge, time, and capacity to control other institutions, and the ex post consequences of policies programs, and projects developed by other institutions subject only to such restrictions as a planning process can with difficulty impose upon them. Plans will be both top-down and bottom-up.

If the planning process is sufficiently strong and rigid to forbid new, nonplanned activities not explicitly approved, everything depends upon the values, knowledge, and available time of the planners. This has many implications. Since planners' time is limited, projects tend to be large to make best use of it. Since wide knowledge implies generalizations, imperfect application to specific situations would seem likely and difficult-to-understand minorities, regions, and activities may frequently be ignored. Private-sector projects would be fewer in number. Since implementors are often regarded as doing what the plan requires rather than what they are doing or wish to do, wide gaps between plan and implementation would seem likely to appear. Since planners tend to be heavily influenced by economists and engineers, they are likely to have high-technology, high-output objectives, and so on.

On the other hand, if the planning process is so weak that it must accept the activities of others, it is simply irrelevant. Project efficiency and effectiveness depend wholly on the appropriateness of the framework within which governmental and nongovernmental instruments take their independent (but interdependent) actions. Since this framework is likely to be weak in less developed countries, public and private projects may be poorly identified and badly implemented.

In either case, an "overall policy for ensuring effective projects" would seemingly strive for a planning policy strong enough to require a project environment – and projects from any sector – that meets overall requirements of societal effectiveness but is sufficiently disbursed and decentralized to take advantage of all of the ideas, initiatives, and capacities available to that society. Such a planning policy would strive to make best use of limited financial and physical resources by enlisting support of human and institutional resources in as wide a range as possible.

THE MONITORING OF POLICY EFFECTS ON PROJECT IMPLEMENTATION

The actual success of project implementation and completion depends upon the establishment of an appropriate organizational structure and set of operating procedures for acquiring and utilizing the needed financial resources, personnel resources, technology resources, and often international resources. Because project demands vary and are often unique to particular situations, this has led to a wide variety of organizational responses and numerous "special" procedures not normally evident in ongoing governmental or private organizations.

Thus, all too often, national policy, or the lack of it, can lead to a setting for project organization and operation that is one of two extremes: a policy so rigid that the lack of flexibility stifles project implementation, or a policy so pliant that a proliferation of structures and exceptions to procedures and standard policies causes dangerous entanglements.

In the first instance, prevailing policies might require that all government projects be embraced within existing governmental or bureaucratic forms, subject to the same procedures for personnel, budget releases, and so on, that are in force within government or corporate agencies. Such a policy might result from desires to regularize and hence simplify overall government management and to treat all government organizations and personnel "fairly" in the same way. But, as we have seen, projects involve new activities. Forcing new activities into old forms and old routines may be inappropriate to the achievement of project objectives.

The other extreme is where a laissez-faire, case-to-case approach is taken to project organization and procedures for acquisition of personnel and finance resources. Individual projects are encouraged to set up structures and procedures as they see fit, either for project expediency or for their own convenience. The result is often the creation of many "special" groups and teams with particularly fast access to funds, to personnel they can pay well, and to exceptions from operating procedures. The existence of these special groups encourages others to mold themselves similarly, so that every time a special project, problem, or activity arises, a new committee, agency, or bureau is set up with special privileges. Instead of reorganizing the agencies originally responsible, they are left to do routine day-to-day tasks, and their competent people are often siphoned off to projects from which new projects in turn are drawn if tasks are not well performed. In this situation, the government tends to lose control of a system that becomes increasingly untidy and without apparent purpose.

The central agency monitoring project implementation should monitor the formation of organizational structures and the introduction of special procedures for project purposes in such a manner as to avoid either of these two extremes. It would be unrealistic, given the unique character of projects, for national policy to uniformly dictate a special structure and mode of resource acquisition and use for all projects. It is possible, however, to articulate certain guidelines and criteria for the governance of project organization.

In the first place, we must state the obvious: The organization must be effective in achieving project goals and results. It is, after all, only the means to an end. For this reason, whatever exceptions or deviations from regulations and operating procedures are necessary to achieve its objectives should be granted provided only that they do not unduly lower outputs elsewhere by fragmenting authority. The crucial issue, of course, is who grants the exception. Obviously, each project staff itself cannot be left to devise its own rules and exceptions, or the resulting excesses and abuses of "special groups" will multiply. It is, therefore, the role of those responsible for the overall policy for ensuring effective projects, discussed earlier as often being the central planning agency, to decide the exceptions necessary to project success and those that need not be given in the interests of project control. The central formulation group can thus maintain the balance between project requirements and standard procedures and policies which continue in force on other agencies and groups.

Second, it is essential that policy ensures the clear definition of vertical and horizontal relationships for projects. The specification of vertical relationships should indicate to which agency – or agencies – the project is responsible and in what way. It should also indicate what kind of reporting is required. Projects that are responsible on the same matters to two or more different agencies with different purposes or expectations are clearly in difficulty. On the other hand, nothing leads to project excesses more quickly than a situation in which the project is accountable to no one. The specification of horizontal relationships should indicate the appropriate techniques – whether these techniques involve formal contracts, coordinating committees, arms-length market transactions, or informal contacts – by which the project acquires inputs (for example, personnel, special services, construction work) or provides outputs to related government units or by which others can benefit from project experience.

Finally, because projects are by definition time-bound, policy must see to it that project organizations do not lose sight of their temporary character. Organizations, like organisms, manifest strong instincts of self-preservation and survival at all costs, even after their usefulness is gone. Thus, clearly defined lifespans and project organization ending dates should be insisted upon by the policy group, not only to keep once-useful teams from becoming creaky and useless bureaucracies, but also to keep project management conscious of the ultimate need to re-channel project resources which may need to be retained.

This does not mean that, in all circumstances, the project organization will cease to exist once the project is completed. Indeed, in many instances the organization created to undertake the construction or establishment of a new institution will continue to live to operate it. (Irrigation authorities, for example, frequently first establish, and then operate, the project.) The shift from establishment to operations, however, should be seen as a distinct one requiring different staffing patterns and managerial techniques.

Formal contracts for projects or, more often, for specific aspects or parts of a project are widely used. Whether the project or subproject is to be done by a private consulting firm, a university research department, another government unit, or even a single individual, a written agreement is often drawn up specifying the outputs promised, the time frame within which the outputs will be delivered, the financial, capital, and human resources required, and often the penalties accompanying noncompliance. Agreement to these specifics is signed by the contracting and contracted parties, and very often becomes a typical building block of a major project. It builds in the methods and procedures and exceptions it requires for success; it defines communication, accountability and control to the point of establishing sanctions; and it is by definition time-bound and temporary. Even in the use of contracts, however, the central agency responsible for projects should establish guidelines to decide, for example, with whom government projects may enter into contracts (other government agencies, private groups), and under what conditions such contracts can be drawn up (competitive bidding, penalty, provision, qualifications on the use of foreign aid or expertise).

In any case, the responsible central agency must create the policy context within which an adequate, but not excessively indulgent, response can be given to several problem areas in public and private project implementation. These problem areas often have to do with policy effects on procedures relative to the acquisition and use of four types of resources required by projects: financial, human, technology, and external or foreign. For this reason, the following major sections deal with each of these four resources, and the specific potential bottlenecks that a central review agency should be alerted to.

POLICIES ON FINANCIAL RESOURCES

Funds in adequate amounts for appropriate purposes must be available in a timely fashion if projects are to be efficiently and effectively implemented. This first of all requires overall policies that ensure the aggregate availability of funds – a tax structure that dependably yields revenues, domestic savings, and investment institutions that encourage savings and make them available to projects, the maintenance of institutions and practices that encourage grants and loans from abroad, and so on. The absence of successful policies of this type will simply abort projects at every stage – and the world is littered with the carcasses (sometimes no more than idea papers, sometimes impressive building shells) of projects that become the victims of poor funding policies.

Budgeting

Assuming that funds can be generated in the aggregate, they must still be allocated and made available to specific projects. This is done by the budget process – the procedures used to decide which activities are to get how much money for what specific purposes and when. Individual projects are subject to the financial constraints of this fundamental process and government decision making.

Financial constraints must be faced very early in the project cycle. If the project is of significant size, activities involved in its formulation and design – immediately following identification – may require a substantial commitment of the time of personnel and of overhead items in existing agencies, or the hiring of new specialized individuals or consulting firms as needed. In either case, funds will need to have been budgeted in advance of the need for project design to cover the costs of personnel and other items in existing agencies or to allow the hiring of new personnel or consulting firms. Budget policies will need to approve sums for this purpose in advance – or to allow additional budget allocations flexibly as the necessity arises. Furthermore, budget policies will influence which identified projects will proceed to formulation and design by determining where the funds for these purposes will be allocated. Allocations of formulation and design funds to agencies interested in industry but not in agriculture, or to central, urban-centered units rather than to provincial, rural-centered units, will bias projects actually formulated toward the industrial/urban sector rather than the agricultural/rural area.

After the project is formulated and designed, its feasibility and its claims to resources must be established. This is done through a budget process through which funds for the project are requested. At this point, a number of problems – and related policies – appear. They include the following: 1) Shall the total cost of the project be considered as a capital cost to be considered in the capital budget? Or should only the purchases of capital items (for example, buildings, machinery, equipment) be considered in the capital budget, with purchases of other items (such as labor, supplies) considered in the recurring budget? If the former, the entire cost is likely to be approved for expenditure over the entire project life. If the latter, necessary funds will be available only subject to the vicissitudes of an annual budget. 2) Shall project management be approved to seek grants or loans to apply against project needs prior to a budget action – or must they await budget approval before seeking such funds or having others do so? If the former, the project will look less desirable since it will seem to be claiming larger, governmentally-provided funds than might prove to be the case and the project may be delayed by subsequent grant or loan negotiations. 3) Shall the budget be submitted on a line-item basis inviting examination with a view focusing on inputs and costs, or on a program basis inviting examination with a view focusing on outputs and benefits? Shall the budget be submitted based on an ad hoc pleas of project supporters or based on a plan demonstrating its relative superiority in terms of net benefits per unit of cost over alternative activities? Clearly, the program emphasis based on a plan is superior for the project (unless it has very strong political support). 4) If the project generates revenues, do these revenues accrue to general government or can they be retained in the project? Clearly, the latter provides added project flexibility. 5) To what extent are citizens – or legislators on behalf of citizens – able to make inputs into budget making and review? What standards. govern the extent to which they can delay, force modifications, or stop specific projects? To the degree to which minorities have procedural or statutory powers to do so, uncertainty and delays are likely.

After project claims to resources are established and the budget approved, there are problems – and related policies – regarding the administration of that budget. They include the following: 1) Is budget approval an authorization to expend funds in accordance therewith or must a separate administrative transaction "release" the funds? (This separate step is used in situations where budget "approvals" frequently exceed cash flows and all cannot be accommodated.) The latter opens the door to costly uncertainty and delays for time-sensitive projects. 2) Is there a preaudit of approved budget expenditures (that is, must all vouchers be individually approved before payments are made), or only a postaudit of such expenditures (that is, a simple accounting for such expenditures after payment has been made)? If the former, bureaucratic delays are again almost inevitable for time-sensitive projects. 3) If budget changes are required (to shift funds from one approved expenditure line to another, to shift funds from one budget period to the next, or to add funds marginally as may be required), are the procedures simple and quick? If they are not, time-sensitive projects, which are by definition operating in new, uncertain areas, are likely to be differentially disadvantaged.

Making Payments

Very closely related to budget procedures are procedures related to the actual disbursement of funds. Problems – and related policies – at this point include the following: 1) Are procedures for the acquisition of equipment, supplies, or contractual services complex and time-consuming – and do they result in the quality and dependability of inputs desired or required? Where complex contracts are required, is legal help promptly and helpfully available? Poor policies leading to poor procedures can mean both poor project quality and delays. 2) Do the procedures whereby vouchers covering goods and services purchased are approved for payment and cash disbursed yield prompt payment to vendors? In part, this relates to the preaudit procedure indicated earlier. But even in the absence of a preaudit, clumsy, overly legalistic, or bureaucratically-excessive procedures open the way for delays, legal tangles, angry vendors whose capacity to operate efficiently is reduced, and outright corruption. This is a major source of project delay and high costs. 3) Are cash flows maintained to allow prompt payments when due? Any government or corporation will receive cash unevenly over the year and may – in the absence of careful planning for short-term borrowing to meet seasonal needs – be faced with the necessity of delaying payments and receiving deliveries of necessary inputs.

This section of "making payments" – and the preceding paragraph dealing with budget administration – both emphasize the negative consequences of inflexible procedures and strongly suggest more flexibility. Yet it must be admitted that these inflexible procedures do put limits on overenthusiastic, poorly organized, or even corrupt project management by subjecting it to bureaucratic discipline. The question is, "Is the cure worse than the disease?" Fortunately, that question does not have to be answered. A better cure is available. It involves responsible budgeting to output-oriented activities with prompt reporting of financial and output results to detect – and allow removal of – faulty management.

Accounting and Auditing

Problems – and related policies – here include the following: 1) Is the accounting system set up to report expenditures promptly by budget authorization categories so that a preaudit is unnecessary, so that project management can anticipate and promptly request necessary budget changes, and so that financial data are routinely available for project reporting and central purposes? If it is not, expensive and time-consuming "back-up" (duplicative) accounting systems will be required both in the preaudit agency and in the project itself. 2) Are audits mechanically focused on detailed examination of adherence to budget categories – with substantial penalties to managers for exceeding detailed authorizations? (This is particularly important if budgets are of a detailed, line-item sort, and if accounting data are late and possibly inadequate.) Or are the audits focused on outputs and evaluation of whether or not managerial uses of funds were, in terms of these outputs, appropriate? Audits that threaten managers (who have had inadequate accounting data) with substantial penalties for small deviations in actual budgeted expenditures, ignoring effective performance, produce new managers who will be formal, pedantic, budgetarily precise − and ineffective in obtaining project goals. 3) If the budget − and audit − agency requires performance reports (and it should!), is it clear what is required, and can the necessary information be routinely produced? If not, inordinate delays, expense, and a lack of cooperation of budget and audit authorities with the project can be predicted.

Relationship to Planning

The relationship between planning and budgeting (as supported by the finance system and the accountants and auditors) is a complex one, rife with possibilities for misunderstandings and inefficiencies. Problems − and related policies − include the following: 1) Planning agencies frequently insist on "approving" activities separate from and prior to budget approvals allocating the necessary funds, rather than developing the procedures and criteria with the budget agency according to which that agency would make decisions appropriate to the plan. This dual practice can give rise to disagreements and delays − and certainly increased expenses. (In some countries, the planning agency has simply taken over the capital budget, which is seen as the development budget. This avoids duplication but raises a serious problem of coordinating the capital and recurrent budgets.) 2) Planning agencies frequently insist on self-auditing of project performance rather than focusing on improving the capacity of the auditors to do so. As they do so, they increase reporting requirements and may fail to recognize major failures in the accounting and auditing system which they might better plan to overcome.

Relationship to Subsequent Operations

It is important that project finance be seen in relation to funds required to meet subsequent, recurring needs. This is particularly important if project finance is provided by external grants and loans, but subsequent operations must be funded locally. In the United States, many governmental units (including, notably, New York City) have been enticed by easy availability of federal funds into projects whose subsequent costs have posed difficult burdens.

In general, then, an agency designed to ensure effective projects should look toward the development of policies that 1) yield an adequate flow of funds to be budgeted to (made available to) projects considered promptly on a multi-year program basis in which the project has considerable flexibility in arranging for grant and loan funds and the use of project-generated revenues, 2) provide approved funds without a separate "releasing" transaction or a preaudit with simple and well-defined procedures for budget modification, 3) allow efficient execution of contracts and prompt payment of vendors without cash-flow problems, 4) provide prompt, useful accounting data facilitating a non-punitive audit focusing on outputs, 5) avoid unnecessary plan-budget conflicts, and 6) take due account of subsequent operating needs.

POLICIES ON HUMAN RESOURCES

Project personnel policies must come to terms with three significant characteristics of projects: 1) That projects are frequently priority activities under pressure to be started – and completed – as soon as possible. Personnel policies appropriate to more leisurely, lower-priority activities may not be desirable for projects. 2) That projects are undertaken by new organizations that are not likely to produce the outlook and ability required of persons who must quickly find effective work assignments and relationships in a substantially new situation. 3) That projects are unique activities of limited duration. Salaries, benefits, and conditions of employment adequate to attract motivated, skilled, and experienced personnel for agencies offering tenure and long-term promotion prospects may not be adequate in limited-term projects.

In this situation, the project – necessarily operating within a larger government or business unit – will be under pressure from two directions. On one hand, a central personnel agency will seek to have project personnel recruited, compensated, promoted, provided benefits, etc., in a fashion consistent with other parts of the organization. It will do so for two reasons: 1) Unequal treatments of employees would violate concepts of "fairness" and lead either (if project employees are favored) to movement of the best employees to projects, or (if project employees are less favored) to inability of projects to recruit qualified people. 2) It will wish to defend a system it feels recruits on merits and guarantees employees protection in matters regarding compensation, promotion, training, benefits, and severance practices while simultaneously providing an effective work force. In other words, the central personnel agency will provide pressure to maintain the integrity of the existing system.

On the other hand, the project management – under pressure to complete its new, unique, priority activity quickly – will be much less concerned with the integrity of the existing personnel system and much more concerned with acquiring the best possible personnel immediately and maintaining them in an environment that keeps them maximally productive.

In this situation, policy at a supraproject level is necessary to provide the guidelines within which individual projects can operate efficiently without destroying the governmental or corporate overall personnel system.

Project Requirements

In this situation, what will a project require?

1. Ability to recruit quickly. Project start-up timetables often do not permit lead time sufficient to enable advertisement for the position and for testing, interviewing, and checking of references of applicants as required by orthodox personnel rules. Projects will wish to acquire directly the services of persons who have demonstrated ability in required specialized fields and in new, yet to be thoroughly defined positions. In short, they will seek competent persons already producing effectively in an existing organization in which they will have to be replaced.

2. Ability to offer attractive compensation. Since personnel will need to be acquired quickly from existing employment for a temporary job, they will be likely to demand higher pay than they (and their counterparts) receive in their existing organization and/or other benefits such as preferred housing, flexible working hours, severance pay agreements, senior management perquisites, and so on. Project management will seek the funds for higher compensation and permission to provide the benefits.

3. Ability to hire expatriates. Sometimes persons of the appropriate competance or experience will not be locally available — or, if available, unwilling to brave the insecurity of the new, short-term project. In this case, hiring of expatriates may provide an answer. Project management frequently seeks this outlet.

4. Minimum training needs. The project — under sharp time and cost pressures — will desire personnel who do not require basic training in the areas of intended responsibilities. Such training as is undertaken will be of an "on-the-job" sort designed to familiarize personnel with project needs and to fully inform all participants about project goals and techniques.

5. Ease of employee termination. The project is of limited duration; employees must be let go as it is completed. Project management will wish to be able to promise minimum difficulties to the employee in this matter as a part of its recruitment package. It will also wish to do so at minimum costs to the project.

6. Freedom to define tasks and provide rewards. Orthodox personnel procedures tend to specify tasks in substantial detail and to provide status as well as financial rewards for faithful performance of these tasks over extended periods. The project will need to set goals that employees must devise methods in unique situations to achieve; thus, the project must be able to reward goal achievement quickly.

Means for Achieving Project Requirements

Projects will seek to achieve these requirements in many ways, including the following:

1. If the project is organized as an identified unit within the traditional government or corporate bureaucracy, it may well move to acquire all of its personnel via secondment from related units in a matrix organization. This practice allows quick recruitment of experienced personnel requiring minimum training and takes care of the termination problem, since employees can simply return to their regular positions upon project completion. If, at the same time, the project is able to provide extra compensation for short-term project work, providing high visibility if successful, the project may well acquire and retain the work force it requires – but, of course, at the expense of existing organizations that will resist (perhaps properly) this temporary outflow of their best people, sometimes by freeing only their least satisfactory employees for project work.

2. By keeping the number of its own personnel to a central coordination minimum and contracting with individuals or agencies (either public or private, local or international) to undertake the detailed tasks of implementation. This transfers personnel problems from the project to the contractor. Since the contractor is likely to be less inhibited by central personnel agency practices, he may be able to quickly hire on attractive terms task-oriented persons (including expatriates) who can be flexibly rewarded while offered prospects of continuing employment via movement from one project contract to another. But, again, this may be at the expense of luring scarce personnel from other important tasks in the country. Moreover, the contractor's efficiency may suffer from lack of familiarity with, or commitment to, the project.

3. By organizing the project as a legally separate unit (for example, a government corporation, a separate corporate subsidiary) with power to set its own personnel policies – modes of selection, compensation, training, job definition and rewards, working conditions, termination, and so on. In this situation, the project becomes a competitor of the central personnel agency in the labor market – perhaps a stiff competitor that will force responses from that agency.

No matter what means the project employs to meet its personnel needs, however, it cannot itself overcome the difficulties stemming from an overall shortage of trained, experienced, skilled persons in the society as a whole. Thus, an agency concerned with ensuring the effective conduct of projects must be concerned with, and supportive of, overall training efforts, particularly as they provide the flexible capacities required by project work.

In general, then, projects require personnel, and their acquisition and maintenance puts them in a conflict situation with central personnel agencies. This conflict must be worked out by means of arrangements that reasonably maintain the integrity of the total personnel system while meeting more important project requirements. On questions of trade-off, efforts should be made to keep damage to the central system less than gains to projects, minimizing the former and maximizing the latter. This conflict – and the trade-offs – will be another area for the development of policy to ensure the effective conduct of projects.

POLICIES ON TECHNOLOGICAL RESOURCES

All projects require a body of technology to be brought in and utilized for project purposes. Some of this technology will be based on the physical and engineering sciences, some on the biological sciences, some on the social sciences, and some on the administrative sciences. All of it will have to be adapted to the needs of the specific project and its special environment.

The extent to which a country can obtain command over technology determines which and how many projects a country can identify, formulate, and implement. Clearly, a country cannot implement projects for which it does not have, and cannot acquire, the necessary know-how.

In addition, however, command over technology also strongly influences the distribution of those increases in real incomes anticipated from successful projects. If, to acquire a necessary body of knowledge, a country must 1) bear the costs of sending its nationals abroad for study to acquire it, 2) pay the salaries of expatriates to claim it, 3) be subject to licensing agreements – and costs – to use it, or 4) give up equity interests in projects as a condition of its acquisition, then to that extent income earned in the country flows to expatriates and local income is reduced. Whether, even with this reduction, the acquisition of technology thereby is desirable depends upon whether or not the diminished increase in real income exceeds local costs. In any case, the project countries are interested in lowering payments made for any given technology. The agency for ensuring effective projects will be interested in lowering these payments without offsetting decline in real incomes.

Actually, much technology is readily available – and countries who have technology subsidize its acquisition by those who do not. Basic technical knowledge is available in all fields in the best graduate schools everywhere – and foundations, international agencies, and bilateral assistance programs provide fellowships to allow attendance. The social and administrative sciences make their findings available in journals easily acquired by interested parties. Much of the technology in the biological sciences – particularly in agriculture – is developed in universities or in international research agencies and is open to all. Indeed, the international agencies highly subsidize the wide distribution of this technology. It is only in the important areas of the physical sciences – and there only with those developments in which proprietary interests protected by secrecy or patents yield monopoly returns – that access to technology is denied or made expensive.

Thus, an agency responsible for ensuring the effective conduct of projects will be interested in participating in the formulation of policies designed to ensure maximum access to technology at minimum costs. In doing so, it will 1) encourage the training of technologists, hold them in the country, and provide them with institutions in which to work, 2) develop individuals and agencies to keep abreast of technological developments in open institutions in such fashion that project opportunities appear, and 3) widen options for limiting costs of using proprietary technologies.

Project Management Techniques as Technology

Clearly, this book discusses a "technology" for the administration of projects. This technology may be primitive, but it is certainly not patented, nor is it secret. Indeed, the Public Policy Implementation and Project Management group is trying as hard as its capacities allow to make it widely available. Similar efforts are being made by the World Bank and other agencies and individuals. Are these offers being taken seriously – and used?

POLICIES ON EXTERNAL RESOURCES

A final word on the use of foreign resources. Projects of major scale, both in developed and developing countries, often resort to acquisition and utilization of financial, human, and technical resources from outside the country. Presumably, the general guidelines on use of these resources – applicable regardless of their source – will be of some assistance. There are, however, additional considerations that cannot be ignored when resources are acquired from another country. These special considerations merit the formulation of special policies governing the limitations and conditions under which foreign resources can optimally be used.

This is a particularly obvious and sensitive factor in the private sector. The use of large amounts of foreign capital investment, and the correspondingly large measure of control by foreign interests, has evoked a variety of policy responses in developing countries, ranging from absolute laissez-faire, not caring about whether foreign interests were in fact exploiting the countries, natural resources and labor force, to strict nationalistic sequestration, blocking capital inflow in crucial areas and sacrificing development progress for patriotism. The issue, faced with equal sobriety by both multinational companies and host developing countries, is a complex one, but each nation must inevitably spell out clearly its policy somewhere between the two extremes.

Not only in the private sector but also in the public sector and in intergovernment cooperation, the question of ulterior purposes can validly be raised, the answers to which should formulate national policy on public foreign assistance, grants, and loans. Further policy can identify priority preferences for the type of outside assistance (consultants or cash, buildings, and equipment for training programs, etc.), the geographical areas into which they should or should not go (for example, urban vs. rural) the field of activity (agriculture, military, industry – and even specific industries), and the national control mechanisms (decision-making authorities, counterpart funding, and so on).

SUMMARY

An overall policy context is vital to the success or failure of development projects. This chapter has identified five important policy factors (articulation of development goals, the perceived role of other socioeconomic institutions, the designation of a central review agency, the generation of projects within a planning framework, and the monitoring of policy effects on project implementation – especially as it affects uses of financial, human, technical and external resources). By reviewing the choice of ways by which governments respond to these policy factors, we can see the immediate and far-reaching effects they have on the generation and management of development projects. Projects succeed or fail only as they draw life from the policy environment.

Index

Completion (task) (cont.)
information system for,
206
preparing schedule for, 206-209
process of, 206-207
three stages of, 206
Completion (task), 205
See also Completion and handover, Completion,
Handover
and failure to terminate projects, 204-205
and failure to prepare completion reports, 205
and use of project outputs, 205
and restriction of project
benefits, 205
common problems of, 204-205
definition of, 204
divestment planning during,
207-210
goal of, 205
phasing in and out of resources
during, 204
prerequisites for success of, 209
transfer from project to
operation during, 209
Completion and handover
and divestment of resources,
210
Computer
role of in projects, 29
Consultants
use of in selection of contractors, 121
Contract(s)
definition of, 120
foreign, in activation stage,
125
variety of, 120
Contract subdivision
example of, 121
Contracting
activities involved in, 118
Control (task)
as distinguished from coordination, 193
definition of, 215
Cooperative curriculum planning,
Intro. xvii

Cooperative networks
development of for curriculum
planning, Intro. xviii
Coordination
as distinguished from control,
193
Cost, 220, 221
in the context of social benefits
and costs, 220
Cost-benefit analysis (c-b), 99,
115, 247
See also Benefit-cost ratio,
Social cost-benefit
analysis
and policy making, 235
definition of, 94-95
Crash cost, 171
Crash time, 171
Critical activity, 161
Critical event, 161
Critical path, 161
Critical Path Analysis (CPA), 150
See also Critical Path Method
Critical Path Method (CPM), 144,
150-161, 163, 166, 168-170,
176, 179, 189
activity as part of, 150-151
activity in, 153
activity duration of, 154
and activity floats, 154-155
and activity slacks, 154-155
and precedence network, 166
and the arrow, 151
backward computing pass of,
155, 159-160
based cost systems, 179
computing scheduling times
of, 154-155
determining activity floats
in, 160
determining basic scheduling
times of, 157
determining the critical path
for, 161
drawing arrow diagrams for,
153
format of, 153
forward computing pass of,
157-159
network, 171
nodes as part of, 151

About the Authors

GENERAL EDITORS AND CONTRIBUTING AUTHORS

LOUIS J. GOODMAN joined the East-West Center Staff in 1971 after serving as a Project Specialist in Engineering Education with the Ford Foundation in the Philippines from 1968-1971. He is Assistant Director of the Resource Systems Institute. Goodman has twenty-two years of national and international experience as an engineering educator, researcher and consultant. He holds degrees from M.I.T. and Harvard University and is registered as a professional engineer to practice in the states of Ohio and New York.

RALPH NGATATA LOVE is currently Director of the Management Education and Development Centre, Massey University, Palmerston North, New Zealand. Before taking up an academic post in 1970, he worked in industry for fifteen years and now serves as director of several private and public corporations. Born in New Zealand, he studied at Victoria University of Wellington and holds degrees in Commerce and Business Administration and a Ph.D. in Policy Formation.

CONTRIBUTING AUTHORS

ROSEMARY M. AQUINO, Adjunct Professor and Director, Project Management Center, De La Salle University, Manila, Philippines. (chapter 11)

CLARK BLOOM, Professor, Department of Public Administration, University of Arizona, Tucson, Arizona. (chapters 2, 3, and 13)

FRANK COTTON, Professor and Head of the Department of Industrial Engineering, Mississippi State University, Mississippi State, Mississippi. (chapter 4)

JOHN HAWKINS, Associate Professor of Education and Director of the Curriculum Inquiry Center, University of California at Los Angeles, Los Angeles, California. (chapter 12 and Introduction to the Curriculum)

TETSUO MIYABARA, East-West Center, Honolulu, Hawaii, Research Fellow, Resource System Institute. (chapter 5)

VICTOR M. ORDONEZ, Special Trade Representative, Ministry of Trade, Republic of the Philippines (seconded by De La Salle University, Manila, Philippines). (chapters 2, 9, 11, and 13)

REZA RAZANI, Professor of Civil Engineering and Director of Planning and Development of Shiraz University, Shiraz, Iran. (chapter 8)

FELISBERTO G.L. REYES, Professor of Civil Engineering, College of Engineering, University of the Philippines, Quezon City, Philippines. (chapter 9)

BINTORO TJOKROAMIDJOJO, Deputy for Administration, National Development Planning Agency (Bappenas), Jakarta, Indonesia. (chapters 6 and 7)

OTHER CONTRIBUTORS

OTHMAN YEOP ABDULLAH, Deputy Director, National Institute of Public Administration, Jalan Ilmu, Malaysia.

GABRIEL IGLESIAS, Professor, College of Public Administration, University of the Philippines, Manila, Phillipines, and currently with the United Nations Asian and Pacific Development Administration Centre, Kuala Lumpur.